Dyer County, Tennessee

Marriages

1860 – 1879

Byron Sistler
and
Barbara Sistler

JANAWAY PUBLISHING, INC.
Santa Maria, California
2012

Dyer County, Tennessee, Marriages 1860-1879

Originally published:
Nashville, 1989

Reprinted by

Janaway Publishing, Inc.
732 Kelsey Ct.
Santa Maria, California 93454
(805) 925-1038
www.JanawayGenealogy.com

2006, 2012

ISBN: 978-1-59641-054-1

Made in the United States of America

DYER COUNTY, TN MARRIAGES

1860-1879

Where two dates appear on an entry, the first one is the date license was issued, the second (in parentheses) the date marriage was solemnized. If only one date, it usually means that the date of execution was the same as the date of license issuance.

Sometimes the execution of the marriage was not reported to the courthouse, and occasionally the clerk failed to note in the marriage book that the license was returned. We would usually make a notation in the entry to indicate the non-execution of a marriage if the book so stated.

The marriages are arranged alphabetically, the first half of the book by groom--the second by bride.

The records included in this book were transcribed by us directly from microfilm of the original marriage books. Error, where it occurs, may be attributed to us, or to the clerks of the period, many of whom did an appallingly sloppy job of entering the information.

If the bride and groom were black, a B is placed at the end of the entry.

It should be remembered that this and other marriage books we have prepared are indexes, and do not include all the information to be found in the original marriage book. Such data as names of bondsmen, ministers, justices of the peace, churches, etc., are omitted. Often such information is helpful to the researcher. Consequently the serious researcher, to obtain this additional information as well as to check on the accuracy of the transcriber, should examine the original marriage record if at all possible.

Byron Sistler
Barbara Sistler

Abbott, Henry to Rebecca Dunston 1-10-1871 (1-13-1871)
Acklin, Thomas to Marenah Robertson 11-9-1870 (11-10-1870)
Adams, Bowlin to Cenus? Tipton 12-15-1870 B
Adams, James M. to Ellen Moseley 1-6-1876
Adams, James M. to Ellen Moseley 6?-6-1876? (with Apr 1876)
Adams, James M. to Sarah F. Mosely 11-7-1872
Adams, John C. to Grisom E. Garrett 6-6-1866 (6-7-1866)
Adcock, Bowling to Elizabeth Shoemake 9-26-1860
Aiken, J. H. to S. J. Carroll 2-28-1871 (3-2-1871)
Aiken, T. H. to Lucinda Thompson 10-29-1868 (no return)
Akin, Christopher to Anna Bumpass 11-29-1870 (12-3-1870) B
Akin, J. G. W. to S. C. Holland 9-4-1876 (no return)
Akin, M. V. to S. A. McCutchen 9-4-1871 (9-5-1871)
Akin, T. R. to M. J. Ward 12-9-1874 (12-10-1874)
Akin, Z. T. to Sarah A. Smith 10-7-1863 (no return)
Albrittain, David to Sarah F. Olds 12-15-1869
Albritton, Sam P. to Martha J. Brown 6-1-1861 (no return)
Alexander, George to Cornelia Faulkner 1-26-1874 (1-28-1874)
Alexander, John D. to Lutitia Mahala Hedin 9-1-1863 (no return)
Alexandra, Sam to Arthena Harris 6-11-1870 (6-10?-1870)
Allen, Benjamin to Susan (Mrs.) Blackburn 12-2-1872
Allen, George to Josafine Cannon 9-13-1870 (no return)
Allen, J. S. to Sarah F. Darden 6-4-1879 (no return)
Allison, Charles to Laura A. McGinn 12-3-1866 (12-4-1866)
Alston, Charles H. to M. A. Leach 11-6-1867
Alston, Nelson to Millie Fowlkes 8-31-1871
Amick, A. J. M. to A. A. Searcy 3-16-1875 (3-17-1875)
Anderson, A. S. to Rachel Estes 10-14-1879
Anderson, Calvin to Emiline Hampton 2-25-1870 (no return)
Anderson, George to Amanda Ferguson 10-15-1873 (10-16-1873)
Anderson, Jack to Margaret Spence 6-2-1866
Anderson, John E. to Randa Weever 6-21-1870
Anderson, John to Mary Wood 1-27-1867 (no return)
Anderson, M. D. to C. C. Singletary 5-18-1863 (no return)
Anderson, Scott to Lucy Fowlkes 1-28-1880
Anderson, Sid to Victoria Twilla 7-16-1870 (7-17-1870)
Anderson, William to Vic Cross 1-23-1867
Andrews, A. C. to Nancy A. Butler 1-24-1871 (no return)
Andrews, J. F. to Margaret Stalcup 6-22-1872 (6-21?-1872)
Andrews, S. P. to Nancy S. T. Parsley 12-13-1870
Anthoney, P. W. to R. J. Niece 2-18-1868 (no return)
Anthony, Fred L. to Celia A. Kent 1-1-1877 (1-2-1877)
Anthony, J. A. to M. A. Anthony 7-11-1877
Applewhite, W. H. to Alice White 12-25-1874 (no return)
Applewhite, W. H. to R. A. Shumaker 6-22-1870 (6-23-1870)
Armstrong, David to Amanda Jones 4-16-1873 (4-17-1873) B
Armstrong, J. F. to Mollie A. Brock 3-14-1867 (3-19-1867)
Armstrong, James to Susan Vaughan 3-20-1871
Arnett, J. W. to Callie Whitley 5-13-1873 (5-14-1873)
Arnett, James T. to Mary E. Dickens 9-11-1872 (9-12-1872)
Arnett, R. M. to M. E. Hunt 5-13-1873
Arnett, W. H. to Nannie Cunningham 1-22-1874
Arnold, J. A. to M. J. Calvin 10-5-1872 (10-6-1872)
Arnold, J. G. to A. J. Radford 11-4-1874 (no return)
Askridge, J. D. to L. R. J. Thetford 8-10-1875 (8-11-1875)
Aspray, H. C. to S. C. Ray 1-15-1872 (no return)
Atkins, Asa A. to Mary M. Walker 12-14-1874 (12-15-1874)
Atkins, J. A. to Mollie Price 3-23-1869 (no return)
Atkins, James to Lavenia Tipton 2-14-1872 (2-4?-1872)
Atkins, John W. to Lucind Helms 1-30-1865
Austin, W. A. to Susan C. (Mrs.) Barker 9-12-1862 (9-13-1862)
Avants, J. T. to A. M. Jackson 1-23-1872 (1-28-1872)
Avery, Henry to Ann Burwell 3-25-1863 (3-25-1863)
Avey, John B. to M. J. G. Gillis 12-27-1871
Avrett, M. A. to M. E. Ward 11-6-1868 (11-8-1868)
Aycock, N. H. to Sarah C. Bell 12-11-1861
Ayers, J. W. to _____ Campbell 3-2-1878 (no return)
Ayrens?, Wilie to Jane Cate 8-7-1871
Bacon, Joseph to Bettie Jones 3-22-1875 (3-24-1875)
Badgett, Zach to Millie Henderson 10-15-1880 (10-24-1880)
Bailey, J. G. to R. T. Brinkley 2-23-1878 (2-26-1878)
Bailey, Jesse to Mary E. Slayton 9-26-1868 (9-27-1868)
Bailey, John B.? to Sarah Ward 9-24-1864 (no return)
Bailey, John C. to Sarah Ann E. Peal 2-3-1862 (no return)
Bailey, John to Sidny Holmes 10-14-1875 (10-15-1875)

Bailey, William A. to Mary Ann Stallcup 7-21-1863 (no return)
Baily, David to Martha Dove 11-29-1869
Bain, James to Martha E. Joslin 4-18-1878 (4-21-1878)
Baines, Frank to Tennessee Bowen 4-15-1872 (4-17-1872)
Bair, Joseph to Sidonia Wilbosern 5-22-1860
Baird, Jo to Mary E. Franklin 6-5-1866 (1?-6-1866)
Baird, Joseph to Susan Smith 2-25-1871 (2-26-1871)
Baird, Lewis to Martha J. Parks 4-12-1871 (no return)
Bairfield, Needham B. to Victoria Faine 5-2-1870
Baker, Duke to Elizabeth Platt 2-11-1863
Baker, E. H. to Lena H. Dawson 12-24-1874
Baker, F. C. to M. E. Marchant 9-18-1866 (9-19-1866)
Baker, George T. to Martha E. Hurt 9-27-1865 (9-28-1865)
Baker, Harris L. to Emma Bet. Dawson 12-25-1872
Baker, Henry W. to Mary L. Kirk 1-20-1863 (1-22-1863)
Baker, J. J. to E. B. Moore 8-24-1867 (8-25-1867)
Baker, Jesse to Martha E. Reynolds 12-4-1869 (12-5-1869)
Baker, Jessee B. to Martha Herril 3-16-1876
Baker, Leonard to Martha A. C. Walker 1-10-1872 (1-11-1872)
Baker, Wily to Lena Lemmons 12-17-1873
Baldrige, George to Eolino Hall 12-20-1866 (12-29-1866)
Baley, Robert? C. to Elizabeth Childers 4-23-1861 (4-25-1861)
Ball, S. H. to M. M. Taylor 1-5-1876
Ball, W. H. to Mary A. Hassell 4-1-1867 (4-3-1867)
Ballentine, W. M. to Harriet A. Stalcup 12-6-1867 (no return)
Balser, W. M. to Nannie Day 3-15-1879 (3-20-1879)
Balser, Wm. S. to Amanda C. Blackburn 2-18-1878
Bandy, James M. to Eliza Rebecca Harrison 3-22-1879 (3-23-1879)
Banker, Joseph to Sallie A. Smith 11-15-1872 (11-17-1872)
Banks, H. to M. J. Gallaher 10-31-1874 (11-3-1874)
Banks, J. L. to E. R. Tucker 9-18-1872
Barger, Christian J. to Julian Skipper 6-30-1860 (7-1-1860)
Barker, Joseph to Frances A. Purdy 6-23-1866 (6-28-1866)
Barker, R. W. to Louisa Chitwood 1-16-1866 (1-17-1866)
Barker, Robt. to Lizzie Darden 1-31-1876 (2-1-1876)
Barnes, James to Eliza Fowlkes 3-1-1877
Barnes, John to Georgia McCutchen 3-7-1873 (3-25-1873)
Barnett, Henry to Lucinda Martin 1-2-1877 (1-3-1877)
Barnett, Jacob to Julia Biggs 12-22-1870 (1-1-1871)
Barnett, Louis to Fannie Tipton 1-3-1877 (1-4-1877)
Barnett, Samuel to Tennessee Spence 8-11-1866
Barr, John to Tabitha Sudberry 1-3-1871 (1-4-1871)
Barrett, A. J. to Finey Gold 1-24-1874 (1-25-1874)
Barrett, J. T. to Ulissus Hopper 6-26-1873
Barrett, James W. to Martha Hopper 2-16-1870 (2-17-1870)
Barrette, J. W. to M. E. Dickey 11-8-1875 (11-10-1875)
Bass, L. H. to Mary B. Dunevant 2-9-1874 (2-11-1874)
Bates, S. D. to Barbara A. Hutson 1-24-1877 (no return)
Bates, Thomas to Fannie Mitchell 12-27-1876 (12-29-1876)
Battle, Jo to Lucinda Easley 7-18-1878
Battle, Lewis to Rebecca Dotson 10-7-1872 (10-14-1872)
Baulch, J. M. to M. L. Perry 11-11-1871 (11-16-1871)
Baxter, Calvin to Rebacca A. Foust 12-25-1866 (12-26-1866)
Baxter, Dave to Zenobia? Tucker 2-1-1877
Baxter, Mit to Arteny Jones 2-17-1871
Baxter, Mit to Eliza Campbell 8-1-1870
Beak, Presley S. to Margaret A. Gammons 3-6-1861
Beakley, James H. to Sarah Jackson 2-19-1876 (2-20-1876)
Beaumont, Alex to Laura Tucker 8-11-1870
Beaumont, Frank to Amanda Clark 1-1-1866
Becket, Charlie to Loula Fowlkes 9-22-1880 (9-23-1880)
Beckett, Letas to Frances Porter 5-30-1871 (6-1-1871)
Beckett, Silas to Bettie Hale 1-3-1877 (1-4-1877)
Bell, Harvey to Martha Bell 1-3-1871 (1-10-1871)
Bell, Henry to Catharine Jones 5-25-1867
Bell, J. P. to M. J. Radford 5-16-1867
Bell, John G. to Mary P. Holland 1-6-1862 (no return)
Bell, John Wesley to Indiana A. Harwell 4-2-1877 (4-4-1877)
Bell, William to Lucy Tucker 11-7-1878 (no return)
Bell, Willis to Lavinia Patterson 1-27-1876
Belton, James to Julia Olds 1-8-1862 (1-9-1862)
Bemis?, L. C. to Helen Spain 12-6-1873 (12-7-1873)
Benham, V. M. to Isabella S. Snow 7-27-1867
Bennett, John to Martha Webb 6-28-1871
Benns, L. C. to Emily Spain 12-6-1871 (12-7-1871)

Bentley, K. H. to P. I. Ferguson 2-25-1861 (no return)
Bentley, W. R. to Martha M. Ferguson 12-14-1860 (12-19-1860)
Benton, R. M. Johnson to Fanny Sawyer 12-22-1869 (no return)
Berry, A. S. to M. F. Hobday 8-4-1877 (no return)
Berry, T. B. to Fannie Pugh 5-6-1871 (5-7-1871)
Bertram, J. W. to Mary Belote 1-10-1872 (1-11-1872)
Bessent, B. A. to Mollie Williamson 12-7-1877 (12-8-1877)
Bessent, James to M. E. Cooper 3-17-1879 (3-18-1879)
Bessent, Plesant R. to E. T. Morris 12-18-1867 (12-19-1867)
Bettis, B. C. to Theodosia Owen 9-11-1871 (9-12-1871)
Bettis, M. V. (Mo?) to L. V. Johnson 11-21-1866 (no return)
Bibb, B. T. to Ann Hawkins 11-11-1867
Bigelow, A. W. to Bettie Nichols 11-4-1875
Biggs, A. R. to Susie Jones 11-30-1870 (12-1-1870)
Biggs, Richard S. to Ellen T. Tisdale 10-17-1874 (10-18-1874)
Biggs, W. H. to Katie A. Jones 7-25-1877
Bills, J. H. to Frankie Davis 12-23-1878 (no return)
Binkley, R. W. to Mary Campbell 11-5-1874 (no return)
Bird, S. J. to Mary F. Olds 12-15-1873 (12-16-1873)
Bishop, Andrew to Amanda Smith 1-27-1869
Bizzel, Stephen V.? to Martha A. Chitwood 11-27-1860
Black, J. F. to S. T. Smith 8-4-1876 (8-5-1876)
Black, James to Mary H. Fonshee 9-26-1867 (no return)
Black, Thomas to Pernissa R. A. Roberson 11-6-1865 (11-7-1865)
Blackbern, J. R. to Mary Ann Privett 10-29-1862 (10-30-1862)
Blackburn, J. A. to E. F. (Mrs.) Parrott 2-9-1869 (no return)
Blackmore, A. J. to F. E. Hufstettler 8-21-1875 (8-23-1875)
Blair, J. R. to Lucy T. Claiborne 6-24-1874
Blair, T. E. to N. C. McCutchen 7-28-1873 (7-31-1873)
Blakemore, J. H. to R. A. Corley 7-27-1878 (7-28-1878)
Bland, Nelson to Fannie Goin 1-4-1876
Blankenship, Colbert to Mary Allen 12-26-1863 (1-21-1864)
Blankenship, J. E. to Mary J. Wright 11-28-1871 (12-20-1871)
Blankenship, Joel to Lou Bessent 2-27-1871 (2-28-1871)
Blankenship, P. L. to Sarah J. Murray 6-15-1872 (6-16-1872)
Blankenship, W. C. to Missouri Murray 10-16-1879
Bledsoe, John to W. E. Gamble 9-8-1877 (9-9-1877)
Bledsoe, M. L. to Sarah Ferrill 5-16-1874 (5-17-1874)
Bledsoe, R. M. to Jennie Finley 2-1-1877
Bledsoe, Thomas A. to Mary Echols 8-31-1876 (9-1-1877?)
Bledsoe, William to S. J. Gamble 11-28-1877 (11-29-1877)
Bloomingdale, Charles B. to Fannie Harton 7-31-1871
Boals, J. W. to Janusy Curtis 3-4-1869 (no return)
Boatwright, C. M. to M. E. Chamberlain 9-1-1870
Boatwright, J. T. to S. J. Davis 10-28-1873 (10-29-1873)
Boatwright, William A. to Etta Chamberlain 4-13-1876
Boaz, Thomas E. to Ella G. Stone 11-19-1872
Bodkin, Daniel to Cordelia Eskew 11-21-1876 (11-22-1876)
Bogguss, Robt. R. to Mary Ann Tucker 9-6-1875 (9-9-1875)
Bogle, R. E. to B. B. (Mrs.) Williams 5-13-1871 (5-14-1871)
Boling, A. J. to Emily Whitteman 12-6-1865 (12-10-1865)
Boling, A. J. to Emily Whittemore 12-6-1865 (12-10-1865)
Bonds, John to Marzella Ballentine 9-3-1862 (9-4-1862)
Bookout, J. F. to H. Ann Lemmon 12-31-1860 (1-1-1861)
Boon, Alexr. to Martha Cross 10-13-1877 (10-14-1877)
Boon, Henry to Frances E. Pierce 3-19-1862
Boon, J. T. to P. E. Hall 10-5-1869
Boon, Wm. A. to Almedia Prichard 1-17-1877 (1-18-1877)
Boone, John to Caroline Cross 1-5-1876
Boone, Marion to Clarissa Ann Magary 12-25-1871 (12-27-1871)
Boose, Andrew to Tennie Ferrill 3-18-1876
Boren, Hosea to E. F. Thurmond 3-20-1878
Borin, Ozy to Elizabeth McFarlin 5-19-1870 (no return)
Borum, J. W. W. to Martha J. Butler 1-2-1869 (1-4-1869)
Bowen, A. C. to M. J. Earle 2-21-1871 (no return)
Bowen, J. P. to Laura Henderson 10-4-1870 (10-6-1870)
Bowen, James to Narcissa Arnold 11-2-1870 (no return) B
Bowen, Jonah to Martha Childers 11-9-1864 (11-10-1864)
Bowen, Marcus to Fannie Porter 12-28-1872 (12-30-1872)
Bowen, Mark to Fanny Rice 10-13-1866 (10-14-1866)
Bowen, Wm. to S. M. Lemons 10-1-1867 (10-2-1867)
Bowlin, Alec. to Amanda Warren 8-30-1862 (9-1-1862)
Bowling, Phillip to Puss Sawyer 12-25-1871 (12-27-1871)
Bowman, G. F. to Amanda B. Duke 5-13-1867 (5-14-1867)
Bowman, J. G. to Nancy Powell 1-5-1870

Bowman, N. L. to Ella McCrackin 4-24-1875 (4-28-1875)
Boyd, Henry Clay to Nannie Edwards 6-28-1867 (6-29-1867)
Boyd, John to M. E. Hendrix 1-30-1866 (1-31-1866)
Boyd, William to Margaret Parnell 12-13-1862 (12-16-1862)
Brackin, J. M. to Georgia A. Stevens 4-10-1878
Bradley, J. D. to K. J. Brashier 3-22-1873 (3-23-1873)
Bradley, J. M. to Sarah A. Lowe 5-25-1873 (5-21?-1873)
Bradley, W. M. to A. F. Singleton 10-23-1866 (10-24-1866)
Bradshaw, A. to Tishie Harris 12-28-1870 (12-29-1870)
Bradshaw, Asa to Frances Smith 2-28-1871 (3-3-1871)
Bradshaw, Geo. to Laura Tucker 11-25-1875
Bradshaw, J. B. to Sarah E. Roper 3-16-1878 (3-17-1878)
Bradshaw, Matt to Milly Foust 8-14-1872
Bradshaw, Matt to Ruth Foust 12-27-1869 (no return)
Bradshaw, Saml. B. to Lenora Powell 9-15-1863 (no return)
Branch, W. M. to L. R. Hoskins 6-18-1875 (6-21-1875)
Brandon, G. L. to C. S. Williams 11-6-1872
Brantlen, J. G. to S. E. Lucas 2-28-1871 (2-29?-1871)
Brashears, John C. to Rebecca J. Hawkins 9-3-1867
Brassfield, E. L. to Fannie Hollins 1-28-1868 (1-29-1868)
Brassfield, Thomas to Charlotte Howell 2-18-1868
Brazier, B. F. to K. J. Caliway 1-26-1870
Brent, William H. to Lethe Jane Mays 4-30-1860 (5-1-1860)
Brewer, A. P. to M. E. Hull 3-27-1877 (3-29-1877)
Brewer, Alfred to Martha A. Reycroft 2-27-1878
Brewer, David to Frances Lanier 2-27-1861 (no return)
Brewer, James to Sarah Pope 2-12-1876 (2-10?-1876)
Brewer, John M. to Emily Cunningham 10-22-1860 (no return)
Brewer, W. B. to M. E. Pate 11-24-1875
Briggs, J. H. to Nancy C. Duncan 5-24-1875
Brigham, D. A. to Ella Bracken 5-1-1878
Briley, James to Mary L. Coble 12-5-1875
Brimen, Geo. to Martha E. Smith 12-28-1878 (no return)
Brimm, George to Amanda A. Harris 12-25-1871
Brinkley, E. W. to Martha Garrison 12-13-1860
Brinkley, J. A. to Margaret Brinkly 9-22-1866 (9-23-1866)
Brinkley, J. S. to Ann Eliza Millican 11-7-1867
Brinkley, J. S. to Mary J. Allen 5-1-1861 (5-2-1861)
Brinkly, T. H. to Amanda Wright 1-7-1868 (1-8-1868)
Britt, Singleton to Charlotte Jones 6-20-1876 (6-22-1876)
Britton, Harrison to _____ no date (with Aug 1867)
Brock, D. to Mattie Singleton 3-29-1875
Brock, S. Frank to Evelyn Green 2-24-1866
Brock, jr., D. to F. A. Dickason 8-13-1872 (8-14-1872)
Brockman, John L. to Martha King 12-27-1865 (12-28-1865)
Brooks, James E. to Bettie Johnson 7-9-1878 (no return)
Brooks, Joseph to Mattie Johnson 10-28-1862 (no return)
Brooks, W. B. to Vina E. Robertson 2-9-1874 (2-11-1874)
Brothers, Jackson F. to Susan F. Miller 1-6-1879 (no return)
Browder, H. H. to M. J. Pate 4-25-1863 (4-26-1863)
Brown, C. F. to M. J. Brown 6-14-1875 (6-17-1875)
Brown, Frank to Ann Henry 12-27-1866 (no return)
Brown, Henry to Susan A. Robbins 8-20-1879 (8-21-1879)
Brown, James to Addie Manning 7-16-1868
Brown, Jefferson to Catharine Lanningham 5-27-1873
Brown, Jesse A. to Bettie J. Essary 9-23-1868
Brown, John A. to Pocahontas Durden 3-12-1879 (3-16-1879)
Brown, John W. to Mary G. Andrews 2-22-1871 (2-23-1871)
Brown, Lot to Amelia Fowlkes 1-24-1879 (1-26-1879)
Brown, Lucius to Nannie Mangrum 11-18-1869 (11-21-1869)
Brown, R. M. to Amanda Arnold 1-7-1875 (1-10-1875)
Brown, Robert F. to Susan E. Parker 10-18-1865 (10-25-1865)
Brown, William to Mary Mangrum 1-19-1867 (1-20-1867)
Brown, William to Matilda A. Landrum 8-5-1873 (8-15-1873)
Brown, William to Renie Perry 5-27-1871 (6-1-1871)
Brown, Wm. R. to Martha A. Barrett 2-12-1875 (2-14-1875)
Brown, Wm. to Amanda Edwards 12-19-1867
Brown?, Silas to Julian Craig 7-22-1869 (7-25-1869)
Bruce, W. W. to Minerva Harris 5-25-1861 (5-30-1861)
Brunston, G. W. to Nancy A. Neules 2-19-1872 (2-20-1872)
Bryant, W. J. to Anna Gibson 3-11-1868 (no return)
Bryant, W. J. to Maggie Gibson 10-28-1871 (10-29-1871)
Buchanan, Harry to Lizzie Bowen 1-8-1872 (no return)
Buchanan, T. C. (Capt.) to Sarah A. Bell 6-28-1875 (6-29-1875)
Buchanan, T. C. to Emma Bell 4-26-1877

Buckingham, J. M. to Lizzie Lewis 3-23-1874 (3-24-1874)
Bugg, Alex to Sarah A. Dock 5-3-1869 (no return)
Bullard, David C. to Jane C. Ferrell 2-4-1867 (2-5-1867)
Bumpass, Amos to Mollie Ward 6-18-1870 (6-19-1870)
Bunnell, Wilson A. to J. T. Tarkington 7-31-1863
Burch, S. to Nancy A. Mills 8-30-1870
Burgess, W. H. to M. C. Taylor 12-14-1876
Burgie, D. S. to J. E. Barnett 10-13-1869
Burkeen, A. J. to Vandelia Meadows 12-21-1870
Burket, J. A. to M. E. Rogers 1-23-1878 (1-24-1878)
Burkett, J. H. to Verginia Robertson 10-6-1870 (no return)
Burkett, John to Mary Ann Dunevant 9-13-1877
Burklen?, Church to Lizzie Connell 5-1-1876
Burkley, Peyton to Dora Ledsinger 5-11-1878 (5-15-1878)
Burks, E. L. to Maggie Clemmons 12-24-1875 (12-26-1875)
Burnam, Joshua to Lou Duncan 11-15-1865 (11-16-1865)
Burnett, J. T. to Mary E. Goodman 1-17-1871 (1-18-1871)
Burnett, Jacob to Nancy C. Poston 1-8-1867 (1-9-1867)
Burnham, G. W. to Nancy P. Brunt 10-19-1872 (10-20-1872)
Burnham, J. H. to M. F. Whitt 12-21-1870 (12-22-1870)
Burnham, W. C. to Tennessee Bailey 9-21-1875 (9-22-1875)
Burns, James to Elizabeth Williams 11-1-1879 (11-2-1879)
Burns, John to Elizabeth Ray 3-29-1869 (no return)
Burnside, H. S. to C. J. Hamilton 1-8-1875 (1-12-1875)
Burrell, Isaac to Eliza F. (Mrs.) Edwards 12-23-1872 (no return)
Burtin, J. W. to Paralee Crow 10-14-1872 (10-17-1872)
Burton, Fley O. to Caroline Bumpasss 2-25-1870 (no return)
Burton, Frank to Fannie Wilkins 12-2-1875
Bush, Ephraim to Rena Cerry 12-24-1870 (no return)
Bush, James D. to Fredericka Anderson 3-10-1874
Butler, M. J. to M. O. Jackson 4-3-1877 (4-4-1877)
Butterworth, R. T. to L. J. Butterworth 2-9-1872 (2-10-1872)
Byassee, Peter to Paris Stallings 4-8-1871 (4-9-1871)
Byrn, R. J. M. to M. E. F. Thacker 3-27-1862 (no return)
Calton, J. L. to M. E. Wherry 9-26-1874 (9-27-1874)
Campbell, Allen to Eadie Harris 1-21-1873 (1-3?-1873)
Campbell, Andy J. to Elmira Hall 3-3-1877 (3-4-1877)
Campbell, J. B. to Tabitha A. R. Cillett 8-6-1878
Campbell, James to Lou Ellen Mitchell 1-26-1877 (1-28-1877)
Campbell, M. F. to M. Tevilla 1-11-1871
Campbell, R. S. to Polly Ann Brush 3-14-1876 (3-17-1876)
Campbell, William H. to L. C. Fuller 2-4-1863 (2-5-1863)
Campbell, William to Mary A. Baker 7-3-1860
Canada, A. B. to Lucy Spoon 12-20-1875 (12-21-1875)
Canada, A. to S. M. Thurmon 8-20-1868 (8-23-1868)
Canada, Isaac to Amanda Harris 9-6-1879 (9-7-1879)
Canada, Isaac to Cordelia Davis 1-20-1877 (1-21-1877)
Canada, William J. to Susan E. Neal 1-15-1873 (1-16-1873)
Canady, Thomas to Elizabeth Herald 11-26-1877
Cannady, John to Martha Jane Norman 1-27-1870 (no return)
Cantlin, Jacob to Julia Ann Hoskins 2-12-1875 (2-25-1875)
Capell, J. T. to Kitty Bessent 10-15-1868
Careley, Martin F. to Elizabeth F. Davis 2-11-1868
Carmack, J. W. to Benny Curtis 1-1-1868 (no return)
Carmack, J. W. to J. A. Dodson 12-17-1875 (12-19-1875)
Carpenter, A. H. to M. E. Churchman 10-27-1874 (10-28-1874)
Carpenter, H. R. to M. S. Ray 5-11-1878 (5-13-1878)
Carpenter, W. C. to Nancy M. Baker 10-2-1868 (10-4-1868)
Carr, B. B. to Mary E. Tharpe 3-22-1876 (no return)
Carroll, B. A. to F. Flack 3-11-1874
Carroll, J. D. to E. M. Harris 1-14-1861 (1-15-1861)
Carroll, S. D. to Julia Ann Akin 11-28-1870 (11-30-1870)
Carroll, W. A. to Mattie Blanton 8-9-1879 (no return)
Carson, Samuel B. to Sarah B. Sampson 3-12-1868
Cart, Andrew to Sarah Jane Ferrell 10-11-1870
Carter, Brooks to Mary Brown 11-30-1878 (12-1-1878)
Carter, J. D. to S. J. Eudaly 1-1-1873
Carter, Perry to Sarah Enochs 5-23-1871 (5-25-1871)
Carter, T. J. to Tennessee Armstrong 12-29-1869 (12-30-1869)
Carter, W. L. to S. A. Gallion 3-6-1871 (3-7-1871)
Carter, William to Mary C. Duke 9-28-1869 (9-29-1869)
Carvin, D. L. to Patsey Dove 11-3-1874 (11-4-1874)
Cate, William to Mary E. Wayson 11-30-1872 (12-4-1872)
Cathcart, W. T. to W. M. Cope 3-5-1879 (3-9-1879)
Cawthon, E. W. to Mollie F. Croom 1-9-1866 (1-11-1866)

Cawthon, J. L. to E. J. McCorkle 2-19-1877 (2-21-1877)
Cerley, J. R. to Mariah (Mrs.) Warren 12-28-1872 (12-31-1872)
Chadwick, Iram to Martha Winberry 9-17-1870 (9-18-1870)
Chamberlain, D. M. to N. E. Farrer 3-10-1868 (no return)
Chamberlain, J. R. to Rosa P. McCombs 2-1-1877
Chamberlain, J. S. to Mary Walker 11-22-1877
Chamberlain, Jo to Lizzie Baxter 6-28-1871 (no return)
Chamberlin, Ed to Parlee McCutchen 5-16-1872
Chambers, C. S. to M. V. Rucker 12-20-1876 (12-21-1876)
Chambers, J. M. to A. R. Rucker 12-18-1872 (12-19-1872)
Chambers, J. N. to D. F. Conklin 9-20-1879 (9-22-1879)
Chambers, James W. to Sarah J. Gibson 1-22-1867 (1-23-1867)
Chambers, James to S. M. Warre 10-12-1868 (12-13-1868)
Chambers, R. T. to Frances E. Davis 9-26-1866 (9-30-1866)
Chambers, R. T. to Sallie R. Johnson 6-8-1878 (6-11-1878)
Chandler, John to Minerva McNeil 9-8-1877 (no return)
Chapman, E. W. to Sarah C. Hawkins 9-13-1867 (no return)
Chapman, William E. to Susie McMillen 12-20-1870
Chappell, J. L. to N. J. Blair 1-6-1874
Cheny, Robert A. to Sarah A. Farmer 9-18-1861 (9-20-1861)
Cherry, G. W. to Florence Albritton 1-5-1872 (1-7-1872)
Childers, Alfred to Sarah Slayton 12-23-1867
Childers, Jno. M. to Mary Childers 12-28-1867 (no return)
Childress, Edward to Pattie Williamson 9-4-1879 (9-7-1879)
Childress, John M. to Elizabeth Simpson 1-12-1871
Childress, W. O. to Mindie? Thompson 6-13-1879 (6-15-1879)
Chitwood, Edmond to Rebecca A. Curtis 6-3-1868 (no return)
Chitwood, J. H. to S. A. Hendricks 11-27-1878 (11-28-1878)
Chitwood, S. A. to M. A. Tatum 8-29-1866 (no return)
Chitwood, S. H. to Emily Pursell 4-16-1867 (no return)
Chrisman, J. L. to Mary E. Laster 10-31-1871 (11-3-1873?)
Chrisman, T. W. to M. E. Bell 2-27-1877
Christie, W. O. to R. E. Reynolds 10-16-1877
Chronister, T. P. to Nancy J. Stevenson 1-7-1868
Chronister, W. C. to Amelia Jones 10-17-1860 (10-8?-1860)
Chronister, Wesley to Sarah Dodson 1-30-1866 (1-31-1866)
Church, Geo. W. to Nannie Vick 9-5-1870 (9-11-1870)
Churchman, H. C. to Eugenie C. Robertson 12-16-1872 (12-17-1872)
Churchman, H. L. to L. H. Oakley 7-31-1869 (8-1-1869)
Churchman, J. R. to M. M. Baker 11-7-1865 (no return)
Churchman, W. J. to E. J. Bell 2-2-1871
Claiborn, C. L. to S. A. Light 12-30-1872 (12-31-1872)
Clark, Bob to Amanda Mulherin 6-13-1867
Clark, Bob to Susan Wynne 1-2-1879
Clark, David C. to Nora A. Young 11-22-1877 (11-25-1877)
Clark, Wm. to Jennie Bowen 1-12-1870 (1-13-1870)
Clarke, J. W. to Sallie J. Hardison 1-26-1874 (1-27-1874)
Clay, Charles to Minerva Lanningham 7-2-1873 (7-3-1873)
Clay, Chas. to Hellen Sorrell 10-6-1864 (no return)
Clayton, John to Jane Foster 1-10-1874 (1-11-1874)
Cleek, Jackson to Tempa N. Pyland 3-23-1868
Clemens, Robt. S. to Martha A. Saddler 7-16-1860
Clement, Paul G. to Martha Goodman 1-11-1865 (no return)
Clements, L. J. to Jennie Applewhite 5-29-1878
Clemmons, J. R. to M. A. Todd 12-29-1875
Clemmons, W. H. to Eliza J. Dudley 3-17-1874
Clendening, W. J. to Martha L. Love 2-4-1867 (2-5-1867)
Cobb, Jackson D. C. to Ann Eliza Kirk 1-30-1861
Cobb, Jacob to Martha Fumbanks? 8-8-1860 (8-9-1860)
Cochran, W. W. to Augustine Neal 12-27-1871 (12-28-1871)
Cochrill, L. J. to Adaline Tate 1-30-1877 (1-31-1877)
Coffman, R. C. to Emma (Mrs.) Nash 12-3-1872 (12-5-1872)
Coker, James Henry to Mary E. Robertson 1-16-1871 (1-17-1871)
Coker, Jas. J. to Susie T. Scales 5-2-1870 (5-3-1870)
Coker, N. to Embra Fowlkes 2-7-1867
Colbert, Frank to Mary Eudaly 12-12-1874
Colbert, James to Lou Mifflin 6-4-1866
Cole, B. G. M. to Margaret Jane Huffine 12-14-1876
Cole, John F. to Jane Shackelton 4-3-1866 (no return)
Cole, W. G. M. to Martha C. Sawyer 2-16-1871
Coleman, Charles to M. E. Hancock 3-31-1879 (4-1-1879)
Coleman, George to Ann Fields 9-14-1869 (no return) B
Collins, F. A. to E. C. Hicks 1-27-1879
Collins, S. C. to Sarah Dockens 10-30-1872
Colvin, Charner B. to Mahala Shelton 12-21-1876 (12-25-1876)

Colvin, J. S. to Jesse Humphrey 9-25-1878 (9-26-1878)
Combs, W. J. to Sarah E. Baker 3-15-1869 (no return)
Comrie?, James to Susan Boggess 6-13-1867
Connell, Alex to Mary Smith 5-27-1871 (5-28-1871)
Connell, Austin to Amanda Mulherin 2-22-1872 (2-23-1872)
Connell, Austin to Nannie Light 10-6-1880
Connell, David to Martha Pell 11-25-1875
Connell, Henry to Ada Harris 5-18-1876 (no return)
Connell, Jack to Helen Light 5-4-1875 (5-5-1875)
Connell, Jack to Hetta Williams 12-2-1869 (no return)
Connell, John F. to Jane Light 2-17-1871 (2-18-1871) B
Connell, Peter to Noon? Tucker 8-9-1877
Connell, W. E. to Mary E. Gold 11-11-1871 (11-12-1871)
Conner, W. to Ellen Blackwood 11-2-1875 (no return)
Conness, John to Mrs. Brown 9-8-1869 (9-9-1869)
Cook, Edward L. to Donie M. Nunn 8-27-1878 (8-28-1878)
Cook, J. R. to Mattie Cunningham 3-2-1876
Cook, John to Jane Dozier 7-23-1862 (7-24-1862)
Cook, Major F. to Lucy Tucker 4-28-1880
Cook, Solomon to Martha A. Hurt 2-25-1861
Cook, T. H. to Neettie Teat 6-13-1874 (6-14-1874)
Cook, Toler to Parthena Fowlkes 1-24-1874
Cook, William to Mollie E. Brown 9-9-1871 (9-12-1871)
Coon, George A. to Julia P. Smith 12-9-1874
Coop, W. A. H. to M. M. Agee 1-7-1871 (1-10-1871)
Cooper, G. G. to Mary E. Mills 7-27-1875 (7-29-1875)
Cooper, J. E. to D. J. Chapman 3-9-1868 (3-12-1868)
Cooper, James H. to Rebeccah C. Barnett 3-23-1865
Cooper, James H. to Susan Southern 6-28-1870
Cooper, P. W. to Sallie Ray 11-20-1875 (11-24-1875)
Cooper, Wm. to Martha A. Barker 10-7-1868 (10-8-1868)
Cope, W. H. to H. E. Hendricks 8-12-1872 (no return)
Copeland, Allen to Lizzie Mitchell 10-12-1872 (no return)
Copeland, Harry to Harriet Doak 1-7-1874 (no return)
Copeland, John to Mollie Copeland 5-8-1877
Corley, N. H. to Martha L. Lamb 6-23-1871 (6-27-1871)
Cotham, Thomas to Mary Pitts 2-21-1869 (no return)
Cothran, Levi to Martha A. Parnell 4-3-1861 (4-4-1861)
Cotton, John to D. A. (Mrs.) Brogden 12-29-1863 (12-31-1863)
Cotton, W. H. to Elizabeth Sanderson 4-5-1871 (4-11-1871)
Couch, Robert to Lucinda Thompson 12-24-1872
Cowell, B. T. to Z. A. Robertson 7-10-1879 (no return)
Cowell, W. H. to M. E. Jones 2-26-1872
Cowles, H. to Martha Howard 12-31-1874
Cowles, Henry to Lucinda Fowlkes 7-17-1869 (no return)
Cox, Jack to Sina Garrison 5-1-1869 (no return)
Cozart, Gilbert to Amanda J. Fuller 12-2-1867 (12-3-1867)
Cozart, J. to S. E. D. Wilkinson 10-2-1871 (10-3-1871)
Cozart, Jasper to Susan Harris 1-13-1866
Crafton, R. L. to Mary E. Purdy 6-18-1866 (6-22-1866)
Craig, David M. to Elizabeth Hart 11-26-1860
Craig, J. O. to E. E. Bell 3-26-1877 (3-28-1877)
Craig, J. Q. to S. S. Bowen 9-17-1866
Craig, James to Mary Garrett 1-8-1867 (1-13-1867)
Crampley, T. R. to Sarah Williams 8-24-1874 (8-25-1874)
Crane, W. H. to Bettie McKani 10-19-1874 (no return)
Craw, Jas. A.? to Emeline Jones 3-23-1864 (no return)
Crawford, J. D. to M. E. Shackleton 1-19-1876
Crawford, J. W. to M. A. Barnett 2-11-1866 (2-12-1866)
Crenshaw, W. J. to Sallie J. Montgomery 12-3-1877 (12-4-1877)
Cribbs, E. G. to R. J. Sawyer 11-18-1869 (11-19-1869)
Cribbs, J. H. to C. C. Wilkins 11-11-1868
Cribbs, J. W. to Josephine McIntosh 10-9-1878
Cribbs, J. W. to Maggie A. McIntosh 11-16-1875 (11-18-1875)
Crichfield, Richard to Martha A. Slayton 1-21-1868
Crisp, Benj. A. to Marinda Garrison 2-16-1870 (2-17-1870)
Crisp, J. E. to M. T. Mote 1-20-1874 (1-21-1874)
Crisp, J. E. to R. A. Boatright 10-13-1869 (no return)
Crocker, J. Y. to Elizabeth Gallaher 7-7-1868 (no return)
Cross, Marcellus A. to America Crow 1-15-1868
Crossnoe, W. C. to Mary Jane Evans 12-13-1870 (no return)
Crow, A. J. to M. C. King 10-14-1872
Crow, James A. L. to N. P. Mills 10-24-1866 (10-25-1866)
Crow, R. S. to Harriet Gleaves 1-17-1872 (1-18-1872)
Crow, R. S. to Mary Ann Ellis 11-28-1870 (11-29-1870)

Crow, W. R. G. to M. A. Hall 1-7-1867 (1-8-1867)
Crow, W. R. to Eliza McBride 1-12-1870 (1-13-1870)
Cummings, Elias D. to Martha A. Cummings 9-22-1873 (9-23-1873)
Cunningham, J. L. to Ellen Greer 12-17-1868 (12-24-1868)
Cunningham, Jno. A. to Polly Taylor 9-10-1861 (no return)
Curby, John W. to Emma James 7-23-1874
Curby, John W. to Paralee Powers 8-8-1876 (8-9-1876)
Currey, James to Emma Bumpass 8-28-1880 (8-29-1880)
Curtis, W. E. to Mary A. Pitts 7-30-1869 (no return)
Curtis, William to Caroline Armstrong 3-6-1861
Dalton, J. T. to Jane (Mrs.) Foster 4-27-1872 (4-28-1872)
Dalton, W. D. to Frances R. Hood 6-14-1879 (no return)
Daniel, J. L. to M. Alice Sinclair 11-25-1869 (11-30-1869)
Daniel, J. W. to N. J. Timms 12-15-1874
Daniel, James to Margaret Thetford 8-16-1875 (8-18-1875)
Daniel, Thomas to Margaret Patterson 2-14-1876
Darden, James H. to Jennie Massey 12-9-1872 (12-12-1872)
Darden, W. B. to Jane Murray 12-25-1872 (12-26-1872)
Davenport, Charles to Susan E. Richardson 12-17-1873 (12-18-1873)
Davenport, Richd. to Margaret King 8-31-1867 (9-13-1867)
David, Eldridge to Emily Landford 1-31-1872 (2-1-1872)
Davidson, George S. to Martha R. Averett 12-30-1867 (12-31-1867)
Davidson, Jack to Mary Hardin 5-29-1866 (6-30-1866)
Davidson, M. V. to R. E. Patton 10-24-1866
Davis, Asa M. to S. J. Hall 5-17-1873 (5-18-1873)
Davis, Daniel to Josie Hamilton 8-16-1878 (8-21-1878)
Davis, I. N. to Nancy E. Barnett 2-20-1863 (2-23-1863)
Davis, J. H. to N. J. Freeman 10-5-1874 (10-6-1874)
Davis, J. L. to Susan Lovett 10-1-1866 (10-10-1866)
Davis, J. W. to J. A. Swayne 1-9-1879
Davis, James A. to Christiana Chandler 7-6-1867 (7-7-1867)
Davis, Jesse to Elizabeth Rowden 11-17-1866 (11-18-1866)
Davis, John C. to Ann Swanner 6-25-1879 (6-28-1879)
Davis, John E. to Asenith Ward 10-12-1868 (10-14-1868)
Davis, John to Julia Margall 7-26-1873 (7-27-1873) B
Davis, John to Julia Mayall 7-26-1873 (no return) B
Davis, John to Margaret Richmond 7-3-1867 (7-4-1867)
Davis, Lee to Phillis Ledsinger 1-25-1877 (no return)
Davis, Marion to Elizabeth Brent 4-20-1865
Davis, Nathan L. to Martha J. Warren 10-7-1869
Davis, Nelson T. to Fannie Justice 4-8-1872 (4-10-1872)
Davis, Reuben to Ann C. Moody 12-17-1870 (12-25-1870)
Davis, W. J. to Sarah Jane Reed 11-27-1866 (11-28-1866)
Davis, W. P. to Mary Wethington 9-27-1869 (9-28-1869)
Davis, W. S. to M. J. Hampton 5-16-1874 (5-19-1874)
Davis, W. T. to Susn Marchant 10-15-1868
Day, Lemuel to Sarah Smith 9-12-1871 (9-13-1871)
Deal, Joseph to Sallie Howell 8-16-1866
Dean, H. A. to S. E. Douglass 10-3-1872 (no return)
Dean, W. M. to M. E. Stallings 3-6-1878 (3-7-1878)
Dearmon, William to Isabela Henry 8-18-1863 (no return)
Dearmore, Ned to Judy Tucker 2-8-1877
Deason, L. to Angeline Gabrel 5-17-1870 (5-19-1870)
Deberry, Joseph to Jane Lee 8-5-1868 (no return)
Degernett, Edwin to Dora Edwards 2-18-1878 (2-21-1878)
Delf, John to Elizabeth Pierce 12-30-1872
Delf, John to Sarah A. Bland 6-14-1869
Delph, John W. to Margaret A. McKelley 3-25-1862
Delph, Philip to Susannah Pierce 8-2-1879 (8-3-1879)
Delph, Phillip to Adeline Sawyer 9-18-1866
Dempsa, Hiram to Elmira McDon 8-27-1868
Denney, S. A. to S. E. Munns? 9-11-1876 (9-17-1876)
Dennis, R. N. to M. A. Gurgett 10-25-1879 (10-26-1879)
Devenport, John to Amanda Goodric 5-14-1870 (5-17-1870)
Dew, Thomas J. to N. L. Redding 10-22-1872
Dewitt?, John to Nora Woods 8-30-1877 (crossed out)
Dickey, H. M. to F. J. Templeton 12-8-1869 (12-10-1869)
Dickey, J. F. to M. H. Archibald 12-8-1869 (12-9-1869)
Dickey, M. H. to Jennie Zarecor? 9-29-1875 (no return)
Dickey, R. C. to N. E. Kennady 10-10-1872
Dickey, R. W. to Millie Stallcup 11-23-1871
Dickey, W. C. to M. J. Radford 10-25-1879 (10-26-1879)
Dickson, A. F. to Laura A. McCutchen 11-26-1866 (no return)
Diggs, J. W. to Mary Parr 2-12-1878 (2-13-1878)
Dillender, John O. to Angeline Randolph 2-24-1864

Dilliard, L. D. to Rachel E. Osborne 11-19-1868
Dillingham, Thomas to Amanda Dunlap 8-5-1870
Dillingham, Wm. to Elizabeth Glenn 10-10-1878
Dillon, J. H. to Manerva Holland 4-7-1870 (no return)
Dillon, James to Mariah Bell 3-23-1874 (3-24-1874)
Ditto, W. N. to Mary R. Saunders 10-9-1866 (10-11-1866)
Dixon, Jesse to Margaret A. Ferrill 2-19-1879 (2-20-1879)
Dixon, O. B. to Billie Hinds 12-11-1878
Doak, Isaac to Julia Ann Copeland 9-27-1877
Doak, John to Florence Fowlkes 3-3-1880
Doak, Robt. L. to Lucy A. Smith 1-20-1862 (no return)
Dobbs, W. J. F. to Amanda J. Winburn 11-4-1869
Dobbs, W. J. F. to Maria (Amanda?) T. Kelley 3-3-1873
Dodd, Isaac Green to Sarah Ann Scalions 4-30-1870 (no return)
Dodd, James A. to Mary J. Pounds 3-25-1869
Dodd, John F. to Elizabeth Robertson 8-2-1862 (8-3-1862)
Dodd, W. R. to P. E. Hook 10-10-1868
Dodd, William R. to Caroline White 10-30-1861
Dodson, John R. to M. J. T. Wiggins 5-21-1878 (5-23-1878)
Doer?, N. L. to Prudence Smithwick 8-20-1860 (8-22-1860)
Doherty, C. to A. C. Tipton 10-15-1868
Donald, James to Hellen Silsby 1-12-1871
Dorherty, Ephraim to Kitsey Swan Cunningham 10-9-1863 (10-11-1863)
Dority, Ephraim to Joanna Pierce 12-13-1871
Dorsey, James to Joella Smith 1-14-1869
Dotsen, David to E. L. Craig 10-1-1867 (10-2-1867)
Dotson, Wat to Lucy F. McBride 9-26-1867
Douglass, Green to Morean Fields 4-1-1878 (4-3-1878)
Douglass, Raphe to Lizzie Jones 12-26-1879
Dove, John to Martha Mills 8-11-1863 (no return)
Doyle, Green to Franky Dickerson 12-28-1866
Doyle, John F. to Ella A. Weakley 9-17-1861 (9-18-1861)
Doyle, William Carroll to Lucy Jennie L. Lauderdale 7-25-1860 (no return)
Dozey, Zach to Susan Jane Smith 8-5-1879 (8-7-1879)
Dozier, D. C. to L. F. Baker 7-13-1866 (7-15-1866)
Dozier, G. W. to Zylpha Warren 2-18-1873 (2-19-1873)
Dozier, H. H. to M. S. Arnett 2-5-1873 (2-6-1873)
Drane, Robt. W. to M. F. Fowlkes 12-2-1874 (no return)
Draper, Walter Scott to Mollie I. Parks 11-24-1870
Driscol, Henry to Mary Higgin 12-27-1866 (12-28-1866)
Drummon, J. M. to Nannie Ledbetter 2-10-1870
Drummonds, S. M. to Ida F. Finley 12-21-1870
Duckworth, James to Rachel Wise 2-9-1876 (2-10-1876)
Duckworth, John B. to Julia Ann Holland 1-18-1875
Dudley, H. W. to Clara Searcey 8-10-1875
Dudley, John D. to M. J. Cook 4-30-1878
Duffee, Marion to Nancy Caroline Poston 11-11-1865 (no return)
Duke, Anthony to E. C. Lack 12-11-1866 (no return)
Duke, George to Martha J. Henderson 2-7-1865
Dumas, John to Alice Jones 10-2-1873 (10-4-1873)
Dumas, Matthew to Josephine Smith 2-16-1874
Dunavan, Peter to Matilda Doyle 8-15-1867
Dunavant, Fernando to Lizzie Bradshaw 2-10-1870 (no return)
Dunavant, Louis to Mary Fowlkes 4-28-1869 (no return)
Dunaway, L. H. to Elizabeth Sawrie 2-28-1866 (3-6-1866)
Duncan, John L. to Nannie Muirhead 11-5-1877 (11-7-1877)
Duncan, Wen. D. L. to Anna M. Lovelace 9-26-1867
Dunevant, Flem to Ann Eliza Smith 12-16-1876 (12-21-1876)
Dunevant, John to Mariah Whitson 12-12-1871 (12-13-1871)
Dunevent, Fernando to Letitia Grimm 5-19-1875 (5-20-1875)
Dunlap, R. W. to Emma E. Daugherty 12-18-1876 (12-24-1876)
Dunn, C. R. to Mary Ivey 4-6-1878 (4-7-1878)
Dunn, Cyrus to Margaret Linton 11-12-1870 (11-15-1870)
Dunn, Samuel M. to Mary Thedford 9-19-1879 (9-30-1879)
Dunnigan, George to Rebecca Binford 10-30-1868 (no return)
Dunnigan, Jeremiah to Nannie Bowen 12-22-1869 (no return)
Dupre, C. A. to Martha E. Finley 11-27-1865
Durden, John to Jane Donald 12-27-1877
Dyer, B. P. to Emily Hosey 10-4-1879 (10-7-1879)
Dyer, B. P. to N. J. Lasiter 10-25-1876 (10-26-1876)
Eady, Hiram to Martha Lane 5-29-1868
Earle, Thomas H. to Sallie J. (Mrs.) Clemons 6-3-1873
Earley, W. E. to E. A. Shofner 4-9-1873 (4-10-1873)

Early, Asbury to Nancy Rooks 11-16-1869 (no return)
Eason, A. to Annie W. Mobley 1-2-1872
Eason, W. C. to Mary Sorrell 1-1-1873
Eatherly, J. R. to Amanda King Reynolds 1-27-1879 (1-29-1879)
Echols, J. B. to R. Candace Lane 1-19-1876
Echols, J. W. to M. F. Smith 12-26-1876 (12-27-1876)
Echols, Joseph W. to Malissie A. Mobley 11-8-1870 (11-9-1870)
Echols, N. to R. J. Bowen 1-27-1877 (1-28-1877)
Edge, George to Frances Douglass 1-23-1878 (no return)
Edney, Allen to Eliza Fumbank 9-23-1869 (no return)
Edney, B. F. to Martha A. Bizzle 1-29-1866 (no return)
Edwards, Barnabas to Martha (Mrs.) Faulkner 11-9-1872 (11-10-1872)
Edwards, G. R. to Susan L. Courtney 2-1-1864 (2-3-1864)
Edwards, James W. to Pocahontas Tansel 3-12-1866
Edwards, N. A. to S. J. Hall 12-21-1864 (no return)
Edwards, Thos. J. to Pricilla B. Brewer 2-6-1865 (2-7-1865)
Edwards, W. W. to Mattie McDavid 9-14-1870
Edwards, William to Nancy A. Swift 7-29-1870 (8-1-1870)
Elliott, Wm. to Mary Jane Hanks 11-30-1864 (no return)
Ellis, A. J. to R. A. Pace 12-18-1876 (12-21-1876)
Ellis, C. W. to Julia Coleman 1-27-1875 (1-28-1875)
Ellis, Edward to Mattie Woods 4-17-1872 (4-18-1872)
Ellis, F. G. to C. J. Nixon 3-2-1863 (3-4-1863)
Ellis, F. G. to Eliza J. Mills 12-1-1866 (12-2-1866)
Ellis, J. N. to Rebecca A. Hamilton 8-26-1868 (8-27-1868)
Ellis, J. T. to M. L. Ellis 2-2-1874 (2-3-1874)
Ellis, J. W. to M. J. Hamilton 2-15-1870 (2-16-1870)
Elmore, Wm. to Mary Hart 6-3-1863
Emerson, Balaam to Alice Huggins 10-25-1876 (no return)
Enoch, Henry to Eliza Jones 7-18-1868 (7-19-1868)
Enoch, W. S. to Rachel E. S. Graves 7-31-1867 (8-1-1867)
Enochs, Edmond to Angeline Wynne 8-19-1870 (no return)
Enochs, J. W. to Eliza A. Fuller 2-20-1861
Enochs, M. P. to Hellen Vaughan 9-22-1874
Enochs, Saml. to Jennie Bell 12-27-1871 (12-28-1871)
Enochs, Samuel to Lucinda Ledsinger 3-20-1873
Enscow, Jas. C. to Mary Ann Fedrick 4-27-1863
Espey, F. C. to May Tinsley 1-20-1875 (1-22-1875)
Espy, J. T. to Rhody J. Pinkston 7-24-1865
Espy, R. R. to Hilly (Mrs.) Brandon 9-23-1863 (no return)
Estes, F. M. to S. F. Phillips 10-13-1875
Ethridge, James P. to S. A. Williams 4-26-1873 (4-27-1873)
Eudaily, M. W. to Laura E. Simmons 6-30-1869 (no return)
Eudaily, William to Louisa Colvin 2-10-1868 (no return)
Eudaley, James T. to Mary B. Mays 11-19-1862
Eudaly, Jo to Jane Beaumont 1-5-1867
Evans, Henry to Martha Scallions 8-16-1867 (9-18-1867)
Evans, Henry to Senia Wright 2-25-1868 (no return)
Evans, J. N. to N. J. Davis 3-10-1863 (3-12-1863)
Evans, James to Matilda Ward 1-6-1869
Evans, Joseph H. to Sarah T. Duncan 4-21-1868 (4-23-1868)
Evans, L. H. to Sarah Reese 9-1-1874 (9-2-1874)
Evans, T. W. to C. F. Carroll 8-24-1869
Evans, W. T. to Sarah Carroll 12-27-1869 (12-29-1869)
Evans, Wallace to Harriet F. Raybern 8-6-1864 (no return)
Fain, R. S. to Bettie Smith 1-17-1872
Fain, Thomas M. to Laura Fuller 3-19-1878 (3-29-1878)
Falkner, H. to Sarah Ann Bull 1-8-1868 (no return)
Farmer, Benj. F. to Emily J. Parrish 11-6-1865
Farmer, J. C. to S. E. Salisbury 11-6-1876 (11-8-1876)
Farris, James M. to Louisa Gammons 4-29-1867 (no return)
Farrow, James to Lucy Crow 12-28-1870 (12-29-1870)
Faulkner, Amos to Martha Warpole 12-21-1863 (no return)
Faulkner, Lafayette to Cornelia O. Boland 4-3-1862
Fautner, David to Lavenia Gammons 8-16-1864 (no return)
Featherston, C. R. to S. E. Moore 9-30-1875 (no return)
Featherston, W. D. to S. A. Oneal 12-20-1865 (no return)
Fedrick, W. W. to Paralee White 5-5-1863 (5-6-1863)
Femzer, William to Nellie Mays 12-7-1872
Fenlen?, Allen to Sarah L. Hardie 9-5-1870 (9-6-1870)
Fenn, J. I. to Josie Smith 2-7-1872
Ferguson, A. T. to Lavina Dunevant 9-18-1879
Ferguson, Fillmore to Maggie Gauldin 9-29-1875
Ferguson, Frank to Jane S.? Fletcher 5-1-1865 (5-4-1865)
Ferguson, Jack to Mary Light 6-27-1866

Ferguson, Jo Green to M. J. Pate 11-30-1870 (nor return)
Ferguson, Lee to Margaret Mays 8-10-1874
Ferguson, Lee to Mary Fields 10-24-1876
Ferguson, Robt. H. to Palmira Spence 10-7-1863
Ferrell, J. M> to Sarah H. Sawyer 12-15-1870
Ferrell, S. A. to Mary J. Steen 2-18-1865 (no return)
Ferrill, Charles to Lucy Foster 12-24-1873 (12-25-1873)
Ferrill, D. P. to M. F. Wilkins 2-22-1866
Ferrill, J. D. to Mary Jane Floyd 7-3-1866 (7-5-1866)
Ferrill, Thomas C. to Addie Walker 1-11-1866
Fielder, Boston to Malinda Johnson 12-21-1868 (12-30-1868)
Fielder, James to Everett May 2-28-1874 (3-1-1874)
Fielder, Jim to Sarah Edwards 5-14-1880 (5-16-1880)
Fields, D. R. to Susan Pierce 9-14-1865
Fields, Henry to Louisa Clay 1-10-1866 (1-13-1866)
Fields, J. T. to Lucy S. Jennings 11-8-1876
Finch, George A. to Mary Badgett 12-31-1864
Findle, Hiram to Emiline Connell 11-19-1869 (no return)
Finley, Allen to Jane Weakly 12-7-1865
Finley, J. Buck to Donie Peery 1-13-1874
Finley, W. B. to Mattie E. James 12-29-1877 (12-30-1877)
Fish, James W. to Frances Crammer? 4-22-1873 (4-27-1873)
Fisher, Allen to Judy Fowlkes 5-13-1874 (5-15-1874)
Fisher, Thos. E. to M. E. (Mrs.) Maury? 9-1-1866 (9-2-1866)
Fitzgerald, George to Corella Brown 7-26-1880 (no return)
Fitzhugh, B. B. to Jane E. Brannon 12-25-1862
Fitzhugh, Bryant to Annariah Delph 3-26-1879
Fitzhugh, Bryant to Sallie Pate 11-18-1867
Fitzhugh, John to Sarah V. McCoy 10-20-1875
Fitzhugh, L. P. to E. J. McFarlin 10-8-1879 (10-9-1879)
Fitzhugh, T. H. to Mary Davis 8-12-1868
Fitzhugh, T. J. to Lou McCoy 2-28-1877 (2-29?-1877)
Fitzhugh, W. C. to J. M. Evans 1-9-1878 (1-10-1878)
Fitzhugh, W. C. to Mary J. Follis 9-29-1869 (9-30-1869)
Fizer, Ed to Jane Muzier? 4-5-1876
Fizer, Edward to Fannie Tipton 7-23-1874 (no return)
Fizer, Green to Alice Prichard 2-24-1875 (2-26-1875) B
Flack, Caleb to Martha Murray 3-11-1874
Flack, J. Y. to Margaret Bruce 5-25-1874 (5-26-1874)
Flack, P. J. to L. M. Wynne 12-17-1872
Fletcher, Richard to M. A. E. Hall 12-20-1865 (12-24-1865)
Flowers, John B. to Margaret A. E. Condor 1-13-1863 (no return)
Flowers, W. A. to S. M. Sorrell 3-19-1867
Floyd, John A. to Susan L. Wright 10-12-1861 (10-20-1861)
Floyd, Miles to Frances Smith 11-30-1865
Follis, W. J. to Julia Peel 10-31-1871
Folson, Daniel to Eliza A. McDaniel 8-26-1869 (no return)
Fonville, John to F. G. Thomas 1-8-1863 (1-12-1863)
Forbes, James to Tiressa Spoon 9-9-1876 (9-15-1876)
Ford, Charles to Angeline Wright 2-13-1867
Foreshee, John to M. C. House 5-28-1867
Forisher, Thomas V. to Marian A. Leetch 6-9-1864
Forshee, F. N. to Nancy Evans 5-13-1866
Forsyth, S. A. to Lucinda Brackin 12-28-1872 (1-7-1873)
Forsyth, W. S. to H. H. Johnson 6-11-1873 (6-15-1873)
Foster, A. J. to Elizabeth Eason 7-29-1865 (8-1-1865)
Foster, Dave to Eliza Walker 12-16-1876 (12-24-1876)
Foster, Henry to Sarah Walker 12-11-1880 (12-17-1880)
Foster, Jacob to Eliza Doyle 1-7-1868
Foster, Jacob to Martha Maggard 9-7-1870 (no return)
Foster, James A. to Montie Ferguson 5-11-1875
Foulkes, Charley to Phillip Pierce 10-30-1880 (10-31-1880)
Foust, Daniel to Hannah Sawyer 4-16-1872
Foust, Mik to Viney Stewart 3-5-1868
Foust, Wm. to Catherine Sawyer 10-23-1867 (no return)
Fowler, W. H. to Emma (Mrs.) Frazier 7-11-1874 (7-12-1874)
Fowlkes, Albert to Martha Southern 12-28-1866
Fowlkes, Base to Easter Neely 12-12-1871 (12-13-1871
Fowlkes, Calvin to Martha Saichern? 10-9-1876
Fowlkes, Daniel to Caroline Crow 10-11-1877
Fowlkes, David to Jane Fumbank 9-8-1866 (no return)
Fowlkes, Frank to Eliza Vinson 11-27-1875
Fowlkes, G. A. to Z. F. Ledsinger 4-4-1865 (4-6-1865)
Fowlkes, Geo. to Jane Corley 1-6-1876 (1-13-1876)
Fowlkes, Green to Amanda Sigrary? 2-14-1880 (2-16-1880)

Fowlkes, Green to Lucy Parker 11-18-1870 B
Fowlkes, H. A. to Z. F. Fowlkes 10-29-1872
Fowlkes, Isaac to Tennessee Light 4-17-1877
Fowlkes, J. A. to A. O. Ledsinger 6-3-1869
Fowlkes, James to Lucy Smith 12-1-1870 B
Fowlkes, Jerry to Lucinda Ferguson 10-4-1873
Fowlkes, Jerry to Mary Connell 11-28-1867
Fowlkes, Jery to Lou Barnett 3-28-1876 (no return)
Fowlkes, Jo to Lucinda Foster 9-22-1877 (9-25-1877)
Fowlkes, John to Laura Copeland 12-29-1880 (12-30-1880)
Fowlkes, Lewis to Rhoda Haskins 7-8-1871 (no return)
Fowlkes, Louis to Candice Fuller 2-6-1878 (2-7-1878)
Fowlkes, Manson to Eliza Davis 7-11-1878
Fowlkes, Matt to Judy Chitwood 12-22-1866 (12-24-1866)
Fowlkes, Mose to Adaline Wallae 9-4-1876
Fowlkes, Parsha L. to Scrappie E. Light 11-12-1874
Fowlkes, Taylor to Nancy Smith 8-14-1868 (8-16-1868)
Fowlkes, William to America Ferguson 6-29-1871
Fowlkes, jr., William P. to Sarah E. Connell 6-15-1863
Fowlks, Boss to Mollie Woods 9-25-1879
Fowlks, Martin to Joanna Wyatt 8-28-1879
Franklin, D. C. to N. B. Van Eaton 10-20-1879 (10-21-1879)
Franklin, John J. to Eliza J. Banks 1-15-1868
Franklin, T. H. to R. A. King 11-9-1869 (11-10-1869)
Frazier, Ephraim to Emma Stephenson 2-1-1868 (2-2-1868)
Frazier, Thos. J. to Mary J. Williamson 5-28-1867
Freedman, Ephram Hart to Parlee Curtis 2-9-1866 (no return)
Freeman, D. A. to N. T. Neely 9-2-1871 (9-3-1871)
Freeman, J. P. to Parilee Burnham 12-23-1873
Freeman, R. F. to Nancy A. F. Brown 12-5-1876
Freeman, Robert to Sallie Cothern 9-5-1870 (9-7-1870)
Frosh, Emanuel to Emily Culwell 2-17-1872 (2-18-1872)
Frosh, Manuel? to Rebecca Smith 3-2-1878 (3-3-1878)
Frost, A. M. to Alice McGarg 12-16-1878 (12-18-1878)
Frost, Wilson to Margaret Byrn 11-18-1867
Fryer, B. N. to M. A. Weakley 11-28-1864 (11-29-1864)
Fugate, James to Verginia Conyers 1-21-1865 (1-22-1865)
Fuller, D. E. to M. F. Tarrant 9-8-1869 (9-9-1869)
Fuller, G. R. to Emma Dickey 12-22-1873 (12-23-1873)
Fuller, Geo. B. to E. J. McGinnis 9-14-1863 (9-17-1863)
Fuller, J. W. to S. A. Crisp 9-7-1868 (9-8-1868)
Fuller, John T. to Mollie J. Justis 1-17-1877
Fuller, John to Mary F. Battle 4-3-1873
Fuller, Robert to Martha Duglas 10-31-1867 (12-5-1867)
Fuller, W. A. to Bettie C. Justis 1-17-1877
Fullerton, A. J. to Nancy J. Reed 9-22-1868
Fumbank, George to Martha Clark 3-1-1867 (3-2-1867)
Fumbanks, A. G. to Elizabeth F. Neely 12-4-1866
Fumbanks, Allen to Lowella Allen 7-5-1879 (7-6-1879)
Fumbanks, C. J. to Harriet Sawyer 2-1-1879 (2-2-1879)
Fumbanks, Jack to Sarah Becket 2-10-1869 (no return)
Fuzzle, Thos. H. to Amanda Nunn 8-1-1861
Fyker, Moses to Elizabeth Colman 1-31-1870 (no return)
Gallaher, L. to Elizabeth Garrison 10-25-1860 (no return)
Galliher, W. T. to M. J. Hinson 2-6-1872 (2-9-1872)
Gammon, Jas. to Fatitia Gammon 5-15-1863 (5-17-1863)
Gammon, John R. to Helen V. Moore 11-12-1866 (11-13-1866)
Gammons, Frank E. to Nancy A. Gammons 4-29-1867 (no return)
Gammons, Jack to Sarah A. Lattimore 1-13-1868
Gammons, Jack to Sarah A. Patterson 3-13-1868 (1?-14-1868)
Gannaway, Nilson to Rosette Belle 7-6-1876
Gannon, W. C. to Amanda Brown 12-6-1871 (12-7-1871)
Gant, John J. to Eliza E. Waits 12-22-1875 (12-23-1875)
Gardner, David A. to J. A. Payne 2-15-1870 (2-16-1870)
Gardner, Wm. to Bettie Parrish 11-12-1867 (11-13-1867)
Garner, Bethnell to M. J. Ellington 10-18-1864
Garret, Isaac to Sarah A. Morris 4-10-1867
Garrett, Alse to Fanie (Mrs.) Smith 9-12-1866 (9-13-1866)
Garrett, E. R. to M. L. Applewhite 2-1-1873
Gaskin, Roy to L. C. Hardican 3-5-1873 (3-10-1873)
Gaulden, J. W. to M. A. Jones 12-20-1864 (12-21-1864)
Gaulden, M. D. to Mollie Capell 9-29-1875 (9-30-1875)
Gaulden, Roland to Malissa Palmer 4-3-1878 (no return)
Gaulden, Roland to Margaret Pierce 3-4-1876 (4-12-1876) B
Gauldin, Willis to Lou Webb 1-21-1870 (1-31-1870)

Gentry, Charles C. to Elizabeth McFarland 12-14-1863
Gentry, Frank to Katie Dougherty 7-20-1865 (no return)
Gentry, John G. to Martha A. A. Young 3-7-1861
Gentry, John to Mary Key 8-22-1865 (8-23-1865)
Gerritt, William to Ann Butterworth 6-1-1867 (no return)
Ghann?, T. B. to Nancy Ann Burnham 9-18-1866 (9-19-1866)
Gibbs, James to Martha Hopkins 3-27-1869 (no return)
Gibbs, R. B. to A. C. Carter 12-7-1860 (11-9-1860)
Gibbs, Walter to Louisa Neal 2-27-1875 (2-28-1875)
Gibson, A. H. to A. G. Roney 11-1-1879 (11-5-1879)
Gibson, George to Lavanda Binkley 4-11-1866 (no return)
Gibson, Harberd to Emma Bradshaw 12-7-1880
Gibson, John to Polly Ann Simmons 2-3-1862 (2-6-1862)
Gibson, Richard P. to Amanda Thompson 8-17-1867 (no return)
Gibson, William H. to M. C. Cooper 5-23-1872 (no return)
Gill, T. N. to S. J. Jostling 3-12-1870 (3-13-1870)
Gilliam, Dell to Ann Fly 1-1-1874
Glassgow, W. J. to Rebecca Lovit 10-10-1871 (10-12-1871)
Gleason, Richd. to Louisa Fowlkes 12-29-1880 (not executed)
Gleason, Samuel L. to Sarah C. Griffin 10-11-1870 (no return)
Gleaves, J. M. to Tennessee Wright 12-21-1876
Gleaves, W. D. to Martha Blair 12-16-1874
Gleaves, Z. T. to H. D. Whittenton 12-20-1871 (12-21-1871)
Gleaves, Z. T. to M. W. Burnham 12-24-1874
Glidewell, W. L. to Amandy Ellis 12-7-1869 (12-8-1869)
Glisson, J. D. to Fannie Thurmond 12-23-1876 (1-4-1877)
Goatley, A. J. to M. J. Baley 7-14-1860 (7-17-1860)
Goforth, Alfred to Mary C. Cowell 9-27-1860
Goforth, Jeff to Amanda Smith 8-5-1879 (8-7-1879)
Gold, J. M. to Missouri Pierce 7-24-1872
Golden, R. T. to L. Evaline Wallan 8-22-1866 (8-23-1866)
Gooch, G. R. to Nancy Todd 7-26-1865 (7-27-1865)
Gooch, Henry A. to Lucinda S. Cobb 1-30-1861 (1-31-1861)
Gooch, W. H. to Marissa Sawyer 12-20-1869
Goodloe, A. H. to Mary W. Cunningham 9-27-1871
Goodloe, M. H. to H. E. Thacker 9-5-1870 (no return)
Goodlow, C. A. to Sallie P. Ward 5-14-1868 (5-16-1868)
Goodman, O. B. to Mary E. Bell 10-19-1860 (no return)
Goodrich, James H. to M. Thompson 7-6-1870
Goodrich, John to Sarah F. Skepper 12-27-1864 (no return)
Goodwin, J. H. to Lizzie V. Goodwin 1-26-1869 (1-28-1869)
Goodwin, W. T. to E. C. Howell? 1-10-1870 (1-12-1870)
Gordan, Jessee to Elizabeth Perry 11-9-1870
Gordon, T. C. to Kate Latta? 6-24-1879 (6-25-1879)
Gowan, M. N. to Pinckney A. McCoy 1-2-1877 (1-4-1877)
Grace, J. C. to Sallie Chrisman 2-8-1877
Grace, Robt. to Elsie Palmer 5-23-1877 (5-24-1877)
Graham, Ben to Elva Foust 11-28-1878
Graham, T. J. to Winnie E. McFarland 10-31-1874
Grant, H. T. to Maggie E. Ledsinger 9-2-1873
Graves, George W. S. to Eliza H. Enoch 7-31-1867 (8-1-1867)
Gray, J. J. to C. J. McCracken 11-2-1870 (11-4-1870)
Gray, J. L. to Martha Ann Redding 11-22-1865 (11-23-1865)
Gray, Jim to Ann Eliza Winchester 10-17-1877 (10-20-1877)
Grayson, Armstead to Frankie Jones 7-4-1876
Grayson, Armstead to Liza Stricklin 4-2-1867
Green, A. M. to Mary J. Hufstetler 6-22-1874 (6-23-1874)
Green, Bob to Luvena Reddick 2-1-1870 (no return)
Green, D. L. to E. M. Summers 12-22-1873
Green, David to Amanda Williams 12-21-1866 (12-22-1866)
Green, E. H. to Ellen J. Kirk 9-6-1860
Green, J. R. to S. J. Blankenship 11-24-1866 (11-25-1866)
Green, James C. to S. E. Hedden 11-18-1862 (11-19-1862)
Green, James R. to F. J. White 12-6-1875 (12-7-1875)
Green, James T. to E. S. Shackleton 6-26-1875 (6-27-1875)
Green, Jesse A. to Sophia E. Scobey 8-1-1877
Green, John N. to M. E. Green 11-11-1875
Green, John to Mollie McKee 1-2-1869 (1-3-1869)
Green, King to Jane Sudberry 1-1-1878
Green, Martin A. to Jamima E. McNeil 12-3-1872
Green, Noah to M. J. Cribbs 12-1-1874
Green, Noah to S. E. (Mrs.) Starrett 3-13-1873
Green, R. T. to Celia A. Dillon 2-5-1874
Green, Thomas to Margaret Young 10-18-1869 (no return)
Greer, C. W. to Sarah Patterson 1-13-1874 (1-18-1874)

Greer, Franklin to Sarah A. Haynes 10-11-1862 (10-12-1862)
Greer, S. A. to Sarah Jane Woods 9-16-1868 (9-17-1868)
Gregory, J. T. to M. L. McCorkle 5-24-1864 (5-25-1864)
Gregory, Wm. C. to Mary C. Grier 2-27-1865 (3-1-1865)
Gregson, P. E. to M. S. Milam 5-4-1871
Griffin, Henry to Louisa Griffin 12-27-1866
Griffin, J. R. to L. J. Watson 9-3-1872 (9-5-1872)
Griffin, John R. to M. L. Lucas 9-3-1867 (no return)
Griffin, T. E. to D. A. Morgan 1-23-1878 (1-24-1878)
Griffin, Thos. J. to Elizabeth V. Garrett 12-20-1870 (no return)
Griffin, W. J. to Elizabeth Warren 11-7-1866 (no return)
Grigsby, Robert to Lizzie Buck 10-8-1868 (no return)
Grills, A. J. to L. E. Gregory 11-14-1871
Grimes, H. F. to Nannie Bradshaw 12-15-1877 (12-19-1877)
Grimm, Amos to Ann Turnage 4-7-1877 (4-9-1877)
Grimm, Amos to Ella Wynne 1-3-1874
Grimm, Edmund to Amanda Douglass 2-19-1873 (2-20-1873)
Grimm, Elijah to Bettie Grimm 1-10-1876 (1-12-1876)
Grimm, Gay to Mourning Grimm 9-26-1877 (no return)
Grimm, Guy to Sallie Fields 3-18-1873 (3-19-1873)
Grimm, Harry to Harriet Tucker 1-3-1872 (1-4-1872)
Grimm, Harry to Martha Harris 6-30-1876
Grimm, Jessup? to Nancy Evans 11-14-1877
Grimm, Ned to Bettie Doyle 12-21-1878 (12-25-1878) B
Groom, Thomas to Sarah A. Crichfield 1-19-1878 (1-23-1878)
Groves, P. W. to Mary A. Swift 11-13-1863 (11-18-1863)
Grugett, M. L. to M. E. Vails 12-16-1874
Grugett?, A. J. to M. A. Wherry 1-15-1874
Guill, John H. to Provie E. Phillips 6-3-1868 (6-4-1868)
Guinn, Jesse to Jane Jackson 1-1-1879 (1-2-1879)
Gwaltney, D. M. to Sarah C. Holland 5-13-1861 (no return)
Gwaltney, W. T. to Stacy A. R. Fuller 4-28-1869 (no return)
Hafford, L. C. to Mary F. Prichard 9-14-1876
Hale, Daniel to Ellen Bradshaw 2-12-1880
Haley, Robt. A. to Mary E. Harrell 10-17-1860
Haley, S. F. to M. S. Fielder 10-26-1867 (no return)
Hall, A. F. to R. F. Leonard 1-9-1878 (1-10-1878)
Hall, A. J. to Jane Finch 8-16-1873 (8-18-1873)
Hall, Henry to Lean Atkins 1-15-1877 (no return)
Hall, Henry to Martha Williams 3-25-1870 (no return)
Hall, J. L. to S. J. Davis 5-9-1878 (5-12-1878)
Hall, J. M. to Susan C. Minton 7-10-1861 (6-11-1861)
Hall, J. S. to E. F. Smith 12-7-1868 (12-8-1868)
Hall, J. W. to E. L. Featherston 3-8-1870 (no return)
Hall, J. W. to Matilda J. Curtis 12-15-1873 (12-18-1873)
Hall, James H. to Adalade Bradshaw 12-14-1864 (12-15-1864)
Hall, James R. to Mary F. Green 11-17-1868 (11-18-1868)
Hall, James to Julia Ann Smith 1-29-1872 (no return)
Hall, John P. to Columbia E. Laster 4-11-1877 (4-12-1877)
Hall, M. A. to Lovey A. Turner 1-25-1869 (no return)
Hall, Seth to Martha J. Courtley 5-18-1864
Hall, Solomon S. to Lenora J. Thetford 3-25-1868 (no return)
Hall, T. W. to Margaret E. Dickey 1-22-1868 (no return)
Hall, Thomas E. to Sarah Killet 2-16-1871
Hall, W. A. to Caifa? Frances Akin 2-25-1869 (no return)
Hall, W. H. to L. C. Brewer 1-29-1877 (no return)
Hall, W. M. to Jane Reynolds 8-1-1871 (8-2-1871)
Hall, Warren to Rebecca Hampton 11-10-1877 (no return)
Hall, Wells W. to Frances Salsberry 1-27-1865 (1-28-1865)
Halliburton, R. H. to Lou Taylor 8-31-1870 (9-1-1870)
Hallum, Morris to Sudie Ray 8-26-1879 (8-28-1879)
Hambrick, F. M. to Tabitha Fowlkes 11-15-1866 (no return)
Hamilton, A. B. to M. J. Hare 2-6-1871 (2-7-1871)
Hamilton, J. J. to V. A. Pitts 1-22-1879 (1-23-1879)
Hamilton, M. C. to Mollie F. Moore 12-18-1876 (12-21-1876)
Hamilton, Ransom to Jane Singleton 7-2-1870 (no return)
Hamlet, Henry to Amarilla Chitwood 4-14-1866 (no return)
Hampton, Albert to Sarah Jane Pritchett 4-16-1870 (4-17-1870)
Hampton, J. L. to Bettie J. Stewart 2-26-1869 (no return)
Hampton, W. H. to Alice Vinson 12-25-1872
Hampton, W. L. to Louisa Jackson 7-1-1867 (7-2-1867)
Hampton, Wade to Martha Johnson 1-29-1877
Hamton, T. L. to Cincinnati Anthony 8-25-1869
Hand, Richard to Hattie Duncans 7-3-1878 (no return)
Harbison, George to Lavina Bryant 11-13-1875 (11-14-1875)

Hardican, J. E. to Mary F. Williams 8-17-1869 (no return)
Hardin, J. G. to S. A. Hollis 5-9-1878 (5-12-1878)
Hardin, John to Mollie Parker 2-12-1869 (no return)
Hardison, J. H. to M. L. Miller 8-29-1876 (8-31-1876)
Hark, M. J. to Mary G. Wood 11-8-1877
Harmon, A. C. to Sarah E. Aiken 8-30-1870 (8-31-1870)
Harmon, B. H. to Lizzie Davis 11-5-1867 (11-7-1867)
Harmon, John H. to Elizabeth Davidson 12-17-1867 (12-18-1867)
Harold, G. G. to Lucinda Reynolds 2-12-1869 (no return)
Harper, Alfred M. to Lucy A. Tucker 11-5-1867 (no return)
Harper, G. W. to Mrs. Thedford 7-22-1874 (no return)
Harper, J. W. to Famie Rudder 10-16-1878
Harper, Robt. L. to Mary Frazier 11-19-1860 (11-27-1860)
Harpole, George D. to Eliza A. Dodd 8-4-1868 (8-6-1868)
Harrell, A. T. to Ida M. Ferguson 12-23-1867
Harrell, Dossey to Lucy E. Tucker 12-22-1862 (12-23-1862)
Harrell, J. K. P. to Sue Doyle 6-16-1868 (no return)
Harrell, Joseph to Malinda J. Goodman 7-22-1861 (no return)
Harrell, Knight? to Malinda Beckett 2-23-1878 (no return)
Harrell, R. G. to Sue Bell 12-19-1866 (12-20-1866)
Harrington, Rewben J. to L. A. Neal 11-28-1876 (11-29-1876)
Harris, Alex to Emma Light 2-19-1880 (no return)
Harris, Andrew to Bettie Gauldin 9-30-1868
Harris, E. G. to M. E. Jordan 10-15-1879 (10-21-1879)
Harris, Granville to Nora Holmes 12-22-1880 (12-23-1880)
Harris, Isaac A. to Jennie Tucker 12-24-1873 (12-25-1873)
Harris, James to Nancy Ann Campbell 9-22-1877 (9-23-1877) B
Harris, James to Parthena Parker 3-5-1874
Harris, Jesse to Martha Jones 7-18-1868
Harris, Jim to Millie Mitchell 11-1-1879
Harris, John C. to Mittie E. Drave 10-18-1866 (no return)
Harris, Jordan to Jane Douglass 9-2-1876 (9-3-1876)
Harris, R. D. to L. M. Haskins 12-21-1869 (no return)
Harris, R. E. to Mary J. Winfred 12-8-1869 (12-9-1869)
Harris, R. to Eliza Palmore 5-18-1871 (5-21-1871)
Harris, Richard to Susan Thornton 1-30-1877 (1-31-1877)
Harris, T. J. to Frances Michaels 1-4-1877
Harris, Tex to Ellen Parker 9-29-1870 (10-1-1870)
Harris, Thomas to _____ 8-24-1866 (no return)
Harris, W. D. to Cyntha Duncen 1-18-1868 (1-22-1868)
Harris, Wm. to Lizzie Paul 2-19-1876 (4-15-1876)
Harrison, A. C. to E. J. McKnight 12-15-1875 (12-17-1875)
Harrison, Henry L. to Frances C. Dunevant 12-3-1878 (12-4-1878)
Harrison, J. H. to L. E. Parker 7-28-1875 (7-29-1875)
Harrison, J. W. to M. R. McAlilley 2-26-1879 (2-29-1879)
Harrison, Joseph to Narcissa Vire 5-15-1866 (5-16-1866)
Harrison, W. H. to Angeline Beaver 1-25-1878 (1-27-1878)
Harrison, W. H. to Jane Williams 10-14-1862
Harrison, Wm. H. to Martha Faulkner 10-26-1870 (10-27-1870)
Hart, Andrew to Sarah C. Turner 4-16-1860
Hart, Andrew to Sarah Jane Ferrell 10-11-1870 (10-12-1870)
Hart, H. C. to D. L. Pope 2-15-1876
Hart, P. W. to Nancy A. Thurmond 9-11-1873
Harton, John W. to Nannie Wheeler 7-31-1869 (8-1-1869)
Harton, M. L. to Lula Landis 12-4-1877
Harvell, L. C. to Puss Giles 3-7-1865 (3-8-1865)
Harvey, T. J. to Sallie Earle 12-30-1878 (12-31-1878)
Harwell, Abner to Martha F. Craig 5-28-1867
Harwell, H. L. to Elizabeth Snow 12-21-1875 (12-22-1875)
Harwell, Neal S. to Verginia Moore 1-17-1871 (1-18-1871)
Harwell, W. F. to Sally Malory 3-17-1865 (3-21-1865)
Haskin, Lafayette to Lucinda Harris 12-30-1878 (1-18-1879)
Haskins, A. B. (Dr.) to M. A. Tucker 5-19-1873 (no return)
Haskins, Alex to Eliza Daugherty 3-15-1877 (no return)
Haskins, Ben to Lucinda Lanier 12-25-1877 (12-26-1877)
Haskins, Haf to Fannie Prichard 8-16-1873 (8-17-1873)
Haskins, Henry to Emma Ledsinger 9-24-1872 (9-26-1872)
Haskins, J. C. to Ann E. Douglass 11-12-1866 (11-13-1866)
Haskins, Richard to Martha Harris 8-19-1874 (8-20-1874)
Haskins, Sam to Amelia Swift 4-30-1874 (5-1-1874)
Hathway, James A. to Martha F. Holland 11-27-1862 (11-30-1862)
Hawkes, J. S. to Adrienne Swift 11-21-1878
Hawkins, E. E. to Harriet L. Ferguson 2-12-1867 (2-13-1867)
Hawkins, G. W. to A. A. Ferguson 10-6-1868 (no return)
Hawkins, S. P. to Sarah A. Hardin 4-5-1870 (4-6-1870)

Hay, G. T. to Rebecca J. Murray 3-9-1874 (3-11-1874)
Hay, H. D. to Mary Bell 7-19-1871 (7-20-1871)
Hay, John H. to Frances E. Taylor 9-13-1867 (no return)
Hayes, Will R. (Dr.) to Sallie Fakes 12-18-1878
Haynes, Isaac N. to Mary T. McKee 8-20-1873 (8-21-1873)
Haynes, Joseph D. to Julia Strawn 11-20-1860 (11-21-1860)
Haynes, W. W. to Eliza C. Haynes 5-3-1870
Haynes, W. W. to Melissa J. Scoby 11-19-1866 (no return)
Haynes, W. W. to P. A. Scoby 12-30-1869 (no return)
Hays, W. P. to M. C. Daugherty 6-25-1879 (6-27-1879)
Hays, W. R. (Dr.) to Louella Chamblin 12-9-1874
Hearn, W. G. to J. A. Trout 6-5-1873
Heath, A. J. to Melissa H. Kirk 11-15-1869 (11-16-1869)
Heath, Danl. W. to Martha V. Kirk 12-21-1864 (12-22-1864)
Heath, Levi T. to Deller M. Self 4-6-1863 (4-8-1863)
Heath, O. to Martha Manning 8-17-1867 (8-18-1867)
Heddin, A. C. to M. F. Fields 5-27-1869 (no return)
Heddin, Elias to Sarah E. Lyon 8-3-1866 (8-7-1866)
Heddin, S. A. to Mollie L. Wright 10-5-1869 (no return)
Helen, William R. to Nancy Espy 3-20-1862
Hellums, Henry to Amanda Bone 3-22-1873 (3-29-1873)
Henderson, E. A. to M. F. (Mrs.) Callahan 8-31-1874 (no return)
Henderson, John to Altonetta Echols 3-17-1866 (3-22-1866)
Henderson, Rufus to Julia Frost 9-7-1867 (9-12-1867)
Henderson, Rufus to Malvina Tumage 3-16-1871 (3-19-1871)
Henderson, T. J. to Earnestine Rodgers 12-23-1870 (12-25-1870)
Henderson, Yancy to Patsy Wood 2-26-1870 (no return)
Hendricks, A. C. to S. A. Lambert 9-21-1875 (9-30-1875)
Hendricks, George W. to Amanda S. A. Hood 2-10-1864 (no return)
Hendricks, H. C. to Tempe Bean 12-8-1873 (12-9-1873)
Hendricks, M. R. to Sallie Pierce 3-23-1874 (3-24-1874)
Hendricks, W. H. to Mary M. Headden 7-24-1877
Hendrix, W. H. to Lucy A. Doak 4-16-1879 (4-17-1879)
Henley, James A. to Ann (Mrs.) Dillahunt 12-19-1877
Henry, A. W. to Martha A. Foster 11-22-1865
Henry, J. H. to Rebecca Lumley 1-1-1872 (1-4-1872)
Henson, Isaac to Susan Brown 1-15-1870 (1-16-1870)
Herrin, Richmond to Martha C. Pace 10-4-1872 (10-6-1872)
Herrin, Samuel to Phoeby Thompson 9-26-1866 (no return)
Herring, Chas. F. to C. L. Sumerow 10-27-1875
Herron, Joseph to Mary Borden 3-21-1876
Hester, James T. to Susan J. Aiken 9-5-1860
Heughan, W. W. to Mattie Landrum 7-27-1877 (8-2-1877)
Hicks, Austin to Rebecca Bowen 12-31-1872
Hicks, Irvin to Elizabeth Robertson 2-22-1878 (2-23-1878)
Hicks, Irvin to Henrietta Robertson 8-25-1877 (no return)
Hicks, Jesse to Parthina Williams 1-9-1867 (1-10-1867)
Hicks, Jo to Louisa Wynne 3-2-1867
Hicks, Monroe to Amanda Dillingham 10-10-1878 (no return)
Hicks, Wiley M. to Caroline Smith 12-24-1866 (12-25-1866)
Higdon, M. H. to Mattie McCrackin 2-14-1874 (2-18-1874)
Higgason, J. T. to Frances Hurt 1-13-1868 (1-15-1868)
Hill, Charley to E. J. Atkins 8-25-1873 (no return)
Hill, George W. to Sarah E. Fuller 11-13-1866 (11-15-1866)
Hill, J. G. to Ann Bessent 12-24-1873
Hill, James to Mahala Williams 1-14-1879 (1-16-1879)
Hill, Louis to Mahulda Porter 5-19-1880 (5-20-1880)
Hill, R. T. to M. L. Griffin 12-21-1870 (12-22-1870)
Hill, William A. to Mary A. Blankenship 12-14-1863 (12-15-1863)
Hines, F. T. to Rebecca Garner 9-19-1870 (9-21-1870)
Hines, W. S. to Frankie (Mrs.) Hall 2-12-1873
Hinton, R. L. to S. B. Montrose 8-22-1860
Hobbs, Emmett to Katie Guinn 1-1-1879 (1-15-1879)
Hobday, B. P. to M. E. Kent 2-29-1876 (3-1-1876)
Hobday, S. M. to Nettie Boone 10-21-1873
Hobday, T. M. to M. E. Kirk 12-18-1876 (12-19-1876)
Hobday, W. R. to M. C. Hicks 11-25-1874
Hobson, W. O. to Nancy E. Wood 4-18-1874 (4-19-1874)
Hodge, H. C. to Barbara F. Via 1-22-1878 (1-24-1878)
Hodge, M. D. to Salina Parrish 12-31-1872 (1-1-1873)
Hodge, Wm. A. to Sarah L. Lanier 10-17-1876
Holland, G. W. to Susan Austin 12-25-1865 (12-27-1865)
Holland, J. K. P. to Ellen Ferrill 8-19-1869
Holland, James to Ruth Ann Kenady 1-14-1865 (1-15-1865)

Holland, LaFayette to E. A. Worship (Bishop?) 12-21-1878 (12-24-1878)
Holland, W. F. to M. J. King 11-18-1867 (11-19-1867)
Holland, W. J. to Kisann Prichard 2-1-1865 (2-2-1865)
Hollingsworth, L. H. to M. J. Palmer 1-31-1877 (2-1-1877)
Hollinsworth, Henry H. to Fannie B. Thetford 5-13-1876 (5-14-1876)
Hollis, Alfred to Chanie Light 12-5-1878 (no return)
Holt, J. C. to M. C. Templeton 4-3-1865 (4-5-1865)
Hood, M. W. to Nancy Smith 2-24-1877 (2-25-1877)
Hood, W. H. to M. S. Telford 3-3-1862 (3-5-1862)
Hooks, J. A. to Sarah E. Neeley 12-18-1871 (12-21-1871)
Hooks, Lewis to Betsy Chrisman 3-4-1867
Horton, A. to M. Amanda Todd 11-26-1874
Horton, Alex to Ella Harris 6-6-1874 (6-11-1874) B
Horton, Thomas to Annie Fowlkes 1-13-1874 (1-14-1874)
Horton, Wm. to Mariah Menzies 9-14-1868 (9-17-1868)
Hoskins, W. M. to Mary Reed 1-17-1874 (1-18-1874)
House, James to Mary M. Prichard 4-16-1867 (no return)
House, S. J. to Josephine Campbell 9-9-1876 (9-10-1876)
Howard, Booker to Sallie Harris 4-2-1873 (3?-2-1873)
Howard, Dock to Amanda Clark 1-10-1870 (no return)
Howard, James to Nancy Hurley 2-1-1870
Howard, Polk to Josephine Sanders 12-22-1876 (1-24-1877)
Howard, Polk to Kisa Walker 1-26-1870 (no return)
Howard, Polk to Millie Harris 12-26-1872
Howard, Stephen S. to Mary Jane Wright 12-9-1863 (no return)
Howard, Stephen to Mary A. Howard 4-21-1860 (4-24-1860)
Howard, Thomas to Mollie Connell 6-3-1871 (6-4-1871)
Howard, Wesley to Malinda Fowlkes 5-26-1871 (5-25?-1871)
Howe, J. S. to Abba Jones 6-22-1866 (6-24-1866)
Howell, A. W. to Elvie G. Yancey 10-1-1878 (10-2-1878)
Howell, John T. to Mary P. Pierce 8-19-1867
Howell, W. C. to R. T. Craig 10-1-1867 (10-2-1867)
Howell, W. H. to Frances Perry 9-3-1869 (9-5-1869)
Howell, Wm. to Dollie Pierce 5-24-1869
Howell?, Dvid to Marian Willis 8-17-1861 (no return)
Hudgens, Wm. to Sarah Fowlkes 5-22-1880
Hudson, E. D. to Martha A. Jones 5-8-1877 (5-14-1877)
Hudson, Thomas to Betty Evans 1-5-1867 (no return)
Hudspeth, R. S. to Elizabeth Slayton 12-25-1867 (12-26-1867)
Huey, J. K. (Dr.) to Sally James 4-7-1869
Hugely, Wm. to Lucy A. Parnell 2-19-1866 (2-20-1866)
Hughes, Fountain E. to Lucy E. Finch 11-12-1863
Huguley, Saml. E. to Lucy E. Scoby 12-13-1864 (12-14-1864)
Huie?, Joseph G. to Frances C. Franklin 7-28-1868 (7-29-1868)
Humbles, J. L. to V. A. Kinley 12-18-1872 (12-19-1872)
Humes, J. A. to Ella Schoolcraft? 12-31-1870 (1-1-1871)
Humphreys, Thomas to Millie Haskins 2-10-1874 (2-12-1874)
Hunt, Thomas to Laura McGaughy 3-19-1874
Hunt, William to R. P. Oakley 9-18-1878 (9-19-1878)
Hunter, J. F. to M. A. Shelton 10-28-1875
Hunter, William T. to Z. S. Pate 11-18-1872 (11-19-1872)
Hurd, James R. to Amanda Hamilton 11-2-1869 (11-4-1869)
Hurt, Geo. T. to Mollie E. Hooper 2-20-1873
Hurt, George T. to Mary E. McKnight 7-28-1874
Hurt, Henry I. to Lucretia Bell 10-24-1870 B
Hutson, William C. to Mattie Williamson 1-9-1877 (1-10-1877)
Ivie, George W. to Mary N. Johnson 2-11-1867 (2-13-1867)
Jackson, Andrew to Charity Martin 3-21-1878
Jackson, Andrew to Sophia Smith 10-12-1870
Jackson, Charles to Evaline James 11-23-1877 (11-24-1877)
Jackson, Ed to Jane Fox 7-28-1875 (7-29-1875)
Jackson, Elisha to Jane Williams 4-17-1872 (4-18-1872)
Jackson, Elisha to Martha Gauldin 12-25-1871 (no return)
Jackson, G. W. to Jane Wilkins 6-10-1876 (6-11-1876)
Jackson, George to Mary Ann Herron 9-20-1860
Jackson, Isaac to Margaret Herron 4-28-1860 (4-29-1860)
Jackson, J. D. to Paralee Brant 2-8-1871 (2-10-1871)
Jackson, J. M. to Annie White 4-29-1868 (no return)
Jackson, J. M. to Hettie Bunks 5-29-1863 (6-2-1863)
Jackson, J. R. to Donie Yates 10-3-1870 (no return)
Jackson, L. H. to T. C. Leath 1-11-1873 (1-12-1873)
Jackson, S. K. to Susan P. Howell 12-14-1870 (12-15-1870)
Jackson, T. M. to L. J. Fuller 12-19-1874 (12-20-1874)
Jackson, William to M. C. Fuller 2-15-1865 (2-16-1865)

Jackson, William to Mariah Parks 11-16-1872 (11-18-1872)
James, David C. to Mollie Gillis 1-16-1867
James, Isham to Lethe E. Golden 8-24-1868 (no return)
James, J. M. to E. P. Reed 4-11-1871 (4-12-1871)
James, Jenning? to Fanny Nash 1-22-1867 (1-20?-1867)
James, John M. to Eliza J. Lankford 4-15-1877
James, John to Nancy Ann Pennington 6-22-1878 (6-23-1878)
James, Madison to Adelphi A. Lankford 12-25-1869 (12-26-1869)
James, Wm. to Elizabeth Hurley 5-18-1863 (5-20-1863)
Jamey?, Geo. W. to Mary Bobett 4-12-1873 (4-16-1873)
Jaycocks, J. T. to A. S. Bettis 4-25-1866 (no return)
Jefferson, Redmond to Eliza White 4-18-1872 (4-22-1872)
Jelks, Solomon to Eliza Moody 10-26-1869 (no return)
Jenkins, Elisha to Margaret Fullerton 12-28-1870 (12-29-1870)
Jennings, J. B. to Laura Jackson 10-23-1868 (no return)
Jennings, W. J. to Julia G. Bradford 8-24-1868 (8-25-1868)
Jetton, R. L. to L. B. Lovett 9-2-1879 (9-10-1879)
Jetton, William A. to Sallie C. Warren 11-23-1874 (11-24-1874)
Jobes, W. H. to Mary J. Vaughan 10-17-1874 (10-18-1874)
Johnson, Albert to M. J. Parker 12-25-1878 (12-26-1878)
Johnson, Allen to Clarissa Wynne 1-4-1873 (no return)
Johnson, Andrew to Alice Murray 1-10-1877 (1-11-1877)
Johnson, Andrew to Annie Smith 7-12-1873 (7-13-1873)
Johnson, B. A. to Sarah J. Kerley 10-9-1860
Johnson, C. G. to A. C. King 7-2-1866 (7-3-1866)
Johnson, C. G. to Mollie Pugh 2-2-1875
Johnson, E. R. to Fannie Eudaly 12-22-1875
Johnson, E. to Elzira Whittenton 8-2-1869 (12-28-1869)
Johnson, Eli to M. W. Frith 12-23-1868 (12-24-1868)
Johnson, Francis M. to Myra V. P. Fielder 9-8-1863 (no return)
Johnson, Geo. T. to Fannie Hurt 11-29-1877
Johnson, George to Emma Light 9-16-1870
Johnson, H. N. to Nancy A. White 10-15-1866 (no return)
Johnson, H. W. to Charlotte A. Christie 1-30-1869 (no return)
Johnson, Henry to Mein? Smith 11-30-1878 (12-1-1878)
Johnson, Isaac to Martha Beard 1-19-1872 (1-20-1872)
Johnson, J. H. to Elizabeth Stewart 6-17-1878
Johnson, J. J. to M. A. White 12-2-1868 (12-3-1868)
Johnson, James to Amanda Wyrick 12-4-1875
Johnson, James to Eliza Fowlkes 10-5-1880
Johnson, John A. to Elvira A. Wilson 1-28-1863 (no return)
Johnson, R. R. to Anna Douglas 6-30-1866 (no return)
Johnson, Richard to Sarah E. Brotherton 7-1-1868 (7-19-1868)
Johnson, S. F. to Martha Collins 1-3-1873 (1-5-1873)
Johnson, S. H. to Malinda E. Rauls 7-28-1868 (7-30-1868)
Johnson, S. L. to Angeline Morris 11-28-1876 (11-29-1876)
Johnson, S. T. to Bettie Street 5-30-1879 (no return)
Johnson, Sam to Martha Whittenton 6-3-1869 (no return)
Johnson, Sherrod to Mary E. Fuller 12-29-1869 (12-30-1869)
Johnson, Thomas to Artelia Light 9-9-1875
Johnson, Thos. H. to Amanda M. Potter 12-21-1867 (12-22-1867)
Johnson, Tom to Eliza Whittington 2-19-1868 (no return)
Johnson, W. M. to Polk Lanier 1-1-1872 (no return)
Johnston, J. F. to Pettie Light 1-27-1869 (1-28-1869)
Jones, Albert to Myra Douglas 5-17-1867 (5-18-1867)
Jones, Albert to Sallie Harris 10-10-1877 (no return)
Jones, Albert to Sarah Snow 8-13-1860 (no return)
Jones, Anderson to Emma Crow 1-2-1879
Jones, Anderson to Rilla Jane Miller 3-30-1876
Jones, Burril to Caroline Cole 1-11-1867
Jones, Butten to Nancy Lacy 8-13-1860
Jones, C. D. to S. E. Sanford 8-18-1869 (8-19-1869)
Jones, Calven to Betcy Ann Baker 2-16-1865 (no return)
Jones, Calvin to M. E. Powers 3-8-1870
Jones, David F. to Sarah F. White 1-16-1863 (no return)
Jones, David to Julia Ann McGinnis 12-15-1866 (12-22-1866)
Jones, E. J. V. to Sallie Applewhite 1-23-1878
Jones, Etheldred to Anne Childress 10-7-1862 (10-8-1862)
Jones, G. F. to N. E. Stults 1-25-1876 (1-26-1876)
Jones, George W. to Sallie Swain 9-21-1871
Jones, Granville to Lizzie Bradford 9-8-1870 (no return)
Jones, Henry to Mary K. Dudley 9-2-1873
Jones, Henry to Retta Horton 10-14-1876 (10-15-1876)
Jones, J. A. to Mary E. Cleek 2-20-1871 (2-26-1873)
Jones, J. A. to Sarah Bullard 10-14-1869

Jones, J. M. to Lizzie Cook ?-19-1878 (with Nov 1878)
Jones, J. P. to Katie Yearwod 5-1-1869 (5-4-1869)
Jones, J. W. to Jane Manning 4-10-1861 (4-11-1861)
Jones, J. W. to Tempy A. Baily 5-14-1868 (5-15-1868)
Jones, Jack to Priscilla Purdle 11-13-1875 (no return)
Jones, James to Hannah Cambell 10-13-1866 (no return)
Jones, James to Martha Ward 9-2-1870 (9-6-1870)
Jones, Jeremiah to S. W. Harrold 2-20-1867 (no return)
Jones, Jo to Agg Fowlkes 5-8-1869 (no return)
Jones, Joel to Elizabeth Cheny 2-23-1864 (no return)
Jones, John to Margaret Robertson 9-6-1867
Jones, L. R. to M. J. Campbell 10-20-1879 (10-21-1879)
Jones, Monroe to Vena Pearce 12-28-1869 (no return)
Jones, Nash to Fanny Clark no date (1-1-1867)
Jones, Nash to Matilda Scroggins 7-24-1875 (7-25-1875) B
Jones, O. A. to Susan J. Johnson 1-28-1868 (1-29-1868)
Jones, Polk to Louisa Fowlkes 7-6-1867 (7-7-1867)
Jones, Reddick to Catharine Baker 5-16-1861
Jones, Richard to Adaline Baxter 7-18-1870 (8-1-1870)
Jones, Robt. to Lou Jackson 4-24-1877 (no return)
Jones, Rupert to Roda Pierce 10-14-1870
Jones, Sam to Mariah Bell 12-29-1879 (no return)
Jones, Samuel J. to Louisa A. Harris 10-26-1869 (no return)
Jones, Sevraves to Isabel Scobey 1-29-1873 (1-30-1873)
Jones, Thomas to Eliza Becket 12-25-1879 (12-26-1879)
Jones, Thomas to Mollie Fowlkes 1-13-1876
Jones, Tobe to Fannie Clark 1-9-1878 (1-10-1878)
Jones, W. H. to Katie C. James 12-22-1874 (12-23-1874)
Jones, W. L. to Elizabeth Anthony 12-22-1869 (12-23-1869)
Jones, W. L. to Lizzie Pace 9-19-1877 (9-20-1877)
Jones, W. N. to Charlotta Ellis 12-15-1870
Jordan, Callis to Nielli Light 12-16-1874 (12-17-1874) B
Jordan, Henry to Leanor Gause 2-28-1868 (no return)
Jordan, John to Mary Ledsinger 5-14-1878 (5-15-1878)
Jordan, W. W. to F. E. Pierce 12-4-1871
Jordan, Wm. to Nannie Hudson 3-26-1880
Kay, C. N. to Nancy A. Tague 2-8-1872
Keath, Joseph D. to Sarah A. Prichard 11-13-1874 (11-14-1874)
Keenan, W. P. to Sallie Hicks 4-18-1878 (4-19-1878)
Kellett, Ethelbert to Evaline Brent 12-25-1866 (12-27-1866)
Kellow, A. A. to Janettie A. Parrish 12-27-1876
Kellow, James to O. D. Moore 8-8-1876 (8-9-1876)
Kellow, John W. to Sallie Echols 11-22-1877
Kellow, Samel J. to L. C. Saunders 10-29-1874
Kellow, Thomas H. to Nancy You 1-20-1875 (1-21-1875)
Kelly, E. Mis? to Martha A. Pool 12-27-1865
Kelso, F. N. to Mary A. Crawford 3-5-1873 (3-6-1873)
Kenley, J. A. to Sarah C. Lankford 9-3-1878 (9-4-1878)
Kent, James W. to M. M. Prichard 2-5-1879 (2-6-1879)
Kerr, Joseph to Jane Beasley 3-7-1871 (3-8-1871)
Kerr, WM. to Kate Stevens 4-6-1869 (no return)
Key, William to Louiza S. Chamberlain 1-31-1861
Kidd, W. T. to Elizabeth Wallace 12-31-1878 (1-1-1879)
Kiger, E. J. to Eliza C. Simpson 12-24-1874
King, J. F. to G. A. Bishop 12-3-1878 (12-4-1878)
King, J. M. to Cynthia Griffin 10-12-1865
King, J. P. to A. G. White 12-18-1878
King, J. T. to M. J. McFarland 3-24-1874
King, J. W. to L. A. Tarrant 7-9-1878 (7-10-1878)
King, James to Lucinda Sawyer 7-29-1880
King, Jethro to Roberta (Mrs.) Thurmond 4-30-1879
King, M. L. to L. A. Tarrant 7-18-1876 (no return)
King, Phillip to Jane Powell 12-10-1878 (12-11-1878)
King, Rufus to M. S. Brimingham 12-3-1874
King, Rufus to Mary Ann Stillman
King, S. H. to M. E. Cavitt 9-3-1878 (9-4-1878)
King, Thomas S. to Willie B. Ripley 9-11-1877 (9-12-1877)
King, W. R. to A. B. Cole 11-23-1872 (11-24-1872)
King, W. T. to Saluda J. King 6-24-1869
King, Wash to Lotta Coleman 7-10-1875 (7-4?-1875)
King, Wash to _____ no dates (with Sep 1875)
King, William T. to Nancy Williams 4-10-1861
King, William to Amanda Roberts 10-27-1879
King, William to Rebecca A. Bowen 12-17-1860 (12-18-1860)
Kingkaid, Robert to Harriet M. Robertson 1-1-1866 (no return)

Kirk, A. H. to Sarah J. Wright 10-3-1867
Kirk, Dick to Mariah Bradford 1-1-1879 (1-2-1879)
Kirk, George to Polly A. Sims 10-23-1871
Kirk, Henry T. to M. L. Fuqua 3-19-1878
Kirk, Henry to Margaret Ellis 8-21-1867 (8-22-1867)
Kirk, J. L. to Mary Clark 9-7-1875 (not executed?)
Kirk, P. T. to S. E. Shoffner 8-13-1866 (8-14-1866)
Kirk, William to T. E. Sanders 10-18-1875
Kirkpatrick, James S. to Manerva E. Meadows 4-11-1864
Kirkpatrick, John A. to Harriet F. Horton 7-29-1863 (8-2-1863)
Knight, W. L. to Amanda E. Michaels 12-26-1872 (no return)
Knight, W. P. to Elvira S. J. Dodd 9-10-1866 (9-11-1866)
Knowles, William J. to Mary E. Butler 6-12-1875 (6-13-1875)
Knowlton, L. to Melissa Blackwell 6-15-1869 (6-16-1869)
Kohnmann?, John to Ida McKenzie 12-4-1878
Lacey, Francis S. to Elizabeth A. Wilkins 7-9-1862
Lacy, W. B. to M. J. Jenkins 9-18-1867 (9-19-1867)
Lamar, W. F. to Margaret V. Linton 11-12-1870 (11-15-1870)
Lamar, W. F. to Mendie Eady 11-12-1870 (11-15-1870)
Lamarr, W. F. to Rachel Aronhart 8-18-1866
Lambert, A. J. to M. H. Armstrong 3-29-1879 (4-1-1879)
Lambert, J. S. to Fannie C. Crawford 2-24-1879 (2-25-1879)
Lambert, Thomas to Susan A. Ellis 5-12-1863 (5-17-1863)
Landrum, Hiram to Susan Dowell 4-26-1872 (5-10-1872)
Landrum, John to Bettie Burch 3-7-1877 (3-8-1877)
Lane, George W. to Sarah P. Killet 9-3-1863
Lane, Jane E. to P. E. Edwards 3-12-1872
Lane, John T. to Mary L. Hampton 1-30-1872
Lane, T. B. to Lucy E. Ferrill 11-18-1878 (11-20-1878)
Lane, W. P. to Mary A. Connell 1-5-1871
Lanier, Aaron to Mary Ward 9-26-1866 (no return)
Lanier, Frank to Laura Burch 1-19-1878 (1-20-1878)
Lanier, J. to Mary J. Echols 7-24-1867
Lanier, L. P. to Cynthia Pruitt 1-1-1868 (1-2-1868)
Lanier, O. E. to Mary E. Pope 10-28-1867 (10-29-1867)
Lanier, Tecumseh to Nannie Lockhart 10-27-1874
Lankford, Champ to Martha Frith 2-13-1872 (2-14-1872)
Lasater, J. C. to M. E. Dyer 7-28-1873 (7-31-1873)
Lassiter, N. T. to M. A. Evans 1-10-1866
Laster, J. A. to R. J. Taylor 1-9-1869 (no return)
Lauderdale, E. B. to Leonora Cobb 12-30-1871 (1-1-1872)
Lauderdale, J. M. to Rebecca Wright 5-4-1869
Lauderdale, John W. to Queen Tipton 11-3-1870
Law, Geo. W. to Louisa Kee 2-27-1873
Law, Umphrey to Dinkie Turnage 4-16-1872 (4-18-1872)
Lea, Isiah to Helen Sorrell 12-27-1862 (1-3-1863)
Leath, G. A. to Leona J. McMackin 12-1-1874 (12-2-1874)
Leath, J. Z. to Emiline Parker 8-16-1872 (8-22-1872)
Ledbetter, J. M. to Jane (Mrs.) Bradford 10-2-1872
Ledbetter, J. W. to S. L. Finley 3-27-1873 (no return)
Ledbetter, Thomas to Lenora Magary 4-4-1873 (no return)
Ledsinger, Boss to Alice Fowlkes 4-26-1876 (4-27-1876) B
Ledsinger, J. Z. to M. J. Johnson 12-2-1868 (no return)
Ledsinger, John to Matta Stewart 12-31-1872 (1-1-1873)
Ledsinger, Thomas F. to Mary Louisa Ferguson 9-27-1865
Lee, John to Susan E. Williams 6-1-1867 (6-3-1867)
Leggett, J. B. to Melissa J. Breece 2-21-1870 (2-23-1870)
Leggit, Noah to Sarah P. Echols 7-11-1862 (7-13-1862)
Lemmons, Thomas to Margaret H. Hardican 3-3-1862 (3-4-1862)
Lemons, J. M. to E. F. Hardican 2-8-1870 (no return)
Lemons, Marion A. to Mary E. Childers 12-30-1867
Leonly?, Henry to Mary E. Howell 4-20-1867 (4-22-1867)
Lester, S. H. P. to Amanda Pierce 6-14-1875 (no return)
Lewelling, A. J. to L. P. Childress 2-25-1873 (2-27-1873)
Lewelling, J. N. to M. F. Boatwright 2-25-1873 (2-27-1873)
Lewellyn, T. E. to Sarah Slayton 3-6-1876 (3-8-1876)
Lewis, James W. to Nancy Jackson 11-14-1878 (11-17-1878)
Lewis, Jerry to Addie Redditt 9-11-1880 (9-12-1880)
Lewis, M. R. to M. E. King 9-10-1875 (9-12-1875)
Liggett, William S. to M. R. Cearce 2-19-1872 (2-21-1872)
Liggin, Daniel to Ellen Dunvegard? 1-26-1867 (no return)
Light, Hiram to Nancy Matthews 4-2-1874
Light, James to Harriet Williams 12-16-1875
Light, Joel E. to Mollie James 12-12-1878
Light, Liss to Winnie Joyner 5-6-1875

Light, Randle to Susan Spence 8-11-1866
Lightfoot, B. D. to Martha M. Burkett 11-14-1877 (11-15-1877)
Lightfoot, M. A. to M. A. Scobey 11-4-1875 (no return)
Lillard, James F. to Mattie E. Kimbrel 5-13-1876 (5-14-1876)
Lillard, Washington to Eliza Wade 11-6-1873
Linnell, Alfred to Mefrinda? Bullard 8-30-1862 (9-11-1862)
Lively, D. C. to M. E. Hall 1-8-1868 (1-9-1868)
Lively, Garland to Martha J. Reynolds 1-29-1866 (no return)
Lock, John Wesley to Nancy Light 7-29-1868 (7-30-1868)
Lockhart, J. S. to Cora I. Massey 12-10-1873 (12-11-1873)
Lockhart, T. J. to Lavina Husband 7-1-1875 (no return)
Logan, William to Manerva Matheny 3-12-1861 (3-14-1861)
Long, Albert to Mary M. Cothan 2-3-1868 (no return)
Louder, Morris to Fannie Fowlkes 1-30-1879
Love, A. L. to Alice Harrison 12-12-1870 (12-15-1870)
Love, John W. to Sarah O. King 12-23-1862
Lovel, James to Didama Campbell 12-7-1872 (12-8-1872)
Lovelace, J. G. to A. B. Bonds 1-24-1871 (1-25-1871)
Lovelace, Wilson to Emma Light 7-10-1880 (7-11-1880)
Loving, D. M. to J. A. Simpson 2-28-1868 (no return)
Lowe, Isaac W. to M. E. Michell 9-4-1872 (9-8-1872)
Lowe, Marvila to Belle J. Roberts 2-25-1878 (2-27-1878)
Lowrance, John H. to M. A. E. Reed 11-15-1863
Lucas, J. A. to Bettie J. Adams 2-8-1872 (2-13-1872)
Lucas, J. M. to Julia C. Everett 12-22-1875 (12-23-1875)
Lucas, Lemuel T. to Missouri J. Lanier 11-6-1867 (no return)
Lumpkins, W. F. to Martha Berry 2-4-1861 (2-5-1861)
Lunsford, S. T. to Frances Ray 5-18-1869 (no return)
Lunsford, W. E. to A. L. Davis 2-14-1877
Lunsford, W. E. to M. E. Davis 1-22-1879 (1-23-1879)
Luntsford, J. A. to P. A. Crow 12-24-1875 (no return)
Luscumbe, Frank W. to Georgia Stevens 9-10-1872
Luster, Stafford to Susan Dearmore 6-19-1860
Lyon, John to Nancy A. Lyons 5-6-1861 (5-9-1861)
Mabin, John to Matilda Ferguson 3-15-1879
Macon, W. H. to Mary Walker 9-28-1871
Madding, Richard to Mary Duke 12-23-1870 (no return) B
Maddrey, Elmore to Mollie Prichard 12-12-1877 (12-13-1877)
Maddrey, Isaac to Malinda Foust 12-21-1868 (no return)
Maddrey, Ricahrd to Adaline Crow 12-18-1866 (12-25-1866)
Maggard, George to Isabella Doyle 8-26-1869 (no return)
Maggard, Jerry to Louisa Foster 7-14-1869 (no return)
Maggard, John to Lucy Wood 12-29-1875 (1-2-1876)
Maggard, Sandy to Lou Parr 1-12-1878
Mahan, Allen to Bette Doak 1-4-1871 (no return)
Mahon, Dallas to Alice Walker 1-28-1868 (2-10-1868)
Mahon, F. E. to E. L. Perry 12-3-1864 (12-13-1864)
Mangrum, James J. to Sarah E. Meter 8-19-1867 (8-20-1867)
Mangrum, Robert to Amanday Rowly 11-16-1867 (no return)
Mangrum, W. H. to Mattie J. Gibson 1-16-1866
Manly, Miles to Emily McCalister 10-19-1867 (10-20-1867)
Mann, Richard to Bettie Grimm 2-8-1876 (no return)
Mann, William to Caroline (mrs.) Singleton 7-19-1873 (7-20-1873)
Manning, E. K. to M. P. (Mrs.) Shipman 12-14-1872 (12-15-1872)
Manning, Ned to Josephine Perry 7-11-1865 (7-17-1865)
Marchant, J. W. to M. J. Rawles 2-9-1876
Marchant, Jerry to Lizzie Fowlkes 7-6-1867
Marcum, Wiley J. to Mary S. Christie 10-22-1867
Marlow, W. H. to Adalaide McCulloch 11-20-1877
Marshall, M. M. to Mary L. Stevens 2-24-1879
Martin, J. M. to Frances W. Carroll 11-22-1873 (11-26-1873)
Martin, Jno. L. to Maggie Nichols 5-2-1866
Mason, F. G. to H. A. Atkins 12-13-1865 (12-14-1865)
Mason, H. J. to Fannie Gannon 11-7-1871 (11-9-1871)
Mason, Henry to Jane Edwards 3-12-1877
Mason, Thomas to Victoria McGaughey 12-27-1876 (12-28-1876)
Massey, James S. to M. A. Johnson 5-10-1860
Massey, John W. to M. E. Walker 3-1-1879 (3-5-1879)
Matheny, Louis to Nancy Patterson 8-17-1861 (8-31-1861)
Mathews, James M. to Emily F. Williams 12-16-1865 (12-18-1865)
Mathews, Miles to Nancy Woods 1-16-1871 (1-19-1871) B
Matthews, Silas to C. A. Moore 9-19-1867 (no return)
Mays, E. P. to N. J. Peery 1-24-1878
Mays, G. D. to S. E. Colvin 2-24-1870
Mays, J. M. to Nancy L. Odom 8-14-1861

Mays, James G. to Louisa Eason 12-16-1861 (12-18-1861)
Mays, N. L. to E. J. (Mrs.) North 6-27-1874 (6-28-1874)
Mays, Thos. J. to Mary J. Frazier 1-4-1879 (1-5-1879)
Mays, W. T. to Susan B. Curtis 4-17-1867
McAfee, John to M. J. (Mrs.) Echols 5-20-1874
McAlister, J. Z. to M. F. Henry 2-7-1872
McBride, Henry to Tresa Ann L. Hood 5-30-1879 (6-1-1879)
McBride, W. F. to Margaret Wayson 4-2-1877 (4-3-1877)
McBride, W. R. to Katie Blanton 6-6-1877
McCallister, A. P. to Sallie F. Pate 10-20-1869 (10-21-1869)
McCann, Stephen to Marian Rudder 10-29-1874
McCarroll, Eli to Elizabeth Cate 5-29-1873
McCarroll, H. L. to L. J. Winters 1-30-1875 (2-3-1875)
McCarroll, James to Lizzie Corvin 3-7-1873
McClanahan, S. G. to Mary E. Davis 2-20-1867 (no return)
McClerkin, James D. to Annie Hill 4-19-1877
McClure, H. H. to Ellen Singleton 5-17-1867 (5-18-1867)
McCon, Jacob to Ruth Pierce 4-15-1873 (4-16-1873) B
McCorkle, J. D. to Etherline Ellis 1-6-1879 (1-8-1879)
McCorkle, J. S. to Mary C. Frazier 8-23-1871 (8-24-1871)
McCorkle, Jo B. to Caroline McCutchen 12-20-1871 (12-21-1871)
McCormack, M. C. to B. Z. Jackson 9-23-1879 (9-24-1879)
McCounts, Thomas to Delia (Mrs.) Hood 1-7-1874 (1-24-1874)
McCoy, J. W. to Anne McFarlin 3-20-1879
McCoy, Jacob to Isabella Butterworth 3-18-1868 (3-19-1868)
McCoy, Jacob to Miss _____ Smith 4-2-1874
McCoy, James L. to Margaretta A. Hufstetler 7-21-1874 (7-27-1874)
McCoy, John to Lundy? Harris 1-22-1878 (1-23-1878)
McCoy, N. W. to N. J. Self 12-23-1875
McCoy, Nathan to Sarah Stevens 5-8-1880 (5-9-1880)
McCoy, W. F. to Virginia H. Latham 10-19-1876
McCoy, W. W. to Alice Z. King 9-13-1871
McCracken, John to Mary F. Haggart 1-21-1862 (1-23-1862)
McCulloch, John to Catherine Hicks 10-25-1865 (10-26-1865)
McCulloch, W. L. to C. Dozier 10-1-1866 (10-4-1866)
McCullough, Hiram to Peggy Connell 2-22-1872
McCutchen, Allen to Ida Norwich 7-8-1878 (8-1-1878)
McCutchen, Frank to Margaret Porter 12-3-1873 (12-4-1873)
McCutchen, Porter to Silla Redley 2-4-1867
McCutchen, W. T. to S. B. Harvey 7-28-1873 (7-31-1873)
McDaniel, Peter to Julia Maggard 8-26-1869 (no return)
McDaniel, Peter to Minerva Swift 4-2-1874
McDaniel, R. Z. to R. E. Wilson 1-4-1869 (1-5-1869)
McDavid, James L. to Victoria Neal 1-29-1868 (no return)
McDavid, S. to Fanni A. Walsin 10-1-1867 (10-2-1867)
McDearman, S. H. to Alvira S. Rucker 12-17-1870 (12-22-1870)
McDearmon, J. M. to S. A. Rucker 12-22-1874 (12-23-1874)
McDearmon, N. E. to M. E. Rogers 1-15-1872 (1-16-1872)
McDonald, Peter to Reddie Horton 1-17-1878 B
McDonnell, George to Mary Brenakin 4-14-1865 (4-17-1865)
McDowell, Wm. to Mary C. Knight 9-16-1871 (9-17-1871)
McElmurry, Phillip to M. L. Shaw 6-22-1870 (6-23-1870)
McFarlan, A. C. to Rebecca J. Cawhon 7-14-1865 (7-16-1865)
McFarland, J. F. to Nancy Rumley 1-6-1872
McFarlane, John W. to Peggy Ann Bettis 12-13-1866 (12-26-1866)
McFarlin, J. W. to Belle Williams 3-20-1879
McGarg, Henry to Lou Frost 1-14-1879 (no return)
McGarg, Peter to Rachel Nash 3-2-1878 (3-7-1878)
McGaughey, George to Jane Lanier 2-21-1873 (4-21-1873)
McGinnis, Thomas J. to Mary E(liza) Gammon 1-24-1866 (1-25-1866)
McGraw, A. A. to Sallie Reynolds 12-31-1872
McGuire, James to Jane Hendren 11-22-1878
McIntosh, Jno. B. to Martha Campbell 12-25-1868 (12-27-1868)
McIntosh, John B. to Margaret Ann Twilla 1-24-1878
McKee, A. H. to C. A. Jones 12-11-1867 (no return)
McKee, R. A. to Samarimus (Sue) Roycroft 1-8-1867 (1-10-1867)
McKennie, Miller to Frances Wynne 5-20-1876
McKenzie, D. M. to Ada B. Love 12-4-1869 (12-7-1869)
McKenzie, Homer to Hattie F. Love 12-12-1870 (12-17-1870)
McKenzie, Homer to L. D. Love 11-26-1877
McKinney, D. V. to Minerva Kerley 10-30-1862
McKnight, Joseph to Frances Beckett 1-29-1872 (1-30-1872)
McKnight, S. A. to Susan M. Kelly 2-28-1865 (3-1-1865)
McKnight, Sam A. to Sarah T. Enochs 10-27-1873 (10-28-1873)
McKnight, William N. to Lucy A. McDavid 1-16-1864 (1-17-1864)

McNeell, A. C. to Mary E. Baker 7-28-1862 (7-29-1863?)
McPherson, Enoch to R. J. Christie 8-16-1866
McSheyn, Charles to Hannah McKinney 12-6-1866
Mead, J. H. to Millie E. Bailey 6-10-1871 (6-11-1871)
Meadows, J. G. to S. E. Jones 10-10-1870 (no return)
Meadows, S. C. to M. L. Mallory 12-22-1870 (no return)
Meadows, William to Sarah Beckett 1-15-1873 (1-16-1873)
Meeks, J. H. to Mary A. Merandy 1-14-1868
Menzies, David to Mary F. Burton 10-31-1872 (no return)
Menzies, George to Ann Buchanan 12-19-1865 (12-22-1865)
Menzies, Isaac to Parthena Parker 10-24-1872 (9?-24-1872)
Meredith, J. S. to Mildred Wesson 7-19-1871 (7-25-1871)
Meredith, Simpson to Amanda Lemon 11-13-1867
Merygin?, William P. to Sally Rodgers 10-16-1866 (no return)
Michell, Crawford to Olive Pate 1-22-1867 (1-24-1867)
Michell, N. J. to Louisa Pugh 12-2-1869 (12-5-1869)
Michell, R. H. to M. F. Hall 8-5-1868 (no return)
Michell, Thos. C. to Lizzie Bell 5-11-1867 (no return)
Mifflin, C. C. to Ellen James 1-8-1870 (1-9-1870)
Mifflin, Caswell C. to Catherine Glisson 1-21-1871 (1-22-1871)
Milam, B. to Eliza White 1-7-1879 (no return)
Milam, G. S. to Nancy J. Wallace 3-15-1865
Milam, S. E. to M. E. Featherston 12-4-1873
Millard, George to Bell Williams 11-12-1873 (11-13-1873)
Miller, Daniel to Margaret Harwell 12-30-1868 (12-31-1868)
Miller, James C. to Gabriella Davis 1-24-1861
Miller, James to Caroline Henderson 12-27-1866 (no return)
Miller, John to Louis Haskin 11-7-1867
Miller, Joseph E. to Sarah E. Montgomery 3-7-1866 (3-8-1866)
Mills, G. W. to M. E. McCracken 5-22-1869 (no return)
Mills, G. W. to Nannie Read 1-9-1877 (1-10-1877)
Mills, J. F. to Bettie King 9-29-1871 (10-3-1871)
Mills, J. J. to P. F. Moody 8-19-1872 (8-21-1872)
Mills, James R. to Martha E. Garner 3-5-1872 (3-7-1872)
Mills, John A. to Prudence (Mrs.) Williamson 12-12-1876 (12-14-1876)
Mills, John A. to Temperance Bessent? 1-1-1867
Mills, Jonathan to Martha Simpson 12-28-1878 (12-29-1878)
Mills, Nat. A. to Almedia C. Ellis 11-6-1866 (11-7-1866)
Mills, Nathaniel to J. E. Edwards 12-30-1873
Miskelly, E. to Martha A. Pool 12-27-1865 (12-30-1865)
Mitchell, Alex to Caroline Radford 1-25-1869 (no return)
Mitchell, B. H. to Finetta Prichard 10-19-1876
Mitchell, Henry to Henrietta Powell 10-19-1877 (10-21-1877) B
Mitchell, J. H. to Martha Hobsen 9-12-1870 (9-13-1870)
Mitchell, Peter to Harriet Griffin 1-6-1874 (1-7-1874)
Mitchell, R. W. to J. E. M. Turney 2-10-1875 (2-19-1875)
Mitchell, Shepard to Julia Nash 12-29-1875 (12-30-1875)
Mitchell, W. R. to Mary V. Kidd 1-26-1878 (1-28-1878)
Modlin, J. H. to M. A. Winters 2-16-1875 (2-17-1875)
Modlin, J. H. to T. S. McCarroll 2-16-1875 (2-17-1875)
Montgomery, A. R. to Frances M. Hall 12-14-1864 (no return)
Montgomery, Green to Alice Robertson 12-30-1865 (no return)
Moody, Eli A. to Sallie Yarington 12-10-1870 (12-11-1870)
Moody, Giles F. to Eliza C. Staggs 10-2-1867 (no return)
Moor, S. H. to Susan C. Shelton 12-30-1878 (1-1-1879)
Moore, A. E. to B. J. Harris 12-24-1872 (12-25-1872)
Moore, A. N. to Elizabeth Sargent 6-7-1879 (no return)
Moore, Charley to Mollie Light 12-25-1877 (12-27-1877)
Moore, F. C. to L. J. Williamson 2-11-1879 (2-12-1879)
Moore, Frank to Eliza Fowlkes 1-6-1872
Moore, Frank to Nancy Beard 12-11-1878
Moore, J. A. to M. E. Thompson 1-14-1868 (1-15-1868)
Moore, J. M. to Mollie Mallory 1-6-1868 (1-8-1868)
Moore, J. S. to Cathie Cook 11-29-1877
Moore, J. S. to Lizzie Shahon ?-?-1867 (4-28-1867)
Moore, Jack to Margaret Wyatt 4-6-1880 (4-8-1880)
Moore, Jefferson to A. M. Pate 12-26-1868 (no return)
Moore, Jo to Susan Foster 1-21-1880 (1-22-1880)
Moore, John R. to Mary A. Clay 2-26-1867 (2-28-1867)
Moore, Jordan to Latitia Howard 8-13-1866 (no return)
Moore, L. D. to Elizabeth Brown 9-13-1867 (9-15-1867)
Moore, Miller to Belle Fowlkes 9-15-1877
Moore, Nick to Nancy Smith 10-28-1880
Moore, Pierce to Margaret Tipton 2-25-1871 (2-26-1871)

Moore, Pierce to Rebecca Horton 9-20-1873
Moore, S. H. to Martha J. Scoby 12-11-1865 (12-13-1865)
Moore, Thos. R. to Mary E. Light 5-20-1869
Moore, Toney to Carrie Smith 3-26-1874 (3-28-1874)
Moore, Wm. W. to S. E. Kellow 11-11-1874 (11-12-1874)
Moorney, M. B. to Amanda Cottam 1-28-1864 (1-29-1864)
Morgan, Henry to Mary Jane Nettles 6-24-1867 (7-25-1867)
Morris, A. J. to S. D. King 7-1-1878 (7-2-1878)
Morris, J. W. to A. J. King 9-23-1873 (9-24-1873)
Morris, J. W. to M. T. Reaves 4-14-1879 (4-18-1879)
Morris, W. H. H. to Mary J. C. Reddin 7-18-1867 (7-17?-1867)
Morris, Z. N. to N. B. Hallet 2-19-1866 (2-20-1866)
Morrison, Thomas to Mary Jane Dove 6-11-1863
Morrow, Samuel to Sarah J. Tucker 10-1-1860 (10-10-1860)
Moseley, J. M. to E. E. Shelton 8-5-1874 (no return)
Moseley, W. H. to Sarah J. Knight 5-5-1870
Mosely, Archer to Mary Mifflin 5-9-1874 (5-10-1874)
Mosely, John E. to Mary Worrels 9-30-1869 (no return)
Moss, John H. to Mahala Shelton 1-27-1863 (1-29-1863)
Motley, Nelson to Fannie Peacock 3-4-1875 (3-5-1875)
Mount, H. N. to Catherine Salisbury 10-18-1866
Mulherin, Frank to Jane Moore 4-6-1880 (no return)
Mulherin, Tom to Mollie Bryant 12-8-1880 (12-9-1880)
Mulherin, William to Nancy Harris 4-22-1875
Mulherin, Wm. to Fannie Connell 10-22-1868
Muns, George W. to Mary A. (Mrs.) Merchant 12-22-1863
Murphey, Jonas to Nancy Stevens 11-1-1871 (11-2-1871)
Murray, J. F. to E. S. Hammel 12-20-1870 (12-22-1870)
Murray, John C. to Amand J. Wessen 12-19-1860 (12-20-1860)
Murray, Thomas M. to Evaline Carrel 6-30-1874 (7-1-1874)
Murray, W. H. H. to Martha E. Pinnon 11-23-1876
Murray, W. H. H. to Mary E. Burnham 10-10-1865 (10-11-1865)
Murray, W. N. to M. S. Hodge 12-17-1873
Murrell, Kelly to Betsy Palmer 8-16-1873 (8-21-1873)
Myett, W. R. G. to Annie Anderson 2-17-1872 (2-18-1872)
Nash, C. T. to Fannie S. Lovelace 5-27-1867 (5-30-1867)
Nash, Geo. to Tennessee Jelks 2-23-1880 (2-25-1880)
Nash, J. N. to Emily Nash 8-7-1865 (8-8-1865)
Nash, John R. to Amanda Miller 11-14-1877 (11-15-1877)
Nash, Luke to Alice Porter 10-8-1877 (10-9-1877)
Nash, R. R. to Emma McDavid 10-11-1860
Nash, Thos. (Dr.) to Harriet McDavid 10-22-1868
Nash, W. B. to Ann Stallings 1-7-1867 (no return)
Nash, W. F. to Merandy G. Morley 7-9-1868 (no return)
Neal, B. F. to Z. A. Carter 12-15-1870
Neal, D. B. to M. M. Ridens 10-5-1871
Neal, J. B. to James Harris 4-7-1879
Neal, James A. T. to Josie Ferril 10-14-1874 (10-19-1874)
Nearn?, J. D. to Mary J. Bolin 6-5-1869 (6-9-1869)
Neeley, M. W. to Elizabeth Dodd 6-5-1873
Neely, James S. to L. T. Brown 11-29-1871 (11-30-1871)
Neely, S. J. to Elizabeth S. Cobb 12-1-1866 (12-4-1866)
Neely, T. G. to P. A. Sorrell 2-20-1866
Neil, J. R. to Mary Elizabeth Horton 9-25-1877
Neil, Sidney R. to Angeline Cresswell 3-12-1879
Nelson, F. M. to L. M. T. Smith 11-22-1877 (11-25-1877)
Nelson, W. H. to Charity Ann Brashier 1-21-1878 (1-22-1878)
Nettles, T. J. to Martha W. Applewhite 8-5-1869
Newnam, J. W. to Martha C. Knowles 12-5-1877 (12-6-1877)
Newton, F. A. to Annie Davis 12-16-1878 (12-17-1878)
Nichol, Moses to Deevy Wagsted 5-25-1860 (no return)
Nicholas, C. to Eliza E. Strother 10-21-1871 (10-22-1871)
Nichols, Alfred T. to Martha Shackleton 4-26-1870 (4-27-1870)
Nichols, James T. to Frances Odom 6-4-1879
Nichols, James W. to Sarah E. Antwine 1-9-1868 (1-12-1868)
Nichols, Jonathan to Amanda Shackleton 4-28-1866 (no return)
Night, Ben M. to Josephine Clark 12-30-1866 (no return)
Nixon, D. C. to Catharine Jones 4-7-1864
Nixon, Thomas F. to Arenia Lunsford 5-30-1868 (no return)
Noe, Bennett to Rachel Burnett 9-3-1870 (9-4-1870)
Nolen, Columbus L. to E. E. Wright 3-9-1874
Norman, George W. to Charlotte Jackson 4-30-1860
Norman, R. T. D. to Charlotte Davis 10-28-1869
Norman, R. T. D. to Mexico Barrett 1-27-1876 (1-28-1876)
Norment, Ben E. to Maggie Craig 9-7-1868 (no return)

Norment, Magor to Julia Connell 4-29-1880
Norsworthy, J. W. to D. J. Prichard 12-18-1878 (12-19-1878)
North, Green to Ella Skipper 10-7-1867
North, J. T. to Nancy Privett 8-18-1877 (8-19-1877)
North, Jesse C. to Eliza Neal 5-27-1868
North, Joseph T. to Leitha Jane Brent 9-1-1862 (9-2-1862)
Nunn, Isaac C. to Maria M. Redick 12-20-1866 (no return)
Nunn, J. H. to Mary J. Perry 10-16-1871 (10-17-1871)
Nunn, J. N. to Margaret C. Jacock 1-30-1867 (1-31-1867)
Nunn, Joseph to Julia Perry 12-28-1867 (no return)
Nunn, Wm. F. to Mary Murray 10-25-1870 (10-26-1870)
Oakley, Ben Jamin to Perry? Warren 8-12-1867 (no return)
Oakley, J. W. H. to Mary A. Shackleton 10-24-1871 (10-25-1871)
Oakley, William to Eliza A. Brewer 11-25-1871 (no return)
Oakly, Richard to Ellen Draw 1-29-1875 (1-31-1875) B
Oaks, John to Missouri Goodrich 7-9-1873
Odel, Albert M. to Almira Williams 9-17-1866 (no return)
Odle, Wm. A. to Melissa C. Renfro 11-1-1869
Oldham, Shack to Susan Goin 3-16-1880
Oldham, Travis to Cherry Brooks 12-15-1866 (no return)
Olds, J. T. to J. P. Only 2-16-1878 (2-19-1878)
Olds, William W. to Fannie T. Marcum 11-16-1876 (11-29-1876)
Olive, J. W. to Mattie Ann Jackson 10-31-1878
Oliver, James to Deliah Fowlkes 12-27-1871 (12-28-1871)
Oneal, Nathaniel C. to Susie A. Warren 9-22-1879 (no return)
Oquinn, E. A. to Mattie Gay 7-28-1874 (7-30-1874)
Osborn, Enoch to Ida Evans 12-24-1869 (12-26-1869)
Osborn, J. F. to Nannie B. Sinclair 10-1-1867 (no return)
Oslin, J. W. to F. E. Wesson 12-20-1871 (12-21-1871)
Overton, Albert to Lou Robertson 12-28-1872 (12-31-1872)
Overton, Albert to Sallie King 12-25-1874
Overton, Scott to amanda Talley 12-21-1874 (12-30-1874) B
Owens, J. J. to Mary Turner 11-11-1876 (11-14-1876)
Pace, A. L. to Elizabeth McKee 8-10-1868 (8-11-1868)
Pace, A. R. to Lucy McCullough 8-20-1875 (8-22-1875)
Pace, B. F. to S. S. Scobey 11-1-1879 (11-4-1879)
Pace, H. J. to M. F. Weatherington 12-9-1874 (12-10-1874)
Pace, J. D. to Fannie Shofner 10-30-1867
Pace, J. D. to Henrietta Sherwood 11-29-1871
Pace, J. T. to L. E. Smith 7-22-1873 (7-24-1873)
Pace, Jo. D. to T. A. Scoby 9-7-1869 (9-8-1869)
Pace, M. R. to S. E. Hamilton 12-17-1878 (12-19-1878)
Pace, W. C. to Rebeccah Cook 4-26-1865
Pace, W. T. to Miley Halum 9-18-1866 (9-20-1866)
Pace, W. T. to Stacy S. Strawn 12-29-1865 (12-30-1865)
Palmer, E. Clark to Elizabeth J. Clark 4-9-1861 (4-10-1861)
Palmer, J. R. to Ellen Grace 10-5-1876 (10-7-1876)
Palmer, J. T. C. to Tennie Stone 11-17-1876 (12-19-1876)
Palmere, James W. to Susanah Aiken 8-31-1868 (9-1-1868)
Palmore, Beng. to Frances E. Little 5-16-1863 (no return)
Palmore, C. C. to S. J. Christian 9-11-1876
Palmore, M. M. to Nancy Ann Warren 7-25-1871 (no return)
Park, W. B. to Martha M. Cliff 10-25-1878 (10-27-1878)
Parker, Dan to Lou Beaumont 2-19-1869 (no return)
Parker, Dennis to Fanny Harris 12-28-1868 (no return)
Parker, J. D. to Nancy A. Richard 11-30-1876
Parker, Jack to Mary Ferguson 1-10-1880 (1-18-1880)
Parker, James A. to E. C. Johnson 4-25-1872
Parker, John to E. Burkett 7-29-1872 (7-31-1872)
Parker, Neid? to Hannah Jones 7-29-1876 B
Parker, R. B. to Mary J. Richards 12-27-1871 (12-28-1871)
Parker, Robert to Tennessee Smith 12-17-1879 (no return)
Parker, Tom to Sarah Johnson 4-17-1869 (no return)
Parks, Andrew S. to M. E. Harris 7-8-1868 (no return)
Parks, Andrew to F. R. Stinnett 4-13-1875 (4-15-1875)
Parks, B. R. to S. A. Douglass 12-24-1872 (12-25-1872)
Parks, Green to Martha Brown 11-26-1873 (11-27-1873)
Parks, James to Malinda J. Harrold 7-29-1867 (no return)
Parks, Jesse to Canda Jones 5-17-1867 (5-18-1867)
Parks, Richard to Milly Jones 2-1-1867 (2-2-1867)
Parks, Sam to Martha Jones 6-8-1867 (6-9-1867)
Parks, Sam to Mary Parks 11-20-1877 (11-23-1877)
Parks, Toney to Martha Griffin 12-17-1879 (12-18-1879)
Parks, jr. 2nd, H. to M. E. Menzies 10-27-1873 (10-28-1873)
Parks, jr., Hamilton to Manie G. Webb 10-5-1878 (10-7-1878)

Parmenter, J. H. to Belle Matheney 2-19-1876 (2-20-1876)
Parnell, J. B. to Sarah Davis 11-13-1867 (11-14-1867)
Parnell, J. H. to S. A. Foggerson 9-8-1860 (9-11-1860)
Parnell, James C. to Rebecca Wright 4-12-1873 (4-13-1873)
Parnell, R. E. to Amelia C. Jones 10-28-1868 (no return)
Parnell, T. F. to R. L. Hamilton 11-30-1869 (12-3-1869)
Parnell, Wiley B. to L. J. Jones 4-19-1873 (4-20-1873)
Parnell, Wm. to Mary Crudup 1-7-1867 (1-10-1867)
Parr, Ben to Luella Fowlkes 3-22-1877
Parr, Columbus R. to Alice Bugg 8-22-1866
Parr, Gantry to Fannie Foster 10-16-1879
Parr, Julian to Josephine Soward 12-23-1875
Parr, Noah to Rosannah McKnight 12-27-1880 (12-30-1880)
Parrish, James B. to Margaret J. Hassell 8-20-1868 (no return)
Parrish, Lawson to Mary Harrison 5-20-1873 (5-25-1873)
Pate, G. W. to Sallie Adams 1-12-1876
Pate, George to Sally Delph 10-3-1864 (no return)
Pate, J. M. to Mollie Cauthorn 9-29-1875 (9-30-1875)
Pate, John C. to M.E. Hurley 8-3-1872 (no return)
Pate, M. D. L. to H. C. Snell 7-21-1874 (7-22-1874)
Pate, M. D. to Elizabeth M. Shelton 12-16-1869
Pate, T. M. to M. E. Curtis 1-2-1878
Pate, W. H. to Sallie Crockett 4-12-1871
Patrick, G. W. to Sarah F. Davis 12-14-1867 (12-23-1867)
Patrick, Page H. to Annie C. Patrick 1-23-1861 (1-24-1861)
Patterson, Henry to Queenie? Ferrill 12-18-1879 (12-25-1879)
Patterson, T. M. to L. C. Ward 1-4-1870 (1-5-1870)
Patterson, W. R. to C. A. Johnson 12-23-1867 (no return)
Patton, G. G. B. to Alcenia A. Rawles 1-9-1861 (no return)
Paul, Wiley to Mariah McGarg 12-30-1878 (no return)
Payne, B. P. to S. A. B. Shelton 8-17-1866
Payne, W. H. to Lou Chatman 11-23-1876
Payne, W. S. to M. E. Sherrod 12-24-1877 (12-25-1877)
Peacock, George to Mariah Talley 3-24-1870 (no return)
Peacock, Jim to Clarasa Bunnell 2-13-1868 (2-19-1868)
Peak, Champ to Puss Harris 12-11-1876 (no return)
Peek, T. D. to H. M. Hart 3-5-1873 (3-6-1873)
Peel, Thomas J. to Mary Jane Griffin 1-6-1874 (1-7-1874)
Peel, W. Riley to M. M. Treadaway 2-22-1873 (2-25-1873)
Peery, A. B. to S. M. C. Gillis 4-4-1871 (4-6-1871)
Peery, B. P. to Pamela R. Para 12-17-1866
Peery, Jerome B. to C. B. Greenwood 5-8-1869 (no return)
Peery, W. A. to Sarah Colevitt 3-16-1875
Peery, W. A. to V. A. Jones 1-31-1872
Pendleton, E. B. to Lucy Rogers 10-12-1869
Pennington, John to Harriet Whit 12-13-1862 (12-14-1862)
Perkins, A. M. to Jane Williams 10-3-1866 (10-4-1866)
Perkins, Abner to Martha Aikens 4-30-1874
Perry, Anthony to Bell McCutchen 3-14-1868
Perry, Craig to Millie Whitson 1-17-1877
Perry, Franklin to L. J. Strahorn 12-23-1867 (no return)
Perry, Henry C. to I. Etta Parker 9-5-1870 (9-7-1870)
Perry, James H. to E. A. Ellington 12-4-1871 (12-6-1871)
Pettis, David to Margaret Atkins 10-4-1871 (10-5-1871)
Pettus, Rufus to Mary Woodson 12-23-1876
Pettus, William to Jane Mayo 12-30-1880
Petty, Henry to Ann Whitworth 8-21-18682
Pew, John to Elosie? Vail 7-28-1869 (7-30-1869)
Phelan, J. W. to Ellen Watson 10-27-1875
Phillips, George to Malinda Enochs 8-23-1879 (no return)
Phillips, H. H. to H. A. H. Miller 1-15-1866
Phillips, H. M. to Rachel C. Edwards 9-24-1870 (no return)
Phillips, Rush to Nancy Clemm 1-3-1866 (1-10-1867)
Pierce, A. G. to Jane Hawk 5-2-1866 (5-3-1866)
Pierce, A. J. to A. C. A. Walker 1-6-1864
Pierce, A. J. to T. J. Westbrook 12-11-1869 (12-12-1869)
Pierce, Ben to Letitia Clark 12-27-1877
Pierce, Ethelbert L. to Ella Walls 11-21-1872
Pierce, G. B. to S. T. Husbands 9-18-1874 (9-20-1874)
Pierce, George P. to H. E. C. Cribbs 1-23-1868 (no return)
Pierce, Henry to Nancy Ann Enoch 9-15-1869 (no return)
Pierce, J. F. to Ozelia Stevenson 3-2-1875
Pierce, J. H. to D. E. Pope 1-19-1876 (no return)
Pierce, Jefferson to Ann Smith 8-27-1868
Pierce, John M. to Ella N. Stevens 4-29-1876 (4-30-1876)

Pierce, Martin to M. A. Tisdale 12-5-1871 (no return)
Pierce, Rily to Fannie Coker 1-1-1873 (12-2-1873)
Pierce, Sam to Angaline Wynne 3-30-1867 (4-1-1867)
Pierce, Sam to Sarah E. McKnight 10-18-1871 (no return)
Pierce, Stephen to Dora B. Leech 12-30-1869 (no return)
Pierce, T. J. to L. E. Harper 1-23-1872 (1-24-1872)
Pierce, William to Margaret Stegall 9-9-1862
Piercy, W. T. to Sarah Parker 11-5-1868
Pike, James D. to Malinda R. Jarrett 8-22-1872
Pile, S. C. to M. J. McElyea 9-21-1866 (9-23-1866)
Pillow, Frank to Amanda Rogers 9-12-1878
Pillow, Peter to Amanda Powell 10-2-1871
Pillow, Peter to Fannie Bell 9-12-1876 (no return)
Pillow, Scott to Eliza Jane Doak 2-8-1877
Pinion, Felix to Lucinda Doak 9-27-1879 (9-29-1879)
Pinner, Joseph C. to Missouri Todd 4-20-1870
Pitt, Levi H. to Frances C. Ferrill 9-30-1868 (no return)
Pitt, Marion to Amanda Fuller 9-2-1867
Pittman, Abell to Sarah A. Colleth 7-13-1860 (no return)
Pitts, Andrew J. to Mary Adelaide Blankenship 9-5-1876 (9-6-1876)
Pitts, Jerry to Fanny Fowlkes 2-2-1867
Pitts, John W. to Mary A. Blankenship 6-24-1873 (no return)
Pitts, Lafayette to Mabel Jones 12-11-1867 (12-12-1867)
Pitts, Theo. to Ann Freeman 5-10-1864 (5-12-1864)
Pitts, W. A. to Caroline Smith 10-23-1860
Platt, D. to Elizabeth Campbell 5-21-1861
Pleasant, Saml. L. to Sarah C. Griffin 10-11-1870 (no return)
Plummer, T. L. to Emma Kellow 12-13-1876 (12-14-1876)
Poarch, J. M. to M. A. Kent 2-29-1876 (3-1-1876)
Polk, James K. to Mollie Moore 12-27-1867 (12-26?-1867)
Polston, J. R. to C. L. Rodgers 10-31-1878 (no return)
Polston, James E. to S. J. Kelly 12-20-1866
Polston, James E. to Susan C. Ray? 6-26-1860
Pomeroy, H. B. to Sallie Ann Reed 1-21-1879 (1-22-1879)
Ponder, R. T. to Sarah E. Parker 10-19-1872 (10-24-1872)
Pope, Alse L. to Malinda Huffine 11-28-1877 (11-29-1877)
Pope, E. P. to A. L. McCorkle 11-5-1873 (11-6-1873)
Pope, H. T. to Sarah C. Huffine 12-4-1878 (no return)
Pope, J. A. to Lucy F. Dozier 12-23-1868
Pope, J. M. to J. L. Gooding 1-19-1878 (1-20-1878)
Pope, James D. to Elizabeth Doak 8-20-1873 (no return)
Pope, John Wesley to Martha Ann Carroll 9-11-1867 (no return)
Pope, John to Sarah Hall 12-21-1878 (no return)
Pope, Wiley to Mollie Cook 10-27-1874
Porter, B. T. to M. A. T. (Mrs.) Clement 1-18-1872
Porter, Danil to Parthena Nash 11-30-1870 (12-3-1870)
Porter, John to Lotta Henderson 3-18-1873 (no return)
Porter, Limus to Susan Nash 12-28-1872 (2-2-1873)
Porter, W. N. to Fannie P. Sharber 8-1-1870
Porter, Wash to Pennie Doyle 11-4-1875
Potter, W. E. to S. C. Nichols 10-8-1867 (10-9-1867)
Powell, A. P. to Josephine Wilkins 1-14-1874 (no return)
Powell, B. A. to Mary Jane Pierce 10-24-1867
Powell, J. D. to Martha A. Dunivant 3-15-1864 (3-16-1864)
Powell, Lewis to Rebacca Mitchell 12-26-1866 (12-27-1866)
Powell, Prince to Missy Peery 8-23-1869 (no return)
Powell, R. P. to M. Michaels 5-4-1872 (5-5-1872)
Powell, R. P. to R. W. Bradshaw 3-16-1861
Powell, Thomas to Frances Wynne 1-8-1880
Powell, Tobe to Elizabeth Crow 10-22-1879 (10-23-1879)
Powell, W. J. to E. S. Rooks 11-22-1866 (11-25-1866)
Powell, W. T. to Mary (Mrs.) Bradshaw 1-8-1867
Powell, William D. to Narcissa J. Henderson 12-3-1861
Powers, Ephraim to Martha Robertson 10-7-1862
Powers, Ephraim to Mary Ann Waters 8-7-1876 (8-9-1876)
Pratt, Nelson T. to Anne Dudley 6-18-1879 (6-19-1879)
Prewet, W. R. to Jamima Winberry 10-11-1871 (10-12-1871)
Price, Doc to Eliza Tucker 12-29-1870 (no return)
Price, F. M. to M. A. Boon 1-17-1870 (1-19-1870)
Prichard, B. R. to J. A. Brewer 12-28-1878
Prichard, Ben F. to Mary E. Hampton 12-21-1872 (no return)
Prichard, G. W. to Sarah A. Prichard 9-7-1868 (no return)
Prichard, Green to Amanda Wyatt 11-29-1877
Prichard, J. R. to A. J. Davis 8-9-1869 (8-10-1869)
Prichard, J. R. to H. (M.?)J. Hall 3-2-1878 (3-7-1878)

Prichard, Jerry to Laura Wyatt 4-2-1877 (4-5-1877)
Prichard, John R. to Sarah E. Williams 12-24-1864 (12-25-1864)
Prichard, John to Paralee Dunevant 12-27-1877
Prichard, Martin to Rosannah Dillard 9-1-1869 (no return)
Prichard, Newton R. to Sarah S. Redding 1-1-1866
Prichard, S. D. to Elizabeth Straine 12-5-1864 (12-7-1864)
Prichard, W. E. to Alice Brewer 9-18-1878 (9-19-1878)
Prichard, W. H. to Mattie Savage 12-18-1878 (12-24-1878)
Prichard, W. J. to Rosa Lee Ledbetter 2-13-1878
Pritchett, N. C. to Susannah Lumley 2-20-1879
Pritchett, Thos. J. to Louisa Milam 2-4-1863 (2-5-1863)
Privett, Riley to Minerva P. (Mrs.) Howard 10-31-1865
Privett, W. R. to Nancy C. Fultcher 4-17-1875 (4-20-1875)
Privett, William to Martha A. Burnett 12-19-1862 (12-25-1862)
Prock, William to Mayville Wallace 8-12-1861 (8-13-1861)
Pugh, J. L. to Bell Swanner 12-11-1877 (12-12-1877)
Pugh, Joel M. to Catharine Williams 1-22-1879 (1-23-1879)
Pugh, Joel to Martha James 8-24-1863 (8-25-1863)
Purcell, Robt. to Margaret Echols 9-20-1879 B
Purdee, Hiram to Frances E. Presgrove 11-17-1863 (no return)
Pursell, H. T. to E. E. Fowlkes 12-9-1873
Pursell, Isaac to Eliza Mauldin 5-25-1867
Pursell, Joel H. to Serena Isibella Mahan 11-3-1862 (11-4-1862)
Pursley, Arnett to Blanchie Chitwood 11-24-1874 (11-25-1874)
Putman, H. G. to F. A. Lovelace 1-23-1870 (1-25-1871)
Pyland, J. F. to S. C. M. Agee 9-30-1867 (no return)
Pyland, J. W. to Disey E. Reddick 8-13-1860 (8-17-1860)
Pyles, J. F. to Mollie Gammons 2-17-1875 (2-18-1875)
Quinn, Zachariah to Susan Pierce 5-9-1867
Radford, O. J. to W. D. Moore 8-2-1871 (8-22-1871)
Rainey, Enos to Amanda C. Norrington 7-7-1865 (7-15-1865)
Rainey, John M. to Martha C. Rives? 7-22-1873 (7-23-1873)
Rainey, R. M. to Nannie Chitwood 10-16-1873
Ralls, J. L. to Elizabeth Hall 9-5-1865 (9-7-1865)
Rambo, James A. to Susan Pennington 4-25-1861
Rambo, Matt to Nancy R. A. Lacy 10-16-1866 (10-20-1866)
Rambo, S. G. to Rebecca F. Saunders 2-24-1863 (2-26-1863)
Randolph, J. H. to Lou Craig 8-9-1871 (no return)
Rankin, James to Charlotte A. Davis 1-6-1868 (1-7-1868)
Rankin, M. J. to M. E. Whittenton 1-30-1867 (2-3-1867)
Ranser, Henry to Nancy Sudberry 1-3-1866 (1-20-1867)
Rasberry, G. W. to Nancy Boatright 12-3-1868 (12-9-1868)
Rasbury, L. G. to Frances A. Winters 11-7-1862
Rawles, W. F. to P. Toombs 8-27-1872
Rawles, W. F. to S. L. Bloar 1-22-1870 (1-23-1870)
Ray, A. F. to Sarah A. Ellis 1-6-1863 (1-8-1863)
Ray, A. F. to Savannah E. Poteet 6-22-1877 (6-24-1877)
Ray, A. L. to Nancy E. Walker 11-5-1860 (11-6-1860)
Ray, J. S. to S. A. Cole 12-29-1875
Ray, John F. to Martha F. Tucker 8-5-1862 (8-19-1862)
Ray, Joseph to Marinaan Laster 8-29-1871 (8-30-1871)
Ray, T. F. to M. E. Pope 1-7-1869
Ray, Thomas to Mary Flowers 10-9-1861 (10-12-1861)
Read, Lewis V. to Elizabeth Wethen 11-27-1867 (11-28-1867)
Read, W. H. to Nannie Mills 12-20-1877
Reagan, Jim to Lucy White 5-25-1877 (5-27-1877)
Reasons, J. C. to Susan Connell 10-18-1879 (10-19-1879)
Reasons, M. C. to Margaret Wheeler 2-9-1878
Reasons, M. G. to M. A. Wheeler 11-17-1877 (11-21-1877)
Reddick, A. J. to M. A. Brewer 10-16-1869 (10-19-1869)
Reddick, Alfred to Delila Freeman 2-2-1869 (no return)
Reddick, Alfred to Martha A. Ferguson 2-10-1866 (no return)
Reddick, Benj. to Armenia Mansfield 1-30-1866 (1-31-1866)
Reddick, Francis to Amanda Reddick 3-9-1864
Reddick, J. K. P. to L. F. Stalling 12-19-1866 (12-20-1866)
Reddick, J. L. to M. F. Brewer 11-28-1866 (11-29-1866)
Reddick, Jessie to Bettie Nunn 2-15-1868
Reddick, M. V. B. to Harriet Stallings 10-26-1860 (10-27-1860)
Reddick, Richard to Ritta Lanier 12-7-1868 (no return)
Reddick, T. T. to Mary J. Farmer 3-30-1864 (no return)
Redding, T. W. to Martha Jane Nash 12-5-1877 (12-6-1877)
Redding, William H. to Mary Murdough 5-4-1863 (no return)
Redick, Humphrey to Frances Bolen 12-27-1864 (12-29-1864)
Reece, Henry Temp to Susan Lane Little 1-5-1865 (1-7-1865)
Reed, H. A. to Martha A. Hendricks 7-15-1878 (no return)

Reed, R. M. to M. L. McBride 12-9-1874
Reed, S. A. to Margaret E. Brewer 12-27-1865
Reeves, Henry W. to Elizabeth J. McCorkle 12-19-1861
Reffington, John S. to Mary A. Lauderdale 11-18-1868
Reycroft, W. T. to Eliza Pope 6-8-1870 (10-5-1870)
Reynolds, D. H. to Mattie Knight 8-23-1873 (8-24-1873)
Reynolds, G. W. to Idella Walker 3-6-1876 (3-8-1876)
Reynolds, Isaac to Lucinda Paine 4-11-1874 (4-12-1874)
Reynolds, J. D. to Amanda J. King 3-30-1875 (4-1-1875)
Reynolds, J. W. to Bettie Shankle 9-26-1878 (9-27-1878)
Reynolds, J. W. to Elmina Cope 9-19-1863 (9-28-1863)
Reynolds, John to Caroline Dodd 6-15-1863
Reynolds, Joseph to Ann Halliburton 1-6-1875 (1-7-1875)
Reynolds, Thos. J. to Eliza King 10-26-1872 (10-27-1872)
Reynolds, Wm. J. to Mary Jane Litte 2-5-1862 (no return)
Reynolds, Z. T. to Sadie Hall 1-7-1879 (1-9-1879)
Rice, T. J. to M. A. Bowen 6-17-1876 (6-20-1876)
Rice, T. J. to N. P. Bowen 4-6-1868 (4-9-1868)
Richards, J. G. to Hellen Spurriers 2-11-1879
Richards, S. M. to Caroline Williamson 2-24-1873 (no return)
Richardson, John to Elizabeth Cearly 9-26-1869 (9-27-1869)
Richardson, John to Mary Jane Ward 6-26-1867 (no return)
Richardson, John to Nancy Jones 8-20-1868 (no return)
Richardson, Jos. S. to Martha A. McDavid 1-6-1864 (no return)
Richardson, Robert to Ann Eliza Saunders 8-8-1868 (8-9-1868)
Richardson, T. J. to M. E. Finley 3-6-1873 (3-5?-1873)
Richie, G. W. to Susan C. Cross 1-9-1867 (1-11-1867)
Richmond, Frank to Elvira Bradshaw 9-19-1864 (no return)
Ridens, Jefferson M. to Mary Lane 9-21-1862
Ripley, J. M. to S. J. Simons 1-24-1876 (1-26-1876)
Ripley, W. P. to Mary E. Roper 2-24-1872 (2-25-1872)
Roads, Danl. to Sarah E. Thompson 4-6-1863 (4-8-1863)
Robbins, J. S. to E. J. Featherston 10-31-1877 (no return)
Robbins, M. A. to Margaret E. Turner 1-5-1876
Robbins, Oscar R. to M. L. Stith 10-11-1869 (10-12-1869)
Robbins, S. C. to Frances S. Lankford 11-17-1877 (11-18-1877)
Robbins, Sylvester to Marian Tarleton 3-5-1879 (3-6-1879)
Roberts, Joseph F. to Dinkie Hassell 3-3-1875
Roberts, Robert C. to Julia Miller 1-24-1861
Roberts, William E. to Elvira Strother 12-24-1869 (no return)
Robertson, Charles to S. E. Grier 9-20-1876
Robertson, D. A. to Mary G. Ledbetter 9-19-1866 (9-20-1866)
Robertson, G. W. to Virginia Neely 7-19-1865 (7-20-1865)
Robertson, Harrison to Tennie Hooper 12-25-1872 (12-26-1872)
Robertson, J. M. to E. A. Lane 12-24-1878 (12-26-1878)
Robertson, J. W. to Pheby Peterson 8-26-1861 (8-27-1861)
Robertson, James to Ann E. Richardson 9-29-1869 (9-30-1869)
Robertson, John W. to Harriet Peterson 1-26-1864 (1-29-1864)
Robertson, L. A. to Malvina Stokes 12-22-1862 (12-23-1862)
Robertson, N. L. to M. J. Montgomery 12-2-1871 (12-3-1871)
Robertson, W. N. to Louisa Hardison 1-15-1879 (1-16-1879)
Robinson, Henry A. to Margaret Light 4-5-1876 (4-6-1876)
Robinson, Jesse S. to Mary A. Salisbury 2-20-1867
Rodgers, C. W. to L. A. Patrick 12-8-1875 (12-9-1875)
Rodgers, J. M. to Dumbilla Polston 8-14-1876 (8-15-1876)
Rodgers, J. S. to A. M. Taylor 11-23-1869 (11-24-1869)
Rodgers, J. W. to Martha Watson 7-22-1879
Rodgers, Polk to Amanda Wood 12-27-1871
Rodgers, Robert to Tennessee Spence 1-1-1880
Roe, James C. to Anna L. Harris 2-20-1867 (no return)
Roe, Robert A. to M. Emma Henderson 1-23-1867 (1-24-1867)
Rogers, Alex to N. T. Hill 9-24-1869 (9-28-1869)
Rogers, G. W. to C. L. Bradley 1-27-1874
Rogers, George to Nannie Tucker 8-7-1874 (8-12-1874)
Rogers, John M. to Nannie Harrison 4-26-1879 (4-27-1879)
Rogers, Lewis M. to Emma Jones 7-8-1878
Rogers, Phillip to Ella Scroggins 10-14-1880
Rollins, Jimmie to Tennessee Sawyer 8-1-1870
Rook, John S. to Tennessee Watson 10-2-1861
Rooks, F. T. to A. A. Brown 1-10-1872 (1-11-1872)
Roper, John to Sallie Staggs 10-10-1863 (11-3-1863)
Rose, James to Jamy Enoch 1-10-1870 (1-11-1870)
Ross, Alexander to Mary Bumpass 2-3-1870
Ross, Caleb to Harriet Robertson 3-3-1862 (3-4-1862)
Ross, John Wm. to Melissa C. Odle 10-30-1875 (10-31-1875)

Ross, M. C. to P. A. Sulivan 9-22-1863 (11-16-1863)
Routly, Matthew to Amanda Stevens 12-1-1866
Rowark, W. H. to Rosaline Rudder 12-4-1867
Rowland, G. M. to L. N. Bettis 10-9-1865 (10-10-1865)
Royster, W. H. to M. W. E. Oneal 7-27-1869 (no return)
Rucker, James M. to Elizabeth Bessent 7-19-1869 (7-21-1869)
Rucker, Neil B. to A. F. McDearmon 3-13-1873
Ruff, Charley to Lutitia Wynne 10-13-1866 (no return)
Ruff, Charley to Penny Ledsinger 12-19-1867
Ruff, Haywood to Lizzie Fizer 1-4-1877 (1-5-1877)
Ruff, Haywood to Lou Moore 9-9-1880 (no return)
Sales, Louis to Susan Hodge 12-27-1876 (or 12-28?)
Sales, Peter to Angelina Pierce 1-10-1878
Salisbury, J. F. to M. M. Brandon 2-25-1879 (2-26-1879)
Sampson, Frank G. to Rebecca Wallace 2-6-1868
Sampson, Wat B. to Maggie J. McGinnis 4-9-1861
Sanders, L. M. to Maggie Church 7-19-1869 (7-20-1869)
Sanders, Stephen to Malinda Maddrey 1-4-1877
Sanders, T. J. to Candis M. Hall 11-19-1860 (11-20-1860)
Sanders, T. J. to M. E. (Mrs.) Moore 9-30-1875 (10-3-1875)
Sanders, W. A. to Cinthia Forester 3-14-1879 (no return)
Sandford, Geo. to Alice Miller 5-18-1878 (5-24-1878)
Sandford, James to Susan Nuirhead 1-13-1877 (1-14-1877)
Sandford, Will to Laura Breasted? 12-28-1880
Sandford, William to Fannie Nash 12-26-1871 (12-27-1871)
Sandlin, E. H. to Sarah C. Vail 3-3-1870
Sanford, Joseph to Sarah A. Finly 11-2-1867 (11-3-1867)
Sanford, Robert to Mary E. Fisher 7-1-1869 (7-4-1869)
Saulsburg, Wm. to Jane Nance 5-22-1879
Saulsbury, James to F. E. Sudberry 12-30-1871
Saunder, J. C. to Maggie Burns 2-2-1870
Saunders, Aleck to Emma Harris 8-22-1874 (9-22-1874)
Saunders, Jo. to Sarah Stanley 2-8-1869 (no return)
Saunders, Murry to Lucinda Parrish 7-15-1867 (7-16-1867)
Saunders, R. B. to Elizabeth Giles 10-1-1866 (10-2-1866)
Saunders, S. L. to E. F. Boyd 1-9-1871 (no return)
Saunderson, J. W. to Darcus Smith 5-4-1872 (5-5-1872)
Sawrie, R. A. to S. E. Harwell 11-4-1868 (no return)
Sawyer, Charles to Fanny Akin 12-26-1868 (12-28-1868)
Sawyer, Charley to Martha Featherston 1-1-1874
Sawyer, Chas. to Mary Bradford 6-29-1868
Sawyer, Daniel to Rhody Williams 5-12-1866 (5-16-1866)
Sawyer, Dennis F. to Joella Webb 8-15-1872 (8-16-1872)
Sawyer, John to Mary Ann Leroy 6-26-1871
Sawyer, Joseph to Anna Light 6-8-1870
Sawyer, Stephen to Martha Jane Ferrill 4-17-1873 (no return)
Scales, S. S. to Lou Burney 11-22-1876 (no return)
Scallions, W. M. to Missouri Harvell 5-17-1869 (5-18-1869)
Scarce, J. H. to Minerva Orr 9-2-1878 (9-5-1878)
Scobey, F. E. to M. E. Smith 12-11-1878 (12-12-1878)
Scobey, L. C. to Parthena Scobey 11-22-1871 (11-24-1871)
Scoby, D. J. to C. R. Hugueley 5-5-1863 (5-6-1863)
Scoby, W. B. to Margaret M. Huguely 2-8-1862 (2-12-1862)
Scott, Abner Tom to Alice Matheny 4-8-1879
Scott, Allen to Sallie Oliver 12-20-1871 (12-21-1871)
Scott, Cornelius to Eliza Douglass 9-28-1872
Scott, David to Missie Applewhite 12-17-1872 (12-18-1872)
Scott, G. A. to A. J. Hurley 2-19-1878 (2-21-1878)
Scott, Geo. E. to Fannie Stevens 4-28-1874
Scott, H. C. to Emma Jordan 1-8-1878 (1-10-1878)
Scott, John to Densi Harris 4-23-1870
Scott, Nelson to Mattie Moseley 2-5-1880
Scott, P. L. to V. A. Humble 5-22-1879 (6-7-1879)
Scott, Samel to Susan Porter 12-24-1872 (12-30-1872)
Scott, W. S. to Ann E. King 1-28-1874 (1-29-1874)
Scott, W. S. to Nancy E. Milam 4-8-1868 (4-9-1868)
Scott, Walter to Amanda Fowlkes 1-6-1866 (no return)
Scruggs, H. H. to S. F. Foster 7-15-1870 (7-18-1870)
Searcy, William to Eliza Talley 7-24-1875 (7-25-1875) B
Searcy, William to Julia Ann Johnson 5-1-1869 (no return)
Seat, J. G. to Lucy Latta 10-18-1871
Segraves?, Jack to Ellen Ledsinger 12-27-1877
Self, J. A. to M. F. Drummonds 11-11-1873 (11-15-1873)
Self, S. J. to Frances Gwaltney 12-5-1860 (no return)
Self, William to Marina Jane Jones 2-12-1873 (2-13-1873)

Seward, J. W. to M. E. Davis 9-11-1871 (no return)
Sewell, Marcus to Frances E. Hines 10-25-1875 (10-27-1875)
Shackleford, Charles (Dr.) to Henrietta (Mrs.?) Cogburn 1-1-1872 (1-2-1872)
Shallow, Ben to Fannie Connell 6-19-1876
Shankle, W. B. to Martha A. Dowell 1-20-1870 (no return)
Sharp, Jo. E. to Mamie Stevens 11-6-1878 (11-7-1878)
Shaw, Craig N. to Parthena Aiken 9-22-1869
Shaw, D. A. to M. J. Cope 8-3-1866 (8-12-1866)
Shaw, D. A. to Mollie Pierce 1-16-1872
Shaw, John A. to Louisa Bledsoe 9-13-1879 (9-14-1879)
Shaw, Judge to Mattie J. Clemmons 12-12-1874 (12-17-1874) B
Shaw, Nelson to Mattie Talley 1-27-1880 (no return)
Shaw, Nelson to Millie Connell 9-12-1872
Shaw, R. L. to Polly Via 12-10-1874
Shaw, W. L. to A. E. Johnson 12-24-1870 (12-25-1870)
Shaw, William to Elizabeth Thomas 1-17-1863 (1-22-1863)
Shekle, A. L. to H. R. Curtis 10-3-1870 (no return)
Shelton, Alfred to Martha Early 2-27-1867 (3-5-1867)
Shelton, Doc to Phillis Branch 7-17-1879 (no return)
Shelton, Elijah H. to Runinia Gurganus 9-29-1865 (10-1-1865)
Shelton, J. E. to H. A. McCormack 12-22-1875
Shelton, J. H. to Susan Payne 10-12-1867 (10-13-1867)
Shelton, J. W. to S. A. M. Gurganus 8-26-1867
Shelton, Thomas to Mary A. H. Phillips 11-30-1874 (12-2-1874)
Shepherd, Levi to Fannie Smith 4-10-1873 (4-11-1873)
Shepley, David to Sarah Jones 2-27-1878 (2-28-1878)
Sherwood, M. to Mollie Peery 6-12-1869 (6-13-1869)
Sheton, John A. to Scelia A. Williams 4-22-1865 (no return)
Shikle, A. L. to H. R. Curtis 10-3-1870 (12-5-1870)
Shirley, Edmond to Nancy Goings 5-2-1878
Shoemake, James to Julia Randolph 10-11-1860
Shofner, W. P. to F. A. Hamilton 3-18-1873 (3-23-1873)
Shorter, Levi T. to Flora Webster 3-31-1868 (no return)
Shurley, Edward to Mariah Musgrave 12-28-1872
Sidney, Sam N. to Laura A. Burton 12-4-1876 (12-14-1876)
Silsby, Louis H. to Harriet Liller Kent 4-28-1860 (4-29-1860)
Simmons, Albert to Letty Stewart 12-24-1873 (12-25-1873)
Simmons, Beng. to Jane Menzies 1-21-1869
Simmons, Berry to Melvina Foust 4-8-1875
Simmons, Dan to Isabella Smith 3-17-1875 (3-18-1875)
Simmons, Ed to Rebecca Asper 8-9-1873 (no return)
Simmons, Samuel to Martha Pope 9-7-1878 (9-17-1878)
Simmons, W. H. to Dicey Ridens 6-17-1869
Simmons, W. S. to Savannah Hastings 8-30-1879 (9-1-1879)
Simmons, W. W. to Arabella C. Walker 10-23-1861 (no return)
Simmons?, Flournoy T. to Mary E. Williamson 12-12-1866 (12-13-1866)
Simons, David C. to Mary E. Rogers 5-9-1868 (5-10-1868)
Simons, Thos. to Letitia Burnett 1-1-1867 (1-3-1867)
Simons, W. B. to Lucy Forbes 4-27-1872 (4-28-1872)
Simpkins, B. R. to Harriet Guinn 10-2-1863 (10-5-1863)
Simpson, G. W. to Susan Jenkins 11-29-1876
Simpson, John to Matilda Topp 6-1-1867 (6-10-1867)
Simpson, M. A. to Sarah E. Fullerton 3-6-1877
Simpson, T. F. to Lucy J. Howard 10-13-1873 (10-14-1873)
Simpson, T. F. to M. J. Singleterry 9-16-1868 (9-26-1868)
Simpson, W. H. to Jennie Chamblin 8-14-1867 (no return)
Simpson, W. K. to Mary A. Henry 12-29-1869 (12-30-1869)
Simpson, W. R. to A. F. (Mrs.) Murphey 11-30-1872 (11-3?-1872)
Simpson, W. R. to Tempe J. Williamson 12-16-1874
Sims, J. C. to Mary Jane Wilson 1-31-1865 (no return)
Sinclair, Ben to Adaline Avery 9-28-1871 (no return)
Sinclair, George to Louella Wynne 2-11-1874 (2-12-1874)
Sinclair, J. D. to Naomi L. Neal 9-26-1866 (9-27-1866)
Skipper, Jerry to Jane Johnson 12-4-1865
Skipper, Silas to Sofrona Hoge 5-2-1865 (5-3-1865)
Skipper, Thomas to Mary Johnson 7-4-1860
Skipper, William to Sarah Johnson 12-25-1860
Skipweth, J. C. to H. B. Chitwood 10-30-1867 (no return)
Slater, F. A. to J. E. Johnson 10-17-1874 (10-18-1874)
Slater, Isaac to Mary Nash 2-19-1867 (3-23-1867)
Slater, L. A. to A. B. Duncan 1-4-1864 (no return)
Slayton, Willis W. to Jane Harris 11-20-1860
Sledge, Robert to Sarah Gammons 3-8-1879 (3-9-1879)

Sledge, William to Beckie Gammons 7-15-1879 (7-16-1879)
Sloan, Martin L. to Isabella T. Weakly 3-9-1868 (3-10-1868)
Smalley, Anderson to Susan Bone 5-30-1871 (5-31-1871)
Smart, Alf? to Tete Mulherin 7-3-1877
Smart, M. W. to R. P. Warren 7-15-1879 (7-17-1879)
Smith, A. H. to S. H. L. Palmer 12-28-1870
Smith, A. M. to Susan Leggett 12-15-1868 (no return)
Smith, Alex to Jane Douglass 3-9-1871
Smith, Alexander to Martha Horton 9-24-1872 (9-25-1872)
Smith, Andrew to Mary Madry 12-26-1867
Smith, Andrew to Susan A. Sawyers 7-13-1872 (no return)
Smith, Armistead to Mollie Beard 11-11-1880
Smith, B. F. to Julia A. Henry 2-22-1869
Smith, Bedford to Tennessee Smith 11-7-1878
Smith, C. A. to L. F. Weatherington 2-24-1879 (2-27-1879)
Smith, C. H. to M. J. Jones 9-24-1869
Smith, D. A. to T. P. Hill 12-18-1868 (12-21-1868)
Smith, Dallis to America Fowlkes 12-8-1873 (no return)
Smith, David F. to Jane E. Butler 10-31-1864 (4-9-1864?)
Smith, Dennis to Charita Walker 1-18-1871 (1-19-1871) B
Smith, Dick to Angaline Fowlkes 1-26-1867 (1-27-1867)
Smith, Dick to Mary A. Howard 12-24-1866 (12-29-1866)
Smith, E. W. to Louanna Harton 2-10-1874 (2-11-1874)
Smith, Elijah to H. F. Morgan 3-2-1866 (3-4-1866)
Smith, F. P. to F. E. Harper 7-22-1876 (7-23-1876)
Smith, Frank to Judy Ann Whitson 1-17-1877
Smith, G. A. to Clem Staggs 4-20-1876
Smith, George to Mollie Smith 8-8-1878
Smith, Green to Susan Bradshaw 3-10-1880 (3-11-1880)
Smith, Hampton to Polly Grimm 12-6-1877
Smith, Henry to Jane Robertson 4-8-1861 (no return)
Smith, Henry to Sarah Bradshaw 9-15-1873 (9-16-1873)
Smith, Hilliard to Bettie Pickard 12-22-1874 (12-23-1874)
Smith, J. A. to M. A. Scobey 12-11-1878 (12-19-1878)
Smith, J. B. to Bettie Lumley 7-27-1872 (8-1-1872)
Smith, J. F. to Rebecca Smith 1-3-1867
Smith, J. H. to Polly Trout 10-4-1871 (no return)
Smith, J. P. to W. M. McDearmon 12-19-1878
Smith, J. R. to Mary (Mrs.) Roberts 3-29-1879 (3-30-1879)
Smith, Jackson to Ann Foust 12-14-1872 (12-26-1872)
Smith, James J. to Jennie A. White 11-6-1876 (no return)
Smith, James K. Polk to Maria Doyle 1-30-1867
Smith, James to Callie Williams 1-8-1874
Smith, James to Caroline Osburn 11-15-1877
Smith, James to Charity Manley 12-26-1870 (12-28-1870)
Smith, James to Maggie Ross 12-21-1876 (12-24-1876)
Smith, Jo. Fletcher to Rebecca A. Mahan 7-25-1867 (no return)
Smith, John D. to T. A. Archibald 2-24-1865 (2-28-1865)
Smith, John to Bettie Fumbanks 3-11-1880
Smith, John to Emily Johnson 2-5-1878
Smith, John to Lou Cobb 10-13-1875
Smith, John to Nora Woods 8-30-1877 (no return)
Smith, John to Sarah Doak 1-20-1871 (1-22-1871) B
Smith, Limerick to Adaline Bendon? 8-3-1867 (8-4-1867)
Smith, Lucien W. to Mary E. Butterworth 8-14-1877 (8-15-1877)
Smith, Monk to Ellen McCorkle 10-27-1875 (10-28-1875) B
Smith, Mose to Lucretia Fumbanks 2-14-1878
Smith, Nathan C. to Eliza Thompson 5-17-1871 (5-18-1871) B
Smith, Nathan to Frances Harris 4-19-1870 (no return)
Smith, Phillip to Malvina Mansfield 7-4-1867
Smith, Pleas to Ann Fowlkes 1-2-1871 (1-8-1871)
Smith, Pompey to Emma Fowlkes 2-16-1879
Smith, R. J. to L. R. Gammon 2-6-1869 (no return)
Smith, Richard to Mollie Spence 3-16-1878
Smith, Robert to Nicey Hodge 8-11-1868 (no return)
Smith, Rufus to Minerva McDaniel 1-22-1880 (1-21?-1880)
Smith, Rupert to Angaline Mahon 5-10-1867 (5-11-1867)
Smith, Sandy to Emiline Williams 7-5-1877
Smith, V. J. to Ann E. Cothran 2-20-1863 (2-24-1863)
Smith, Vincent to Tennessee McGary 12-27-1880 (12-29-1880)
Smith, W. B. to Mary B. Walker 2-6-1861 (2-7-1861)
Smith, W. M. to Julia Meadows 6-1-1867 (no return)
Smith, W. M. to Lizzie Simms 3-3-1873
Smith, Wesley to Emma Morgan 8-28-1880 (8-29-1880)
Smith, Will to Bettie McNail 1-5-1880 (1-15-1880)

Smith, Willis to Dollie Tucker 10-19-1870 (10-10?-1870) B
Smith, Wm. to Dollie Daniel 12-1-1877 (12-2-1877)
Smith, Wm. to Margaret Anderson 3-23-1875 (3-25-1875)
Smith, Wm. to Millie Silsby 6-14-1876 (6-15-1876)
Smith, Wyatt to Alice Ledsinger 4-13-1871 (4-14-1871)
Smither, Jos. H. to Verginia L. Richardson 10-10-1870 (10-11-1870)
Snead, Israel to Mary Jordan 11-17-1874 (11-18-1874)
Snow, Elijah to Martha Helen Jones 5-10-1862 (5-18-1862)
Snow, J. F. to Dicey E. Grills 10-31-1873 (11-4-1873)
Sollis, B. L. to Jane Boone 12-14-1867 (12-15-1867)
Sollis, Geo. D. to M. Amanda Lowe 2-1-1879
Sorrell, A. C. to Leonie Yow 9-12-1870 (9-13-1870)
Sorrell, Albert B. to Mary L. Neely 4-21-1866
Sorrell, J. H. to M. R. Yowe 12-22-1870
Sorrell, Jeptha O. to Rachael Eeson 3-28-1865
Sorrell, N. W. to Mattie Page 1-3-1872
Sorrell, S. C. to E. F. Lovelace 7-29-1868 (no return)
Sorrell, W. W. to Viola Turnley 10-23-1877 (10-24-1877)
Southerland, James B. to Jane Spain 10-29-1860 (no return)
Southern, Louis to Isabella Pierce 12-?-1865 (12-30-1865)
Southern, Millard to Julia Talley 4-6-1878 (4-7-1878)
Soward, Bird to Mollie Miller 2-7-1878
Soward, John to Edwina? Parr 2-24-1876 (no return)
Sowers, J. P. to M. E. Williams 8-1-1871
Spain, W. W. to M. E. Miller 5-23-1860
Spain, William D. to Jennie Nichols 7-12-1875 (7-13-1875)
Speight, J. H. to Fannie Hilliard 11-10-1873 (no return)
Spence, Charles to Tennessee Anderson 8-23-1866 (8-24-1866)
Spence, G. E. to Lucinda Thompson 10-1-1867 (no return)
Spence, Henry to Lizzie Bell 6-30-1876
Spence, Wm. to Frances Smith 2-22-1878 (2-23-1878)
Spence, Wm. to Susan Fields 1-15-1868
Spencer, Isaac to May F. Lyons 5-11-1874
Spencer, J. P. to Elizabeth Jackson 9-19-1878 (9-20-1878)
Spencer, Jacob to Rebecca Reynolds 1-18-1870 (1-16?-1870)
Spoon, W. R. to E. T. Cochrane 12-1-1876 (12-3-1876)
Spoon, William R. to L. E. Jones 7-20-1878 (7-21-1878)
Spradlin, William to Amanda I. Johnson 4-3-1876 (4-12-1876)
Spraggins, H. T. to Annie Williams 1-25-1879 (1-26-1879)
Spraggins, W. F. to Mary Edwards 5-5-1877
Staggs, Etheridge to Sarah M. Hood 1-11-1877
Staggs, Henry to Martha Ann Redding 12-23-1863 (no return)
Staggs, Henry to Martha Davidson 12-24-1864 (1-2-1865)
Staggs, R. to Darcus (Mrs.) Swann 4-3-1871 (4-9-1871)
Stagner, J. W. to Eugene Mitchner 3-2-1878 (3-23-1878)
Stalcup, B. S. M. to H. I. Hall 1-19-1871
Stalkup, J. F. to M. A. Lawhorn 1-27-1870 (1-28-1870)
Stallcupp, W. J. to Sarah J. Taylor 4-10-1869
Stamp, J. T. to S. A. Bui? 12-6-1865 (12-13-1865)
Stamps, J. T. to S. A. Bell 12-6-1865 (12-13-1865)
Stamps, Nathan to Margaret Willis 7-17-1867 (8-10-1867)
Stanfield, Wm. H. to Roxana O. Davis 11-4-1868 (no return)
Stanley, Henry to Nancy Rogers 8-24-1878 (8-25-1878)
Starks, Pharaoh to Angeline Wynne 12-23-1879
Statum, George to Josephine Livingstone 10-25-1877
Steart, T. W. to Hellen T. Brown 10-18-1871 (no return)
Steele, W. F. to M. E. Ayers 1-10-1876 (1-12-1876)
Stephens, D. H. to S. E. Gillis 3-11-1875
Stephens, D. M. to Lizzie Hobson 1-14-1878 (1-16-1878)
Stephens, John to Mary A. Halbrooks 8-11-1863
Stephens, Mortimer to S. B. Robbins 1-30-1878 (no return)
Stephenson, W. C. to Susan Gentry 1-12-1876
Stevens, A. M. to Julia A. Brackin 12-19-1865 (12-21-1865)
Stevens, Henry to Eliza Sinclair 3-8-1870 (no return)
Stevenson, J. B. M. to Mary F. Viah? 1-3-1866 (no return)
Stevenson, N. K. to Emma Brown 1-1-1863
Steward, George to Amanda Wood 1-1-1878
Stewart, James to Eliza Ledsinger 12-28-1870 (12-29-1870)
Stewart, John M. to Nancy Elizabeth Crews 10-12-1870 (10-13-1870)
Stinson, David to Mary Parker 12-28-1868 (12-29-1868)
Stockton, J. S. to M. A. Scobey 12-2-1878 (12-5-1878)
Stockton, J. T. to Jennie Pace 9-15-1874 (9-17-1874)
Stone, W. A. to M. C. Manley 10-17-1874 (no return)
Strawn, J. A. to S. J. Minton 3-31-1865 (4-1-1865)
Strayhorn, S. H. to Sarah M. Biggs 12-8-1868 (12-9-1868)

Strayhorn, Willis to Fannie Blair 1-31-1872 (2-1-1872)
Stricklan, Jackson to Hasentine Thurmond 2-18-1871 (2-19-1871)
Strickland, William to Amanda Watkins 5-8-1875 (5-9-1875)
Stricklen, Janus M. to Amanda J. Strange 3-10-1868
Stricklin, James to Virginia D. Drummond? 7-5-1869 (no return)
Strong, Morris to Franky Williams 1-1-1868 (1-2-1868)
Strong, Osborne to T. S. Talley 12-27-1876
Strother, Henry to Ann Ferguson 12-24-1868
Strother, Henry to Harriet Ann Beard 7-18-1873 (no return) B
Strother, Hesikiah to Eliza Smith 10-4-1880 (10-17-1880)
Strother, Hezekiah to Mollie Maddra 7-18-1873 (10-31-1873)
Stull, R. D. to Joseph Isabella Staggs 1-30-1877
Sudberry, James F. to M. E. Smith 11-25-1873 (no return)
Sullivan, B. H. to Anna Stephens 2-23-1876
Sumrow, R. W. to Nancy Warren 1-7-1867
Suttlemore, James to Jennie Colvin 12-29-1875 (1-2-1876)
Swanner, J. G. to Jennie Jackson 10-26-1871
Swayne, Adam to Ann Odum 5-11-1867 (no return)
Swift, James to Eliza Curtis 8-2-1871 (8-19-1871)
Swift, Willie to Victoria McGaughey 7-26-1873 (no return)
Swift, Willis to Victoria McGaughen 7-26-1873 (8-27-1873)
Swindle, A. R. to Fannie Taylor 2-6-1873
Swindle, E. H. to I. J. Bruithwick 2-26-1866
Talley, J. Thomas to M. E. Harrison 12-24-1873
Talley, James to Adaline Harris 4-29-1876 (4-30-1876) B
Talley, T. S. to Lola Jones 6-20-1878
Tancel, A. L. to Sarah A. Spence 6-18-1868
Tansel, Thomas E. to Mary McBride 10-12-1871
Tansil, M. to Mollie Jones 1-13-1874
Tansil, Sain A. to Dolly Wherry 5-7-1875
Tarkington, A. W. to E. R. Tipton 1-5-1867 (1-7-1867)
Tarkington, Wm. D. to Fannie Sorrell 4-3-1878 (4-4-1878)
Tarrant, John H. to M. A. S. Graw (McGraw?) 9-24-1866 (9-25-1866)
Tarrant, N. B. to S. V. Smith 1-4-1870 (1-5-1870)
Tatam, George W. to Rachael Aronhart 5-25-1865
Tate, W. G. to Elizabeth Peoples 9-20-1872 (9-29-1872)
Tatum, Andy to Harriett Palmer 12-26-1870 (12-29-1870)
Tatum, George M. to Eunice Bloomingdale 11-27-1877 (11-28-1877)
Tatum, P. B. to Emma A. Wood 4-24-1866
Taylor, C. A. G. to A. L. Hall 9-19-1867
Taylor, Crofford to Katharin Duncan 5-16-1865
Taylor, D. F. to Margaret E. Wilkinson 6-2-1879
Taylor, D. F. to S. J. Hawkins 1-7-1879 (1-8-1879)
Taylor, Duncan D. to Nancy Ellis 10-14-1868 (10-15-1868)
Taylor, Granville to Sarah Tucker 12-25-1877 (12-27-1877)
Taylor, H. M. to L. C. Rainey 2-4-1875
Taylor, Henry to Caroline Alexander 8-3-1870 (8-4-1870)
Taylor, Henry to Lizzie Glevur? 11-30-1872 (12-1-1872)
Taylor, Henry to Mary Crow 11-21-1874 (11-24-1874) B
Taylor, Henry to Nancy E. Ayers 1-28-1874 (1-29-1874)
Taylor, J. B. to Susan Anna Jones 12-27-1876 (12-28-1876)
Taylor, James N. to Margaret E. Taylor 10-16-1866 (10-18-1866)
Taylor, John S. to M. A. K. Enoch 12-23-1865 (12-27-1865)
Taylor, John to Martha Stegall 2-2-1864 (2-3-1864)
Taylor, Powell S. to Margaret E. Spain 7-18-1867
Taylor, S. J. to Mollie E. Crenshaw 10-13-1873 (10-15-1873)
Taylor, W. N. to Miranda G. Nash 11-25-1878 (11-27-1878)
Taylor, W. N. to Rebecca L. Harton 11-14-1870 (11-15-1870)
Taylor, William D. to C. A. Garrison 8-7-1878 (8-8-1878)
Taylor, William to F. E. Enochs 10-8-1872 (10-9-1872)
Teater, B. W. to Margaret M. Hendricks 10-30-1867 (no return)
Templeton, R. F. to S. A. Akin 1-21-1868 (1-22-1868)
Templeton, S. G. to S. E. Williams 8-21-1865 (8-22-1865)
Terry, Pleasant to Matilda Ferguson 12-14-1864
Tevilla, E. P. to T. A. Peery 11-10-1868
Tevilla, H. C. to Sarah Edwards 11-28-1868 (11-30-1868)
Thacker, Moses to Rachel Lovelace 12-21-1868 (no return)
Therman, E. S. to Alice Nichols 10-14-1868 (10-15-1868)
Thetford, J. C. to Mary E. Canada 12-12-1868 (12-13-1868)
Thitford, J. A. to P. J. Aikin 1-8-1867 (1-9-1867)
Thogmodden, J. D. to Lucra Price 2-19-1867 (3-22-1867)
Thomas, Isaac to Rachel Walker 12-27-1876
Thomas, John H. to Alice Silsby 12-28-1872
Thomas, Levin to Elizabeth A. Goodrich 3-7-1861
Thomas, Pate to Lou Enochs 1-3-1878

Thomas, Robt. H. to Margaret M. Teater 7-27-1878 (7-28-1878)
Thomas, W. A. to Hattie (Mrs.) Martin 12-26-1870
Thomason, H. M. to M. A. Seals 8-14-1869 (no return)
Thomason, James G. to Mary E. Knowles 11-13-1878
Thomasson, Osborn to Lucy Ferrill 12-27-1880 (no return)
Thompson, Anely to Sarah Holland 11-27-1860
Thompson, Columbus W. to Elizabeth F. Moore 1-17-1871
Thompson, F. H. to Sarah A. Wheeler 8-14-1860 (no return)
Thompson, J. B. to Lizzie Spain 2-25-1878 (2-27-1878)
Thompson, J. S. to M. F. Smith 8-12-1867 (8-13-1867)
Thompson, J. S. to Mary McCutchen 12-30-1868 (no return)
Thompson, J. W. to Mollie Edwards 2-23-1876
Thompson, Jarret to Martha A. R. Thompson 5-15-1865
Thompson, M. to L. C. Parks 12-10-1872 (12-11-1872)
Thompson, S. F. to M. L. Baker 11-5-1873 (11-6-1873)
Thompson, Stephen S. to Sarah E. McBride 5-25-1867 (5-27-1867)
Thompson, Thomas to Amanda R. Moseley 12-24-1873
Thompson, William H. to Susan M. Gibson 8-1-1863 (8-2-1863)
Thompson, William to Abby Green 4-6-1870 (4-7-1870)
Thornton, John H. to Sarah J. Olds 12-2-1868
Thornton, S. L. to M. A. King 11-18-1874 (11-19-1874)
Thornton, Seth L. to Lillian C. King 12-3-1867 (no return)
Thornton, T. H. to M. R. Griffin 1-16-1878
Thorp, S. A. to Jennette Hitchcock 5-16-1866 (5-20-1866)
Thurman, Wm. M. to M. A. Nash 3-9-1866 (3-11-1866)
Thurmond, J. N. to Emiline Johnson 9-11-1873
Thurmond, J. P. to C. A. Wood 2-15-1865
Thurmond, Richard to Callie Grace 8-28-1877 (8-29-1877)
Tigrett, A. B. to Lutie A. Parks 5-14-1873 (5-15-1873)
Tilman, J. F. to M. O. T. West 6-10-1879 (6-11-1879)
Tiner, W. H. R. to Ellen Green? 10-29-1867
Tinkle, S. A. to J. A. Petty 6-1-1874 (no return)
Tinkle, Thos. W. to Sarah A. Moore 2-2-1861 (2-3-1861)
Tinsley, Charles A. to Amanda L. Simms 3-17-1868 (no return)
Tinsley, G. P. to Callie Maxwell 5-7-1873 (5-8-1873)
Tinsley, J. W. to Claudia Lovelace 3-21-1877
Tipton, Alex to Jane Hutson 2-20-1878 (no return)
Tipton, Alex to Lucy Smith 6-3-1879
Tipton, Alex to Mary Spence 5-30-1866 (6-2-1866)
Tipton, Fillmore to Caroline Ruff 2-28-1877
Tipton, H. T. to Mattie E. Tipton 2-20-1866
Tipton, J. Cas to Mamie J. Want? 6-5-1870
Tipton, J. D. B. to Ella F. Pate 8-15-1874 (8-16-1874)
Tipton, J. H. to M. J. Smith 4-12-1871 (no return)
Tipton, Lee to Sarah Frazier 10-10-1874 (10-19-1874)
Tipton, P. L. to Sallie A. Light 10-3-1874 (10-4-1874)
Tipton, P. M. to Barbary Walker 11-16-1865
Tipton, Pleasant to Mary E. Tarkington 11-3-1868
Tipton, Preston M. to Mollie P. Leight 2-6-1878
Tipton, William to Clary Spence 5-8-1879 (5-9-1879)
Tipton, William to Mariah Ruff 10-31-1874
Tipton, Wm. M. to Nancy Pooch 12-25-1866
Tipton, jr., Wiley B. to Rebecca A. McDavid 10-9-1866
Todd, A. F. to Sallie Armstrong 9-6-1866
Todd, C. W. to S. A. Carter 10-1-1879
Tolbert, W. S. to Mollie Blackman 2-27-1876 (2-28-1876)
Topp, Ben to Phillip Johnson 2-21-1868 (2-22-1868)
Topp, Wash to Amanda Edwards 12-28-1870 (12-29-1870)
Torrence, James M. to Emma M. Brown 4-26-1870
Tower, George A. to E. M. Hull 7-6-1870
Townsend, Henry to Octavy Peacock 11-3-1880 (11-4-1880)
Townsend, J. C. G. to Nancy E. Adams 9-13-1860
Townsend, John to Lizzie Enochs 12-29-1873 (12-30-1873)
Townsend, Stephen to Lou Beaumont 8-16-1877
Trafford, J. V. to Frances Richardson 6-11-1870 (6-12-1870)
Trail, Valentine to Martha E. Dickey 4-23-1864 (4-26-1864)
Travis, Geo. to Bettie Copeland 1-28-1874 (1-29-1874)
Travis, John to Amanda Swanner 12-12-1877
Treadwell, Albert to Septimus Dunnegan 1-31-1874 (2-8-1874)
Trew, Robert to Ada Jones 8-26-1870 (8-29-1870)
Trimble, J. L. to T. C. Scott 2-26-1873 (2-27-1873)
Tripp, George to Malinda Gaskins 6-4-1879 (6-22-1879)
Trotter, William A. to Annie Todd 4-29-1861 (5-2-1861)
Trout, Daniel H. to Mary Cox 10-15-1870 (10-16-1870)
Trout, J. B. to E. C. Tucker 3-25-1867 (2?-28-1867)

Trout, J. W. to M. E. Turrentine 12-20-1866 (12-23-1866)
Trout, J. W. to N. L. Hendricks 12-24-1876 (12-26-1876)
Trout, W. E. to Maggie Simons 12-31-1878 (1-1-1879)
Trout, W. S. to Susan A. Wood 11-20-1866 (no return)
Troutt, E. H. to Lonesome Howard 1-28-1870 (1-29-1870)
Troy, Edgar to Margaret Burnham 2-10-1869 (no return)
Troy, F. A. to M. A. Crow 12-11-1872
Troy, J. P. to M. J. Smith 9-14-1863 (9-15-1863)
Troy, James F. to E. A. King 8-25-1866 (8-26-1866)
Troy, William E. to Harriet Garrison 5-27-1862 (no return)
Troy, Zach T. to S. A. Crow 12-28-1867 (12-29-1867)
Trusty, Thomas T. to Mary F. Cooper 8-21-1872
Trusty, W. T. to Rebecca Wright 2-7-1872 (no return)
Tucker, Daniel S. to M. L. (Mrs.) Walker 2-19-1872 (2-20-1872)
Tucker, J. B. to Eudora Parker 4-1-1879 (4-2-1879)
Tucker, Jno. B. to Mozella Perry 10-1-1866 (10-10-1866)
Tucker, Stephen to M. A. T. Bean 10-25-1870 (no return)
Tunely?, H. L. W. to N. (Mrs.) Conwell 8-3-1868 (8-4-1868)
Turfim, Wm. to Nancy Ann Wright 2-17-1863 (2-18-1863)
Turnage, Green to Alice Stevens 8-23-1872 (8-25-1872)
Turner, Frank to Margaret Arnold 12-21-1870
Turner, J. M. to Lucinda Lumley 1-31-1877 (2-1-1877)
Turner, James to Eliza Jane Craig 1-28-1864 (no return)
Turner, James to Jane Goodrich 12-23-1864
Turner, John to Bettie Wynne 8-21-1878 (8-28-1878)
Turner, Thomas to Mariah Wilson 6-12-1878 (6-13-1878)
Turner, W. S. to Laura J. McIntosh 4-8-1867
Turner, William to Jane Pinkston 6-1-1861 (no return)
Turner, Wm. to Martha Walker 5-12-1869 (no return)
Turpin, Joseph to Juntha J. Steward 12-5-1860 (12-26-1860)
Turpin, Richmond to Ann Eliza Harris 9-22-1863 (9-23-1863)
Turpin, Richmond to Louisa T. Hassell 6-13-1864 (no return)
Tyler, H. A. to Bettie Fowlkes 4-1-1868 (4-2-1868)
Tyler, Mark to Mary Jane Watson 5-12-1879
Underwood, Wm. to Sarah Waters 12-14-1877 (12-20-1877)
Vail, LJ. N. to D. E. Bettis 8-5-1871 (no return)
Vail, W. M. to D. A. Timmes? 12-19-1878
Vann, J. C. to Sue M. Fuller 10-28-1868 (11-29-1868)
Vaughan, J. H. to Anne Colvin 9-7-1878 (9-8-1878)
Vaughan, Wm. H. to M. E. Olive 9-10-1872 (9-11-1872)
Vernon, E. R. (Dr.) to Sallie Clark 12-25-1867
Vernon, John E. to Mary E. Wesson 9-22-1871 (9-25-1871)
Via, Pleasant to Louisa A. Webb 11-14-1876
Via, Stephen A. to Nancy J. Jarrett 7-19-1871 (no return)
Viar, R. F. to Martha E. Pitts 8-22-1866 (8-23-1866)
Viar, Thomas to Melissa E. Viar 11-16-1865 (no return)
Vican, John A. to Jennie Williams 6-6-1879 (6-15-1879)
Vick, Wm. S. to Susan A. Brimingham 11-16-1864
Vincent, N. P. to Sarah J. Ball 3-10-1866 (no return)
Vinyard, W. F.? to Nancy J. Humphreys 12-24-1868 (no return)
Vire, M. R. to Ann Gammons 12-21-1866 (12-27-1866)
Waddy, William to Annie Turner 12-23-1871 (12-24-1871)
Wade, J. E. to M. R. Crudup 8-20-1878 (8-21-1878)
Wade, R. P. to Charlotte L. Jackson 12-20-1867 (12-28-1867)
Wade, R. P. to Nancy J. Forshee 11-12-1868
Wade, Tinzel to H. Mitchuer 1-20-1872 (1-21-1872)
Wadlingford, John W. to Julia Anderson 1-31-1878 (2-3-1878)
Wadlington, Ben C. to M. T. Enochs 9-24-1877 (9-27-1877)
Waggoner, David to S. E. Cobb 10-22-1879 (10-23-1879)
Waggoner, G. W. to Angeline Chitwood 1-20-1869 (1-21-1869)
Waggoner, Leonard to Jennie Green 12-13-1878 (12-18-1878)
Wagster, R. A. to S. E. Corley 2-28-1867
Waldren, J. H. to Adaline Featherston 2-12-1873 (no return)
Waldron, J. W. to Mollie Wofford 1-1-1877 (1-4-1877)
Walker, A. C. to M. A. Walker 8-3-1869 (8-4-1869)
Walker, Archer to Letheann Fowlkes 12-25-1877 (no return)
Walker, Bailey to Cheney Fowlkes 6-22-1872 (6-30-1872)
Walker, Ben T. to Ellen Pinyan 11-3-1877 (11-4-1877)
Walker, David B. to Martha A. McKane 3-17-1868 (no return)
Walker, G. W. to Julia Colvin 4-13-1876
Walker, G. W. to S. E. Shelton 3-5-1879 (3-6-1879)
Walker, H. S. to Elizabeth Gammons 12-14-1870 (12-15-1870)
Walker, H. S. to L. C. Harrison 12-24-1862 (1-8-1863)
Walker, Henry Ray to Mary Ann Light 6-5-1866
Walker, J. A. to M. M. Shelton 10-16-1869 (10-17-1869)

Walker, J. P. to Emma Harris 10-29-1873
Walker, Mose? to Mary Jane Jones 7-23-1873
Walker, Moses to Josephine Johnson 9-12-1866 (9-27-1866
Walker, P. A. to E. C. Milam 10-16-1866 (no return)
Walker, T. J. to L. E. Price 1-14-1867 (1-20-1867)
Walker, Uriah to Huldah Porter 12-12-1876 (12-13-1876)
Walker, W. A. J. to Mary A. Smith 9-7-1870 (no return)
Walker, W. S. to Martha J. King 8-12-1869 (8-13-1869)
Walker, W. T. to Bettie E. Jones 7-25-1877
Walker, W. W. to Myra McGaughy 7-31-1867
Walker, Washington to Sarah Word 12-23-1871 (12-26-1871)
Wall, J. W. to M. A. Lovett 9-28-1868 (no return)
Wallace, J. A. to Susana Wallace 3-25-1873 (3-27-1873)
Wallace, James A. to Mary C. Jack 11-11-1862 (11-13-1862)
Wallace, W. A. to M. Reed 3-9-1863 (3-25-1863)
Walls, James M. to Polly McCrackin 9-11-1861 (no return)
Walls, James to Matilda Sevier? 10-24-1866
Walton, C. J. to Jane Nichols 5-3-1879
Walton, Charles C. to Mary K. Phillips 7-30-1879 (7-31-1879)
Walton, Daniel to Emiline Webster 1-20-1872 (2-1-1872)
Walton, George to Ann Haskins 7-14-1877 (7-15-1877)
Walton, J. H. to Sallie C. Bell 12-7-1868 (no return)
Walton, Stephen to Mollie Davis 3-5-1873 (3-6-1873)
Walton, T. H. to Elizabeth F. Payne 6-23-1862 (no return)
Ward, Charles to Harriet Rice 2-21-1872 (2-23-1872)
Ward, Henry to Mary Silsby 12-20-1865 (12-24-1865)
Ward, J. B. to M. J. Hampden 9-7-1872 (no return)
Ward, J. H. to Annie Miller 10-1-1877 (no return)
Ward, J. S. to Mary E. Thompson 1-27-1868
Ward, John to Martha Cearley 8-12-1867
Ward, R. M. to A. Oneal 10-21-1867 (10-24-1867)
Ward, Willis to Ann Powell 12-2-1869 (no return)
Warmack, James to Mary Shelton 11-28-1873 (12-11-1873)
Warmack, William to Lavina Grayum 8-17-1870 (8-29-1870)
Warren, James to Martha J. Stucken 11-22-1865
Warren, Joseph to Caroline Bell 4-14-1868 (no return)
Warren, Nathaniel W. to Harriet R. Vail 4-2-1864 (4-4-1864)
Warren, W. S. to Mariah O. Striclin 2-19-1869 (no return)
Washington, Lewis to Fannie White 5-17-1877
Waters, F. M. to Frances Simpson 1-1-1870 (1-3-1870)
Waters, J. N. to Eliza A. Murray 6-13-1868
Waters, L. H. to Hattie Nash 4-10-1880 (4-18-1880)
Watkins, Newton P. to Martha J. Watson 2-6-1869 (no return)
Watkins, W. L. to Mary K. Weakley 2-14-1866
Watkins, Will M. to Eliza A. Phillips 9-27-1860
Watkins, Zach to Fannie Stevens 10-11-1876 (10-12-1876)
Watson, Albert to Mary J. Simpson 11-20-1868 (11-22-1868)
Watson, W. H. to Mary Jones 11-27-1871 (11-28-1871)
Wayson, Alex to Nancy Stricklin 1-15-1878
Weakley, D. R. to Sallie E. Curtis 3-8-1872
Weakley, Henry to Agnes Hale 8-1-1877
Weakley, M. H. P. to Mary Morris 12-24-1870 (3-15-1871)
Weakly, James to Mary Hall 5-22-1867
Weaver, Charles to Martha Turner 11-26-1860
Weaver, W. J. to Cerilla J. Parteet 2-18-1869 (no return)
Webb, Asberry to Louiza A. Robbins 9-12-1860
Webb, E. W. to E. F. Baker 10-18-1879 (10-19-1879)
Webb, G. W. to Ann B. Tatum 8-12-1868 (8-20-1868)
Webb, J. R. to Mary E. Chitwood 9-30-1865 (no return)
Webb, James F. to Malissa C. Gowan 7-31-1878 (8-1-1878)
Webb, John to Ella (Mrs.) Tucker 12-24-1866 (12-25-1866)
Webb, Thos. H. to M. S. Macomb 9-4-1867 (no return)
Webb, W. A. to Mollie Grace 8-22-1877
Webber, James A. to Martha A. Simons 5-3-1875 (5-4-1875)
Webster, J. M. to M. A. Gentry 1-10-1872
Webster, John to Chincy Norment 7-3-1867
Weddington, W. B. to Josaphine McMackin 2-15-1871
Welch, Esquire to Rachel Jones 6-19-1877
Welch, S. J. to M. L. E. Johnson 8-18-1870
Welch, W. G. to M. F. Rainey 10-29-1870 (10-30-1870)
Welch, William to Florence Claiss 7-29-1874
Wells, Lee to Dinkie Light 10-26-1871
Wells, T. Lee to Ella Pell 2-26-1879
Wells, Thomas to Mary Smith 2-17-1866 (2-18-1866)
Wesley, J. W. to Mattie Williams 12-25-1874 (no return)

Wesson, J. D. to P. A. Dickey 2-3-1875 (2-4-1875)
Wesson, J. W. to M. M. Dodd 5-24-1869 (5-27-1869)
Wesson, Nat to Mary F. Williams 12-24-1867 (no return)
Wheeler, J. E. to M. J. Hart 2-17-1872 (2-18-1872)
Wheeler, J. T. to F. M. Hart 1-14-1879 (1-15-1879)
Whichard, J. W. to Susan Ann Woods 3-25-1879 (3-28-1879)
White, A. S. to Julia A. Archer 9-6-1875 (9-8-1875)
White, Aaron to Susan Ward 11-30-1878 (12-1-1878)
White, Bryant to Margaret Walker 3-24-1870 (no return)
White, C. B. R. to Amanda Yow 10-20-1874 (10-21-1874)
White, Henry W. to Sarah E. Edwards 12-2-1861
White, J. A. to Sarah E. McAfee 7-5-1869 (7-7-1869)
White, J. E. to J. L. Jackson 3-15-1877
White, J. E. to J. L. Jackson ?-?-1877 (no return)
White, J. M. to F. L. Dodd 9-10-1865 (9-11-1865)
White, James Henry to Margrett E. Jones 2-8-1870 (2-9-1870)
White, M. V. to E. P. C. Curtis 5-22-1867 (5-23-1867)
White, Patrick Y. to Sarah J. Hibbitts 2-6-1866 (2-7-1866)
White, Wm. to Dilsy Allen 7-9-1866 (6?-10-1866)
Whitehorn, W. W. to Lizzie Reasons 7-9-1872 (7-15-1872)
Whitis, Benjamine to Amanda Lanier 2-5-1861 (2-20-1861)
Whitlock, William to C. F. Jones 3-6-1874 (3-7-1874)
Whitlock, Wm. to Nancy Watson 1-19-1867 (1-21-1867)
Whitman, John F. to Louisa Neal 11-29-1862
Whitson, G. W. to Mary E. Cooper 5-6-1871
Whitson, John T. to Emaline Wynne 4-4-1861
Whitson, John T. to Mary L. McKnight 7-24-1879
Whittaker, Orange to Mollie Patterson 1-17-1876 (no return)
Whitten, James W. to Jennie Wright 6-16-1874 (no return)
Whitten, M. H. to Dora Wiseman 5-30-1874 (no return)
Whittenton, J. R. to M. Troy 8-26-1869 (8-27-1869)
Whittington, John to Viny M. King 10-30-1865 (10-31-1865)
Whittle, M. (Rev.) to Mary Foard 1-3-1863 (no return)
Wicks, G. A. to Mary Gibson 1-4-1875 (1-5-1875)
Wicks, Tobe to Cynthia A. Ledsinger 12-27-1875
Wigfall, R. F. to Margaret McCutchen 7-23-1875 (7-24-1875)
Wiggin, J. R. to Sarah Jane Arnold 4-12-1871 (4-13-1871)
Wilborne, George to Sallie A. Finch 1-5-1876
Wilcox, W. L. to S. J. Hendrix 10-22-1867 (no return)
Wilkins, Henry to Harriet Ann Deak 4-14-1880 (4-15-1880)
Wilkins, Newton Benjamin to Lucinda Elizabeth A. Campbell 12-20-1873 (12-21-1873)
Wilkinson, James F. to Mary E. Spain 3-19-1878 (3-25-1878)
Wilkinson, R. B. to Louisa Drane 5-16-1878 (5-17-1878)
Williams, A. B. to Sally Ann Harrison 1-4-1866
Williams, A. L. to Susan Kirk 11-18-1874 (no return)
Williams, A. M. to Zylphia J. Williams 6-24-1873
Williams, Alex to Mary E. Norton 9-3-1867
Williams, Alex to Sylvia Mays 2-15-1877
Williams, Ben to Cynthia Stedman 11-16-1870 (11-18-1870)
Williams, Benj. F. to Dortha A(labama) Smith 12-12-1865 (12-13-1865)
Williams, Edward to Lyd A. Gillaland 1-30-1861 (no return)
Williams, H. B. to Martha Hardican 10-19-1863
Williams, J. H. to A. M. Nelson 12-14-1877 (12-16-1877)
Williams, J. R. to Callie Odle 8-22-1870 (8-28-1870)
Williams, J. W. to Soprona E. Whitt 5-8-1869 (no return)
Williams, Jno. A. (Dr.) to Harriet J. Wynne 3-27-1877 (no return)
Williams, Jo. to Martha Olds 2-10-1872 (2-19-1872)
Williams, John S. to Mary C. Adams 2-9-1870 (no return)
Williams, Joseph to Elizabeth Haskins 6-11-1879 (6-12-1879)
Williams, Luke to Martha Johnson 11-23-1870 (11-24-1870)
Williams, M. J. to Martha J. Cunningham 10-12-1869
Williams, M.? J. to Jane Fisher 9-3-1867 (no return)
Williams, N. to Elizabeth A. Reece 1-9-1871 (1-11-1871)
Williams, S. R. to A. R. Stalkup 10-17-1878 (10-18-1878)
Williams, Sam A. to Linnie Fields 11-23-1876
Williams, Samuel H. to Eddy Carter Haskins 12-23-1874 (12-24-1874)
Williams, W. A. to E. P. Thetford 10-11-1877 (no return)
Williams, Wesley to Elizabeth Johnson 11-19-1869 (11-21-1869)
Williams, William to Mary Patrick 4-2-1873 (4-3-1873)
Williamson, F. M. to Alice A. Nash 9-16-1868
Williamson, George to Mary Ray 9-23-1865 (9-24-1865)
Williamson, Hardy to Emiline McClusky 12-4-1867 (12-5-1867)
Williamson, J. F. to Susan E. Coleman 8-31-1860

Williamson, J. M. to Callie Boo 10-21-1879 (10-23-1879)
Williamson, Jeff to Harriet Maggard 1-20-1872 (1-21-1872)
Williamson, Spencer to Delilah Carpenter 5-2-1878
Williamson, W. C. to F. E. Lawhorn 1-20-1863 (1-21-1863)
Willis, Edward to Margaret M. Hommel 12-31-1860 (1-1-1861)
Willis, George W. to Efarilla Swanner 12-23-1863 (no return)
Willis, Thomas to Malinda Enochs 2-23-1872 (2-24-1872)
Williva, Washington to Nancy T. Etheridge 8-12-1862
Wilson, Dan T. to Lizzie Chadwick 6-6-1869 (no return)
Wilson, James to Nancy Vinson 4-23-1872 (4-24-1872)
Wilson, John T. to Julia A. Sparkman 7-13-1867 (7-14-1867)
Wilson, John W. to Lou Harris 10-21-1867 (no return)
Wimberley, B. F. to Nancy E. Stewart 4-27-1868
Winberry, Alfred to Mima Edwards 11-3-1869
Winberry, R. M. to Mary L. James 1-3-1871 (1-5-1871)
Winchester, Henry to Eliza Johnson 3-7-1874 (3-11-1874)
Winchester, Henry to Martha Ann King 12-24-1867 (12-25-1867)
Wood, Dock to Rebecca Richardson 12-18-1866 (1-20-1867)
Wood, Henry to Sarah McGary 5-6-1876 (5-7-1876)
Wood, James H. to Mary C. Porter 10-23-1876 (10-24-1876)
Wood, Minor to Lucy Smith 1-20-1869
Wood, Robert F. to Eliza Jane Whitson 12-23-1869 (no return)
Wood, S. A. to Dona Chitwood 5-11-1875
Wood, S. A. to Mary E. Coker 10-16-1879
Wood, Stephen to Alice Barnett 12-30-1874 (12-31-1874)
Wood?, James to Mary E. Davis 8-15-1867 (8-16-1867)
Woodard, Amos to Maryline Mills 4-30-1861
Woodburry, Henry to Charlotte L. Bradley 1-31-1861 (1-30?-1861)
Woods, Daniel to Emma Fowlkes 1-6-1872 (no return)
Woods, David to Delia Walker 12-6-1879 (12-8-1879)
Woods, Robert to Nancy Chitwood 12-16-1879 (no return)
Woods, Thomas to Sarah T. Harmon 1-11-1862 (1-12-1862)
Woods, W. H. to J. P. Green 10-2-1869 (10-6-1869)
Woods, W. to Susan Herald 3-6-1878 (3-7-1878)
Woods, Will to Rachel Harris 4-5-1879 (4-7-1879)
Woods, William T. to Susan Goodloe 11-28-1862 (12-?-1862)
Woodside, Amaziah to Frances Montgomery 10-3-1860 (no return)
Woodsides, J. M. to Alice Jackson 8-23-1875 (8-25-1875)
Woodson, Richard to Fannie Smith 2-12-1874
Wooley, D. W. to Maryline E. Moody 11-28-1874 (12-1-1874)
Word, Henry to Della Fields 12-25-1879
Works, Alex to Provie Clark 9-8-1877
Works, Frank to Jane Oldham 2-10-1872 (2-15-1872)
Worrel, Caswell to Nancy Williams 1-2-1866 (no return)
Wright, A. N. to Sallie Sandlin 10-20-1874 (10-22-1874)
Wright, Bascom to Alice Locke 7-28-1875 (no return)
Wright, James W. to Elizabeth Talley 5-14-1861
Wright, Jo? to Eva Ann Cole 3-11-1871 (3-12-1871)
Wright, John B. to Sarah M. Landrum 3-28-1877 (3-29-1877)
Wright, W. L. to Dennis Stone 10-16-1865 (10-18-1865)
Wright, William S. to Martha T. Smith 6-26-1863 (7-2-1863)
Wright, Wm. W. to Martha M. Headen 1-16-1871 (1-18-1871)
Wyatt, Geo. to Anna Bonds 2-28-1877 (no return)
Wyatt, Geo. to Henrietta Jane Chamberlain 1-14-1880 (1-17-1880)
Wyatt, J. N. to Parena V. Parks 12-13-1864 (no return)
Wyatt, W. L. to Harriet Hendricks 10-3-1871 (10-4-1871)
Wynn, Jeff to Berchie Crook 10-18-1880 (10-19-1880)
Wynn, Thomas to Mollie Doyle 9-25-1879
Wynn, V. G. to Agnes V. Tipton 12-20-1865
Wynne, B. F. to A. A. Dunevant 3-5-1873 (3-6-1873)
Wynne, Balsam to Abigial? Johnson 3-2-1867
Wynne, J. G. to M. T. Dunnevant 2-6-1868
Wynne, James Newton to Catharine Ledsinger 9-24-1869 (no return)
Wynne, Jeff to Jane Wynne 12-26-1867 (no return)
Wynne, Tom to Becky Wyett 12-24-1867 (12-26-1867)
Yates, J. S. to Belle Dickerson 12-13-1877 (12-18-1877)
Yates, James M. to Sarah F. Steen 3-29-1866 (no return)
Yates, L. H. to Polly Niece 12-4-1869 (12-5-1869)
Yates, S. J. to N. E. Sudbury 11-14-1866
Yates, W. H. to A. M. Foster 6-27-1860
Yeargin, George W. to Mary Ann Leroy 12-30-1862
York, Eugene to Susan F. Adcock 7-24-1875 (no return)
York, George W. to Fannie Watkins 4-18-1870 (no return)
York, John B. to V. C. McGill 10-18-1870 (10-20-1870)
York, W. B. (Dr.) to Mollie Parker 1-14-1867 (1-15-1867)

Young, B. F. to Laura A. Hopper 3-20-1878 (3-21-1878)
Young, C. M. to Margaret Brandon 8-30-1870 (9-1-1870)
Young, Charlie to Lucy White 10-21-1870 (1-22-1871)
Young, J. M. to Mary R. E. Walker 9-4-1876 (9-6-1876)
Young, Louis to Louisa Prato 9-17-1868 (no return)
Young, Thomas E. to S. C. Richie 12-22-1877 (12-23-1877)

Adams, Bettie J. to J. A. Lucas 2-8-1872 (2-13-1872)
Adams, Mary C. to John S. Williams 2-9-1870 (no return)
Adams, Nancy E. to J. C. G. Townsend 9-13-1860
Adams, Sallie to G. W. Pate 1-12-1876
Adcock, Susan F. to Eugene York 7-24-1875 (no return)
Agee, M. M. to W. A. H. Coop 1-7-1871 (1-10-1871)
Agee, S. C. M. to J. F. Pyland 9-30-1867 (no return)
Aiken, Parthena to Craig N. Shaw 9-22-1869
Aiken, Sarah E. to A. C. Harmon 8-30-1870 (8-31-1870)
Aiken, Susan J. to James T. Hester 9-5-1860
Aiken, Susanah to James W. Palmere 8-31-1868 (9-1-1868)
Aikens, Martha to Abner Perkins 4-30-1874
Aikin, P. J. to J. A. Thitford 1-8-1867 (1-9-1867)
Akin, Caifa? Frances to W. A. Hall 2-25-1869 (no return)
Akin, Fanny to Charles Sawyer 12-26-1868 (12-28-1868)
Akin, Julia Ann to S. D. Carroll 11-28-1870 (11-30-1870)
Akin, S. A. to R. F. Templeton 1-21-1868 (1-22-1868)
Albritton, Florence to G. W. Cherry 1-5-1872 (1-7-1872)
Alexander, Caroline to Henry Taylor 8-3-1870 (8-4-1870)
Allen, Dilsy to Wm. White 7-9-1866 (6?-10-1866)
Allen, Lowella to Allen Fumbanks 7-5-1879 (7-6-1879)
Allen, Mary J. to J. S. Brinkley 5-1-1861 (5-2-1861)
Allen, Mary to Colbert Blankenship 12-26-1863 (1-21-1864)
Anderson, Annie to W. R. G. Myett 2-17-1872 (2-18-1872)
Anderson, Fredericka to James D. Bush 3-10-1874
Anderson, Julia to John W. Wadlingford 1-31-1878 (2-3-1878)
Anderson, Margaret to Wm. Smith 3-23-1875 (3-25-1875)
Anderson, Tennessee to Charles Spence 8-23-1866 (8-24-1866)
Andrews, Mary G. to John W. Brown 2-22-1871 (2-23-1871)
Anthony, Cincinnati to T. L. Hamton 8-25-1869
Anthony, Elizabeth to W. L. Jones 12-22-1869 (12-23-1869)
Anthony, M. A. to J. A. Anthony 7-11-1877
Antwine, Sarah E. to James W. Nichols 1-9-1868 (1-12-1868)
Applewhite, Jennie to L. J. Clements 5-29-1878
Applewhite, M. L. to E. R. Garrett 2-1-1873
Applewhite, Martha W. to T. J. Nettles 8-5-1869
Applewhite, Missie to David Scott 12-17-1872 (12-18-1872)
Applewhite, Sallie to E. J. V. Jones 1-23-1878
Archer, Julia A. to A. S. White 9-6-1875 (9-8-1875)
Archibald, M. H. to J. F. Dickey 12-8-1869 (12-9-1869)
Archibald, T. A. to John D. Smith 2-24-1865 (2-28-1865)
Armstrong, Caroline to William Curtis 3-6-1861
Armstrong, M. H. to A. J. Lambert 3-29-1879 (4-1-1879)
Armstrong, Sallie to A. F. Todd 9-6-1866
Armstrong, Tennessee to T. J. Carter 12-29-1869 (12-30-1869)
Arnett, M. S. to H. H. Dozier 2-5-1873 (2-6-1873)
Arnold, Amanda to R. M. Brown 1-7-1875 (1-10-1875)
Arnold, Margaret to Frank Turner 12-21-1870
Arnold, Narcissa to James Bowen 11-2-1870 (no return) B
Arnold, Sarah Jane to J. R. Wiggin 4-12-1871 (4-13-1871)
Aronhart, Rachael to George W. Tatam 5-25-1865
Aronhart, Rachel to W. F. Lamarr 8-18-1866
Asper, Rebecca to Ed Simmons 8-9-1873 (no return)
Atkins, E. J. to Charley Hill 8-25-1873 (no return)
Atkins, H. A. to F. G. Mason 12-13-1865 (12-14-1865)
Atkins, Lean to Henry Hall 1-15-1877 (no return)
Atkins, Margaret to David Pettis 10-4-1871 (10-5-1871)
Austin, Susan to G. W. Holland 12-25-1865 (12-27-1865)
Averett, Martha R. to George S. Davidson 12-30-1867 (12-31-1867)
Avery, Adaline to Ben Sinclair 9-28-1871 (no return)
Ayers, M. E. to W. F. Steele 1-10-1876 (1-12-1876)
Ayers, Nancy E. to Henry Taylor 1-28-1874 (1-29-1874)
Badgett, Mary to George A. Finch 12-31-1864
Bailey, Millie E. to J. H. Mead 6-10-1871 (6-11-1871)
Bailey, Tennessee to W. C. Burnham 9-21-1875 (9-22-1875)
Baily, Tempy A. to J. W. Jones 5-14-1868 (5-15-1868)
Baker, Betcy Ann to Calven Jones 2-16-1865 (no return)
Baker, Catharine to Reddick Jones 5-16-1861
Baker, E. F. to E. W. Webb 10-18-1879 (10-19-1879)
Baker, L. F. to D. C. Dozier 7-13-1866 (7-15-1866)
Baker, M. L. to S. F. Thompson 11-5-1873 (11-6-1873)
Baker, M. M. to J. R. Churchman 11-7-1865 (no return)
Baker, Mary A. to William Campbell 7-3-1860
Baker, Mary E. to A. C. McNeell 7-28-1862 (7-29-1863?)
Baker, Nancy M. to W. C. Carpenter 10-2-1868 (10-4-1868)

Baker, Sarah E. to W. J. Combs 3-15-1869 (no return)
Baley, M. J. to A. J. Goatley 7-14-1860 (7-17-1860)
Ball, Sarah J. to N. P. Vincent 3-10-1866 (no return)
Ballentine, Marzella to John Bonds 9-3-1862 (9-4-1862)
Banks, Eliza to John J. Franklin 1-15-1868
Barker, Martha A. to Wm. Cooper 10-7-1868 (10-8-1868)
Barker, Susan C. (Mrs.) to W. A. Austin 9-12-1862 (9-13-1862)
Barnett, Alice to Stephen Wood 12-30-1874 (12-31-1874)
Barnett, J. E. to D. S. Burgie 10-13-1869
Barnett, Lou to Jery Fowlkes 3-28-1876 (no return)
Barnett, M. A. to J. W. Crawford 2-11-1866 (2-12-1866)
Barnett, Nancy E. to I. N. Davis 2-20-1863 (2-23-1863)
Barnett, Rebeccah C. to James H. Cooper 3-23-1865
Barrett, Martha A. to Wm. R. Brown 2-12-1875 (2-14-1875)
Barrett, Mexico to R. T. D. Norman 1-27-1876 (1-28-1876)
Battle, Mary F. to John Fuller 4-3-1873
Baxter, Adaline to Richard Jones 7-18-1870 (8-1-1870)
Baxter, Lizzie to Jo Chamberlain 6-28-1871 (no return)
Bean, M. A. T. to Stephen Tucker 10-25-1870 (no return)
Bean, Tempe to H. C. Hendricks 12-8-1873 (12-9-1873)
Beard, Harriet Ann to Henry Strother 7-18-1873 (no return) B
Beard, Martha to Isaac Johnson 1-19-1872 (1-20-1872)
Beard, Mollie to Armistead Smith 11-11-1880
Beard, Nancy to Frank Moore 12-11-1878
Beasley, Jane to Joseph Kerr 3-7-1871 (3-8-1871)
Beaumont, Jane to Jo Eudaly 1-5-1867
Beaumont, Lou to Dan Parker 2-19-1869 (no return)
Beaumont, Lou to Stephen Townsend 8-16-1877
Beaver, Angeline to W. H. Harrison 1-25-1878 (1-27-1878)
Becket, Eliza to Thomas Jones 12-25-1879 (12-26-1879)
Becket, Sarah to Jack Fumbanks 2-10-1869 (no return)
Beckett, Frances to Joseph McKnight 1-29-1872 (1-30-1872)
Beckett, Malinda to Knight? Harrell 2-23-1878 (no return)
Beckett, Sarah to William Meadows 1-15-1873 (1-16-1873)
Bell, Caroline to Joseph Warren 4-14-1868 (no return)
Bell, E. E. to J. O. Craig 3-26-1877 (3-28-1877)
Bell, E. J. to W. J. Churchman 2-2-1871
Bell, Emma to T. C. Buchanan 4-26-1877
Bell, Fannie to Peter Pillow 9-12-1876 (no return)
Bell, Jennie to Saml. Enochs 12-27-1871 (12-28-1871)
Bell, Lizzie to Henry Spence 6-30-1876
Bell, Lizzie to Thos. C. Michell 5-11-1867 (no return)
Bell, Lucretia to Henry I. Hurt 10-24-1870 B
Bell, M. E. to T. W. Chrisman 2-27-1877
Bell, Mariah to James Dillon 3-23-1874 (3-24-1874)
Bell, Mariah to Sam Jones 12-29-1879 (no return)
Bell, Martha to Harvey Bell 1-3-1871 (1-10-1871)
Bell, Mary E. to O. B. Goodman 10-19-1860 (no return)
Bell, Mary to H. D. Hay 7-19-1871 (7-20-1871)
Bell, S. A. to J. T. Stamps 12-6-1865 (12-13-1865)
Bell, Sallie C. to J. H. Walton 12-7-1868 (no return)
Bell, Sarah A. to T. C. (Capt.) Buchanan 6-28-1875 (6-29-1875)
Bell, Sarah C. to N. H. Aycock 12-11-1861
Bell, Sue to R. G. Harrell 12-19-1866 (12-20-1866)
Belle, Rosette to Nilson Gannaway 7-6-1876
Belote, Mary to J. W. Bertram 1-10-1872 (1-11-1872)
Bendon?, Adaline to Limerick Smith 8-3-1867 (8-4-1867)
Berry, Martha to W. F. Lumpkins 2-4-1861 (2-5-1861)
Bessent, Ann to J. G. Hill 12-24-1873
Bessent, Elizabeth to James M. Rucker 7-19-1869 (7-21-1869)
Bessent, Kitty to J. T. Capell 10-15-1868
Bessent, Lou to Joel Blankenship 2-27-1871 (2-28-1871)
Bessent?, Temperance to John A. Mills 1-1-1867
Bettis, A. S. to J. T. Jaycocks 4-25-1866 (no return)
Bettis, D. E. to LJ. N. Vail 8-5-1871 (no return)
Bettis, L. N. to G. M. Rowland 10-9-1865 (10-10-1865)
Bettis, Peggy Ann to John W. McFarlane 12-13-1866 (12-26-1866)
Biggs, Julia to Jacob Barnett 12-22-1870 (1-1-1871)
Biggs, Sarah M. to S. H. Strayhorn 12-8-1868 (12-9-1868)
Binford, Rebecca to George Dunnigan 10-30-1868 (no return)
Binkley, Lavanda to George Gibson 4-11-1866 (no return)
Bishop, G. A. to J. F. King 12-3-1878 (12-4-1878)
Bizzle, Martha A. to B. F. Edney 1-29-1866 (no return)
Blackburn, Amanda C. to Wm. S. Balser 2-18-1878
Blackburn, Susan (Mrs.) to Benjamin Allen 12-2-1872

Blackman, Mollie to W. S. Tolbert 2-27-1876 (2-28-1876)
Blackwell, Melissa to L. Knowlton 6-15-1869 (6-16-1869)
Blackwood, Ellen to W. Conner 11-2-1875 (no return)
Blair, Fannie to Willis Strayhorn 1-31-1872 (2-1-1872)
Blair, Martha to W. D. Gleaves 12-16-1874
Blair, N. J. to J. L. Chappell 1-6-1874
Bland, Sarah A. to John Delf 6-14-1869
Blankenship, Mary A. to John W. Pitts 6-24-1873 (no return)
Blankenship, Mary A. to William A. Hill 12-14-1863 (12-15-1863)
Blankenship, Mary Adelaide to Andrew J. Pitts 9-5-1876 (9-6-1876)
Blankenship, S. J. to J. R. Green 11-24-1866 (11-25-1866)
Blanton, Katie to W. R. McBride 6-6-1877
Blanton, Mattie to W. A. Carroll 8-9-1879 (no return)
Bledsoe, Louisa to John A. Shaw 9-13-1879 (9-14-1879)
Bloar, S. L. to W. F. Rawles 1-22-1870 (1-23-1870)
Bloomingdale, Eunice to George M. Tatum 11-27-1877 (11-28-1877)
Boatright, Nancy to G. W. Rasberry 12-3-1868 (12-9-1868)
Boatright, R. A. to J. E. Crisp 10-13-1869 (no return)
Boatwright, M. F. to J. N. Lewelling 2-25-1873 (2-27-1873)
Bobett, Mary to Geo. W. Jamey? 4-12-1873 (4-16-1873)
Boggess, Susan to James Comrie? 6-13-1867
Boland, Cornelia O. to Lafayette Faulkner 4-3-1862
Bolen, Frances to Humphrey Redick 12-27-1864 (12-29-1864)
Bolin, Mary J. to J. D. Nearn? 6-5-1869 (6-9-1869)
Bonds, A. B. to J. G. Lovelace 1-24-1871 (1-25-1871)
Bonds, Anna to Geo. Wyatt 2-28-1877 (no return)
Bone, Amanda to Henry Hellums 3-22-1873 (3-29-1873)
Bone, Susan to Anderson Smalley 5-30-1871 (5-31-1871)
Boo, Callie to J. M. Williamson 10-21-1879 (10-23-1879)
Boon, M. A. to F. M. Price 1-17-1870 (1-19-1870)
Boone, Jane to B. L. Sollis 12-14-1867 (12-15-1867)
Boone, Nettie to S. M. Hobday 10-21-1873
Borden, Mary to Joseph Herron 3-21-1876
Bowen, Jennie to Wm. Clark 1-12-1870 (1-13-1870)
Bowen, Lizzie to Harry Buchanan 1-8-1872 (no return)
Bowen, M. A. to T. J. Rice 6-17-1876 (6-20-1876)
Bowen, N. P. to T. J. Rice 4-6-1868 (4-9-1868)
Bowen, Nannie to Jeremiah Dunnigan 12-22-1869 (no return)
Bowen, R. J. to N. Echols 1-27-1877 (1-28-1877)
Bowen, Rebecca A. to William King 12-17-1860 (12-18-1860)
Bowen, Rebecca to Austin Hicks 12-31-1872
Bowen, S. S. to J. Q. Craig 9-17-1866
Bowen, Tennessee to Frank Baines 4-15-1872 (4-17-1872)
Boyd, E. F. to S. L. Saunders 1-9-1871 (no return)
Bracken, Ella to D. A. Brigham 5-1-1878
Brackin, Julia A. to A. M. Stevens 12-19-1865 (12-21-1865)
Brackin, Lucinda to S. A. Forsyth 12-28-1872 (1-7-1873)
Bradford, Jane (Mrs.) to J. M. Ledbetter 10-2-1872
Bradford, Julia G. to W. J. Jennings 8-24-1868 (8-25-1868)
Bradford, Lizzie to Granville Jones 9-8-1870 (no return)
Bradford, Mariah to Dick Kirk 1-1-1879 (1-2-1879)
Bradford, Mary to Chas. Sawyer 6-29-1868
Bradley, C. L. to G. W. Rogers 1-27-1874
Bradley, Charlotte L. to Henry Woodburry 1-31-1861 (1-30?-1861)
Bradshaw, Adalade to James H. Hall 12-14-1864 (12-15-1864)
Bradshaw, Ellen to Daniel Hale 2-12-1880
Bradshaw, Elvira to Frank Richmond 9-19-1864 (no return)
Bradshaw, Emma to Harberd Gibson 12-7-1880
Bradshaw, Lizzie to Fernando Dunavant 2-10-1870 (no return)
Bradshaw, Mary (Mrs.) to W. T. Powell 1-8-1867
Bradshaw, Nannie to H. F. Grimes 12-15-1877 (12-19-1877)
Bradshaw, R. W. to R. P. Powell 3-16-1861
Bradshaw, Sarah to Henry Smith 9-15-1873 (9-16-1873)
Bradshaw, Susan to Green Smith 3-10-1880 (3-11-1880)
Branch, Phillis to Doc Shelton 7-17-1879 (no return)
Brandon, Hilly (Mrs.) to R. R. Espy 9-23-1863 (no return)
Brandon, M. M. to J. F. Salisbury 2-25-1879 (2-26-1879)
Brandon, Margaret to C. M. Young 8-30-1870 (9-1-1870)
Brannon, Jane E. to B. B. Fitzhugh 12-25-1862
Brant, Paralee to J. D. Jackson 2-8-1871 (2-10-1871)
Brashier, Charity Ann to W. H. Nelson 1-21-1878 (1-22-1878)
Brashier, K. J. to J. D. Bradley 3-22-1873 (3-23-1873)
Breasted?, Laura to Will Sandford 12-28-1880
Breece, Melissa J. to J. B. Leggett 2-21-1870 (2-23-1870)
Brenakin, Mary to George McDonnell 4-14-1865 (4-17-1865)

Brent, Elizabeth to Marion Davis 4-20-1865
Brent, Evaline to Ethelbert Kellett 12-25-1866 (12-27-1866)
Brent, Leitha Jane to Joseph T. North 9-1-1862 (9-2-1862)
Brewer, Alice to W. E. Prichard 9-18-1878 (9-19-1878)
Brewer, Eliza A. to William Oakley 11-25-1871 (no return)
Brewer, J. A. to B. R. Prichard 12-27-1877
Brewer, L. C. to W. H. Hall 1-29-1877 (no return)
Brewer, M. A. to A. J. Reddick 10-16-1869 (10-19-1869)
Brewer, M. F. to J. L. Reddick 11-28-1866 (11-29-1866)
Brewer, Margaret E. to S. A. Reed 12-27-1865
Brewer, Pricilla B. to Thos. J. Edwards 2-6-1865 (2-7-1865)
Brimingham, M. S. to Rufus King 12-3-1874
Brimingham, Susan A. to Wm. S. Vick 11-16-1864
Brinkley, R. T. to J. G. Bailey 2-23-1878 (2-26-1878)
Brinkly, Margaret to J. A. Brinkley 9-22-1866 (9-23-1866)
Brock, Mollie A. to J. F. Armstrong 3-14-1867 (3-19-1867)
Brogden, D. A. (Mrs.) to John Cotton 12-29-1863 (12-31-1863)
Brooks, Cherry to Travis Oldham 12-15-1866 (no return)
Brotherton, Sarah E. to Richard Johnson 7-1-1868 (7-19-1868)
Brown, A. A. to F. T. Rooks 1-10-1872 (1-11-1872)
Brown, Amanda to W. C. Gannon 12-6-1871 (12-7-1871)
Brown, Corella to George Fitzgerald 7-26-1880 (no return)
Brown, Elizabeth to L. D. Moore 9-13-1867 (9-15-1867)
Brown, Emma M. to James M. Torrence 4-26-1870
Brown, Emma to N. K. Stevenson 1-1-1863
Brown, Hellen T. to T. W. Steart 10-18-1871 (no return)
Brown, L. T. to James S. Neely 11-29-1871 (11-30-1871)
Brown, M. J. to C. F. Brown 6-14-1875 (6-17-1875)
Brown, Martha J. to Sam P. Albritton 6-1-1861 (no return)
Brown, Martha to Green Parks 11-26-1873 (11-27-1873)
Brown, Mary to Brooks Carter 11-30-1878 (12-1-1878)
Brown, Mollie E. to William Cook 9-9-1871 (9-12-1871)
Brown, Mrs. to John Conness 9-8-1869 (9-9-1869)
Brown, Nancy A. F. to R. F. Freeman 12-5-1876
Brown, Susan to Isaac Henson 1-15-1870 (1-16-1870)
Bruce, Margaret to J. Y. Flack 5-25-1874 (5-26-1874)
Bruithwick, I. J. to E. H. Swindle 2-26-1866
Brunt, Nancy P. to G. W. Burnham 10-19-1872 (10-20-1872)
Brush, Polly Ann to R. S. Campbell 3-14-1876 (3-17-1876)
Bryant, Lavina to George Harbison 11-13-1875 (11-14-1875)
Bryant, Mollie to Tom Mulherin 12-8-1880 (12-9-1880)
Buchanan, Ann to George Menzies 12-19-1865 (12-22-1865)
Buck, Lizzie to Robert Grigsby 10-8-1868 (no return)
Bugg, Alice to Columbus R. Parr 8-22-1866
Bui?, S. A. to J. T. Stamp 12-6-1865 (12-13-1865)
Bull, Sarah Ann to H. Falkner 1-8-1868 (no return)
Bullard, Mefrinda? to Alfred Linnell 8-30-1862 (9-11-1862)
Bullard, Sarah to J. A. Jones 10-14-1869
Bumpass, Anna to Christopher Akin 11-29-1870 (12-3-1870) B
Bumpass, Emma to James Currey 8-28-1880 (8-29-1880)
Bumpass, Mary to Alexander Ross 2-3-1870
Bumpasss, Caroline to Fley O. Burton 2-25-1870 (no return)
Bunks, Hettie to J. M. Jackson 5-29-1863 (6-2-1863)
Bunnell, Clarasa to Jim Peacock 2-13-1868 (2-19-1868)
Burch, Bettie to John Landrum 3-7-1877 (3-8-1877)
Burch, Laura to Frank Lanier 1-19-1878 (1-20-1878)
Burkett, E. to John Parker 7-29-1872 (7-31-1872)
Burkett, Martha M. to B. D. Lightfoot 11-14-1877 (11-15-1877)
Burnett, Letitia to Thos. Simons 1-1-1867 (1-3-1867)
Burnett, Martha A. to William Privett 12-19-1862 (12-25-1862)
Burnett, Rachel to Bennett Noe 9-3-1870 (9-4-1870)
Burney, Lou to S. S. Scales 11-22-1876 (no return)
Burnham, M. W. to Z. T. Gleaves 12-24-1874
Burnham, Margaret to Edgar Troy 2-10-1869 (no return)
Burnham, Mary E. to W. H. H. Murray 10-10-1865 (10-11-1865)
Burnham, Nancy Ann to T. B. Ghann? 9-18-1866 (9-19-1866)
Burnham, Parilee to J. P. Freeman 12-23-1873
Burns, Maggie to J. C. Saunder 2-2-1870
Burton, Laura A. to Sam N. Sidney 12-4-1876 (12-14-1876)
Burton, Mary F. to David Menzies 10-31-1872 (no return)
Burwell, Ann to Henry Avery 3-25-1863 (3-25-1863)
Butler, Jane E. to David F. Smith 10-31-1864 (4-9-1864?)
Butler, Martha J. to J. W. W. Borum 1-2-1869 (1-4-1869)
Butler, Mary E. to William J. Knowles 6-12-1875 (6-13-1875)
Butler, Nancy A. to A. C. Andrews 1-24-1871 (no return)

Butterworth, Ann to William Gerritt 6-1-1867 (no return)
Butterworth, Isabella to Jacob McCoy 3-18-1868 (3-19-1868)
Butterworth, L. J. to R. T. Butterworth 2-9-1872 (2-10-1872)
Butterworth, Mary E. to Lucien W. Smith 8-14-1877 (8-15-1877)
Byrn, Margaret to Wilson Frost 11-18-1867
Caliway, K. J. to B. F. Brazier 1-26-1870
Callahan, M. F. (Mrs.) to E. A. Henderson 8-31-1874 (no return)
Calvin, M. J. to J. A. Arnold 10-5-1872 (10-6-1872)
Cambell, Hannah to James Jones 10-13-1866 (no return)
Campbell, Didama to James Lovel 12-7-1872 (12-8-1872)
Campbell, Eliza to Mit Baxter 8-1-1870
Campbell, Elizabeth to D. Platt 5-21-1861
Campbell, Josephine to S. J. House 9-9-1876 (9-10-1876)
Campbell, Lucinda Elizabeth A. to Newton Benjamin Wilkins 12-20-1873 (12-21-1873)
Campbell, M. J. to L. R. Jones 10-20-1879 (10-21-1879)
Campbell, Martha to Jno. B. McIntosh 12-25-1868 (12-27-1868)
Campbell, Mary to R. W. Binkley 11-5-1874 (no return)
Campbell, Nancy Ann to James Harris 9-22-1877 (9-23-1877) B
Campbell, _____ to J. W. Ayers 3-2-1878 (no return)
Canada, Mary E. to J. C. Thetford 12-12-1868 (12-13-1868)
Cannon, Josafine to George Allen 9-13-1870 (no return)
Capell, Mollie to M. D. Gaulden 9-29-1875 (9-30-1875)
Carpenter, Delilah to Spencer Williamson 5-2-1878
Carrel, Evaline to Thomas M. Murray 6-30-1874 (7-1-1874)
Carroll, C. F. to T. W. Evans 8-24-1869
Carroll, Frances W. to J. M. Martin 11-24-1873 (11-26-1873)
Carroll, Martha Ann to John Wesley Pope 9-11-1867 (no return)
Carroll, S. J. to J. H. Aiken 2-28-1871 (3-2-1871)
Carroll, Sarah to W. T. Evans 12-27-1869 (12-29-1869)
Carter, A. C. to R. B. Gibbs 12-7-1860 (11-9-1860)
Carter, S. A. to C. W. Todd 10-1-1879
Carter, Z. A. to B. F. Neal 12-15-1870
Cate, Elizabeth to Eli McCarroll 5-29-1873
Cate, Jane to Wilie Ayrens? 8-7-1871
Cauthorn, Mollie to J. M. Pate 9-29-1875 (9-30-1875)
Cavitt, M. E. to S. H. King 9-3-1878 (9-4-1878)
Cawhon, Rebecca J. to A. C. McFarlan 7-14-1865 (7-16-1865)
Cearce, M. R. to William S. Liggett 2-19-1872 (2-21-1872)
Cearley, Martha to John Ward 8-12-1867
Cearly, Elizabeth to John Richardson 9-26-1869 (9-27-1869)
Cerry, Rena to Ephraim Bush 12-24-1870 (no return)
Chadwick, Lizzie to Dan T. Wilson 6-6-1869 (no return)
Chamberlain, Etta to William A. Boatwright 4-13-1876
Chamberlain, Henrietta Jane to Geo. Wyatt 1-14-1880 (1-17-1880)
Chamberlain, Louiza S. to William Key 1-31-1861
Chamberlain, M. E. to C. M. Boatwright 9-1-1870
Chamblin, Jennie to W. H. Simpson 8-14-1867 (no return)
Chamblin, Louella to W. R. (Dr.) Hays 12-9-1874
Chandler, Christiana to James A. Davis 7-6-1867 (7-7-1867)
Chapman, D. J. to J. E. Cooper 3-9-1868 (3-12-1868)
Chatman, Lou to W. H. Payne 11-23-1876
Cheny, Elizabeth to Joel Jones 2-23-1864 (no return)
Childers, Elizabeth to Robert? C. Baley 4-23-1861 (4-25-1861)
Childers, Martha to Jonah Bowen 11-9-1864 (11-10-1864)
Childers, Mary E. to Marion A. Lemons 12-30-1867
Childers, Mary to Jno. M. Childers 12-28-1867 (no return)
Childress, Anne to Etheldred Jones 10-7-1862 (10-8-1862)
Childress, L. P. to A. J. Lewelling 2-25-1873 (2-27-1873)
Chitwood, Amarilla to Henry Hamlet 4-14-1866 (no return)
Chitwood, Angeline to G. W. Waggoner 1-20-1869 (1-21-1869)
Chitwood, Blanchie to Arnett Pursley 11-24-1874 (11-25-1874)
Chitwood, Dona to S. A. Wood 5-11-1875
Chitwood, H. B. to J. C. Skipwith 10-30-1867 (no return)
Chitwood, Judy to Matt Fowlkes 12-22-1866 (12-24-1866)
Chitwood, Louisa to R. W. Barker 1-16-1866 (1-17-1866)
Chitwood, Martha A. to Stephen V.? Bizzel 11-27-1860
Chitwood, Mary E. to J. R. Webb 9-30-1865 (no return)
Chitwood, Nancy to Robert Woods 12-16-1879 (no return)
Chitwood, Nannie to R. M. Rainey 10-16-1873
Chrisman, Betsy to Lewis Hooks 3-4-1867
Chrisman, Sallie to J. C. Grace 2-8-1877
Christian, S. J. to C. C. Palmore 9-11-1876
Christie, Charlotte A. to H. W. Johnson 1-30-1869 (no return)
Christie, Mary S. to Wiley J. Marcum 10-22-1867

Christie, R. J. to Enoch McPherson 8-16-1866
Church, Maggie to L. M. Sanders 7-19-1869 (7-20-1869)
Churchman, M. E. to A. H. Carpenter 10-27-1874 (10-28-1874)
Cillett, Tabitha A. R. to J. B. Campbell 8-6-1878
Claiborne, Lucy T. to J. R. Blair 6-24-1874
Claiss, Florence to William Welch 7-29-1874
Clark, Amanda to Dock Howard 1-10-1870 (no return)
Clark, Amanda to Frank Beaumont 1-1-1866
Clark, Elizabeth J. to E. Clark Palmer 4-9-1861 (4-10-1861)
Clark, Fannie to Tobe Jones 1-9-1878 (1-10-1878)
Clark, Fanny to Nash Jones no date (1-1-1867)
Clark, Josephine to Ben M. Night 12-30-1866 (no return)
Clark, Letitia to Ben Pierce 12-27-1877
Clark, Martha to George Fumbank 3-1-1867 (3-2-1867)
Clark, Mary to J. L. Kirk 9-7-1875 (not executed?)
Clark, Provie to Alex Works 9-8-1877
Clark, Sallie to E. R. (Dr.) Vernon 12-25-1867
Clay, Louisa to Henry Fields 1-10-1866 (1-13-1866)
Clay, Mary A. to John R. Moore 2-26-1867 (2-28-1867)
Cleek, Mary E. to J. A. Jones 2-20-1871 (2-26-1873)
Clement, M. A. T. (Mrs.) to B. T. Porter 1-18-1872
Clemm, Nancy to Rush Phillips 1-3-1866 (1-10-1867)
Clemmons, Maggie to E. L. Burks 12-24-1875 (12-26-1875)
Clemmons, Mattie J. to Judge Shaw 12-12-1874 (12-17-1874) B
Clemons, Sallie J. (Mrs.) to Thomas H. Earle 6-3-1873
Cliff, Martha M. to W. B. Park 10-25-1878 (10-27-1878)
Cobb, Elizabeth S. to S. J. Neely 12-1-1866 (12-4-1866)
Cobb, Leonora to E. B. Lauderdale 12-30-1871 (1-1-1872)
Cobb, Lou to John Smith 10-13-1875
Cobb, Lucinda S. to Henry A. Gooch 1-30-1861 (1-31-1861)
Cobb, S. E. to David Waggoner 10-22-1879 (10-23-1879)
Coble, Mary L. to James Briley 12-5-1875
Cochrane, E. T. to W. R. Spoon 12-1-1876 (12-3-1876)
Cogburn, Henrietta (Mrs.?) to Charles (Dr.) Shackleford 1-1-1872 (1-2-1872)
Coker, Fannie to Rily Pierce 1-1-1873 (12-2-1873)
Coker, Mary E. to S. A. Wood 10-16-1879
Cole, A. B. to W. R. King 11-23-1872 (11-24-1872)
Cole, Caroline to Burril Jones 1-11-1867
Cole, Eva Ann to Jo? Wright 3-11-1871 (3-12-1871)
Cole, S. A. to J. S. Ray 12-29-1875
Coleman, Julia to C. W. Ellis 1-27-1875 (1-28-1875)
Coleman, Lotta to Wash King 7-10-1875 (7-4?-1875)
Coleman, Susan E. to J. F. Williamson 8-31-1860
Colevitt, Sarah to W. A. Peery 3-16-1875
Colleth, Sarah A. to Abell Pittman 7-13-1860 (no return)
Collins, Martha to S. F. Johnson 1-3-1873 (1-5-1873)
Colman, Elizabeth to Moses Fyker 1-31-1870 (no return)
Colvin, Anne to J. H. Vaughan 9-7-1878 (9-8-1878)
Colvin, Jennie to James Suttlemore 12-29-1875 (1-2-1876)
Colvin, Julia to G. W. Walker 4-13-1876
Colvin, Louisa to William Eudaily 2-10-1868 (no return)
Colvin, S. E. to G. D. Mays 2-24-1870
Condor, Margaret A. E. to John B. Flowers 1-13-1863 (no return)
Conklin, D. F. to J. N. Chambers 9-20-1879 (9-22-1879)
Connell, Emiline to Hiram Findle 11-19-1869 (no return)
Connell, Fannie to Ben Shallow 6-19-1876
Connell, Fannie to Wm. Mulherin 10-22-1868
Connell, Julia to Magor Norment 4-29-1880
Connell, Lizzie to Church Burklen? 5-1-1876
Connell, Mary A. to W. P. Lane 1-5-1871
Connell, Mary to Jerry Fowlkes 11-28-1867
Connell, Millie to Nelson Shaw 9-12-1872
Connell, Mollie to Thomas Howard 6-3-1871 (6-4-1871)
Connell, Peggy to Hiram McCullough 2-22-1872
Connell, Sarah E. to William P. Fowlkes, jr. 6-15-1863
Connell, Susan to J. C. Reasons 10-18-1879 (10-19-1879)
Conwell, N. (Mrs.) to H. L. W. Tunely? 8-3-1868 (8-4-1868)
Conyers, Virginia to James Fugate 1-21-1865 (1-22-1865)
Cook, Cathie to J. S. Moore 11-29-1877
Cook, Lizzie to J. M. Jones ?-19-1878 (with Nov 1878)
Cook, M. J. to John D. Dudley 4-30-1878
Cook, Mollie to Wiley Pope 10-27-1874
Cook, Rebeccah to W. C. Pace 4-26-1865
Cooper, M. C. to William H. Gibson 5-23-1872 (no return)

Cooper, M. E. to James Bessent 3-17-1879 (3-18-1879)
Cooper, Mary E. to G. W. Whitson 5-6-1871
Cooper, Mary F. to Thomas T. Trusty 8-21-1872
Cope, Elmina to J. W. Reynolds 9-19-1863 (9-28-1863)
Cope, M. J. to D. A. Shaw 8-3-1866 (8-12-1866)
Cope, W. M. to W. T. Cathcart 3-5-1879 (3-9-1879)
Copeland, Bettie to Geo. Travis 1-28-1874 (1-29-1874)
Copeland, Julia Ann to Isaac Doak 9-27-1877
Copeland, Laura to John Fowlkes 12-29-1880 (12-30-1880)
Copeland, Mollie to John Copeland 5-8-1877
Corley, Jane to Geo. Fowlkes 1-6-1876 (1-13-1876)
Corley, R. A. to J. H. Blakemore 7-27-1878 (7-28-1878)
Corley, S. E. to R. A. Wagster 2-28-1867
Corvin, Lizzie to James McCarroll 3-7-1873
Cothan, Mary M. to Albert Long 2-3-1868 (no return)
Cothern, Sallie to Robert Freeman 9-5-1870 (9-7-1870)
Cothran, Ann E. to V. J. Smith 2-20-1863 (2-24-1863)
Cottam, Amanda to M. B. Moorney 1-28-1864 (1-29-1864)
Courtley, Martha J. to Seth Hall 5-18-1864
Courtney, Susan L. to G. R. Edwards 2-1-1864 (2-3-1864)
Cowell, Mary C. to Alfred Goforth 9-27-1860
Cox, Mary to Daniel H. Trout 10-15-1870 (10-16-1870)
Craig, E. L. to David Dotsen 10-1-1867 (10-2-1867)
Craig, Eliza Jane to James Turner 1-28-1864 (no return)
Craig, Julian to Silas Brown? 7-22-1869 (7-25-1869)
Craig, Lou to J. H. Randolph 8-9-1871 (no return)
Craig, Maggie to Ben E. Norment 9-7-1868 (no return)
Craig, Martha F. to Abner Harwell 5-28-1867
Craig, R. T. to W. C. Howell 10-1-1867 (10-2-1867)
Crammer?, Frances to James W. Fish 4-22-1873 (4-27-1873)
Crawford, Fannie C. to J. S. Lambert 2-24-1879 (2-25-1879)
Crawford, Mary A. to F. N. Kelso 3-5-1873 (3-6-1873)
Crenshaw, Mollie E. to S. J. Taylor 10-13-1873 (10-15-1873)
Cresswell, Angeline to Sidney R. Neil 3-12-1879
Crews, Nancy Elizabeth to John M. Stewart 10-12-1870 (10-13-1870)
Cribbs, H. E. C. to George P. Pierce 1-23-1868 (no return)
Cribbs, M. J. to Noah Green 12-1-1874
Crichfield, Sarah A. to Thomas Groom 1-19-1878 (1-23-1878)
Crisp, S. A. to S. J. W. Fuller 9-7-1868 (9-8-1868)
Crockett, Sallie to W. H. Pate 4-12-1871
Crook, Berchie to Jeff Wynn 10-18-1880 (10-19-1880)
Croom, Mollie F. to E. W. Cawthon 1-9-1866 (1-11-1866)
Cross, Caroline to John Boone 1-5-1876
Cross, Martha to Alexr. Boon 10-13-1877 (10-14-1877)
Cross, Susan C. to G. W. Richie 1-9-1867 (1-11-1867)
Cross, Vic to William Anderson 1-23-1867
Crow, Adaline to Ricahrd Maddrey 12-18-1866 (12-25-1866)
Crow, America to Marcellus A. Cross 1-15-1868
Crow, Caroline to Daniel Fowlkes 10-11-1877
Crow, Elizabeth to Tobe Powell 10-22-1879 (10-23-1879)
Crow, Emma to Anderson Jones 1-2-1879
Crow, Lucy to James Farrow 12-28-1870 (12-29-1870)
Crow, M. A. to F. A. Troy 12-11-1872
Crow, Mary to Henry Taylor 11-21-1874 (11-24-1874) B
Crow, P. A. to J. A. Luntsford 12-24-1875 (no return)
Crow, Paralee to J. W. Burtin 10-14-1872 (10-17-1872)
Crow, S. A. to Zach T. Troy 12-28-1867 (12-29-1867)
Crudup, M. R. to J. E. Wade 8-20-1878 (8-21-1878)
Crudup, Mary to Wm. Parnell 1-7-1867 (1-10-1867)
Culwell, Emily to Emanuel Frosh 2-17-1872 (2-18-1872)
Cummings, Martha A. to Elias D. Cummings 9-22-1873 (9-23-1873)
Cunningham, Emily to John M. Brewer 10-22-1860 (no return)
Cunningham, Kitsey Swan to Ephraim Dorherty 10-9-1863 (10-11-1863)
Cunningham, Martha J. to M. J. Williams 10-12-1869
Cunningham, Mary W. to A. H. Goodloe 9-27-1871
Cunningham, Mattie to J. R. Cook 3-2-1876
Cunningham, Nannie to W. H. Arnett 1-22-1874
Curtis, Benny to J. W. Carmack 1-1-1868 (no return)
Curtis, E. P. C. to M. V. White 5-22-1867 (5-23-1867)
Curtis, Eliza to James Swift 8-2-1871 (8-19-1871)
Curtis, H. R. to A. L. Shekle 10-3-1870 (no return)
Curtis, H. R. to A. L. Shikle 10-3-1870 (12-5-1870)
Curtis, Janusy to J. W. Boals 3-4-1869 (no return)
Curtis, M. E. to T. M. Pate 1-2-1878

Curtis, Matilda J. to J. W. Hall 12-15-1873 (12-18-1873)
Curtis, Parlee to Ephram Hart Freedman 2-9-1866 (no return)
Curtis, Rebecca A. to Edmond Chitwood 6-3-1868 (no return)
Curtis, Sallie E. to D. R. Weakley 3-8-1872
Curtis, Susan B. to W. T. Mays 4-17-1867
Daniel, Dollie to Wm. Smith 12-1-1877 (12-2-1877)
Darden, Lizzie to Robt. Barker 1-31-1876 (2-1-1876)
Darden, Sarah F. to J. S. Allen 6-4-1879 (no return)
Daugherty, Eliza to Alex Haskins 3-15-1877 (no return)
Daugherty, Emma E. to R. W. Dunlap 12-18-1876 (12-24-1876)
Daugherty, M. C. to W. P. Hays 6-25-1879 (6-27-1879)
Davidson, Elizabeth to John H. Harmon 12-17-1867 (12-18-1867)
Davidson, Martha to Henry Staggs 12-24-1864 (1-2-1865)
Davis, A. J. to J. R. Prichard 8-9-1869 (8-10-1869)
Davis, A. L. to W. E. Lunsford 2-14-1877
Davis, Annie to F. A. Newton 12-16-1878 (12-17-1878)
Davis, Charlotte A. to James Rankin 1-6-1868 (1-7-1868)
Davis, Charlotte to R. T. D. Norman 10-28-1869
Davis, Cordelia to Isaac Canada 1-20-1877 (1-21-1877)
Davis, Eliza to Manson Fowlkes 7-11-1878
Davis, Elizabeth F. to Martin F. Careley 2-11-1868
Davis, Frances E. to R. T. Chambers 9-26-1866 (9-30-1866)
Davis, Frankie to J. H. Bills 12-23-1878 (no return)
Davis, Gabriella to James C. Miller 1-24-1861
Davis, Lizzie to B. H. Harmon 11-5-1867 (11-7-1867)
Davis, M. E. to J. W. Seward 9-11-1871 (no return)
Davis, M. E. to W. E. Lunsford 1-22-1879 (1-23-1879)
Davis, Mary E. to James Wood? 8-15-1867 (8-16-1867)
Davis, Mary E. to S. G. McClanahan 2-20-1867 (no return)
Davis, Mary to T. H. Fitzhugh 8-12-1868
Davis, Mollie to Stephen Walton 3-5-1873 (3-6-1873)
Davis, N. J. to J. N. Evans 3-10-1863 (3-12-1863)
Davis, Roxana O. to Wm. H. Stanfield 11-4-1868 (no return)
Davis, S. J. to J. L. Hall 5-9-1878 (5-12-1878)
Davis, S. J. to J. T. Boatwright 10-28-1873 (10-29-1873)
Davis, Sarah F. to G. W. Patrick 12-14-1867 (12-23-1867)
Davis, Sarah to J. B. Parnell 11-13-1867 (11-14-1867)
Dawson, Emma Bet. to Harris L. Baker 12-25-1872
Dawson, Lena H. to E. H. Baker 12-24-1874
Day, Nannie to W. M. Balser 3-15-1879 (3-20-1879)
Deak, Harriet Ann to Henry Wilkins 4-14-1880 (4-15-1880)
Dearmore, Susan to Stafford Luster 6-19-1860
Delph, Annariah to Bryant Fitzhugh 3-26-1879
Delph, Sally to George Pate 10-3-1864 (no return)
Dickason, F. A. to D. Brock, jr. 8-13-1872 (8-14-1872)
Dickens, Mary E. to James T. Arnett 9-11-1872 (9-12-1872)
Dickerson, Belle to J. S. Yates 12-13-1877 (12-18-1877)
Dickerson, Franky to Green Doyle 12-28-1866
Dickey, Emma to G. R. Fuller 12-22-1873 (12-23-1873)
Dickey, M. E. to J. W. Barrette 11-8-1875 (11-10-1875)
Dickey, Margaret E. to T. W. Hall 1-22-1868 (no return)
Dickey, Martha E. to Valentine Trail 4-23-1864 (4-26-1864)
Dickey, P. A. to J. D. Wesson 2-3-1875 (2-4-1875)
Dillahunt, Ann (Mrs.) to James A. Henley 12-19-1877
Dillard, Rosannah to Martin Prichard 9-1-1869 (no return)
Dillingham, Amanda to Monroe Hicks 10-10-1878 (no return)
Dillon, Celia A. to R. T. Green 2-5-1874
Doak, Bette to Allen Mahan 1-4-1871 (no return)
Doak, Eliza Jane to Scott Pillow 2-8-1877
Doak, Elizabeth to James D. Pope 8-20-1873 (no return)
Doak, Harriet to Harry Copeland 1-7-1874 (no return)
Doak, Lucinda to Felix Pinion 9-27-1879 (9-29-1879)
Doak, Lucy A. to W. H. Hendrix 4-16-1879 (4-17-1879)
Doak, Sarah to John Smith 1-20-1871 (1-22-1871) B
Dock, Sarah A. to Alex Bugg 5-3-1869 (no return)
Dockens, Sarah to S. C. Collins 10-30-1872
Dodd, Caroline to John Reynolds 6-15-1863
Dodd, Eliza A. to George D. Harpole 8-4-1868 (8-6-1868)
Dodd, Elizabeth to M. W. Neeley 6-5-1873
Dodd, Elvira S. J. to W. P. Knight 9-10-1866 (9-11-1866)
Dodd, F. L. to J. M. White 9-10-1865 (9-11-1865)
Dodd, M. M. to J. W. Wesson 5-24-1869 (5-27-1869)
Dodson, J. A. to J. W. Carmack 12-17-1875 (12-19-1875)
Dodson, Sarah to Wesley Chronister 1-30-1866 (1-31-1866)
Donald, Jane to John Durden 12-27-1877

Dotson, Rebecca to Lewis Battle 10-7-1872 (10-14-1872)
Dougherty, Katie to Frank Gentry 7-20-1865 (no return)
Douglas, Anna to R. R. Johnson 6-30-1866 (no return)
Douglas, Myra to Albert Jones 5-17-1867 (5-18-1867)
Douglass, Amanda to Edmund Grimm 2-19-1873 (2-20-1873)
Douglass, Ann E. to J. C. Haskins 11-12-1866 (11-13-1866)
Douglass, Eliza to Cornelius Scott 9-28-1872
Douglass, Frances to George Edge 1-23-1878 (no return)
Douglass, Jane to Alex Smith 3-9-1871
Douglass, Jane to Jordan Harris 9-2-1876 (9-3-1876)
Douglass, S. A. to B. R. Parks 12-24-1872 (12-25-1872)
Douglass, S. E. to H. A. Dean 10-3-1872 (no return)
Dove, Martha to David Baily 11-29-1869
Dove, Mary Jane to Thomas Morrison 6-11-1863
Dove, Patsey to D. L. Carvin 11-3-1874 (11-4-1874)
Dowell, Martha A. to W. B. Shankle 1-20-1870 (no return)
Dowell, Susan to Hiram Landrum 4-26-1872 (5-10-1872)
Doyle, Bettie to Ned Grimm 12-21-1878 (12-25-1878) B
Doyle, Eliza to Jacob Foster 1-7-1868
Doyle, Isabella to George Maggard 8-26-1869 (no return)
Doyle, Maria to James K. Polk Smith 1-30-1867
Doyle, Matilda to Peter Dunavan 8-15-1867
Doyle, Mollie to Thomas Wynn 9-25-1879
Doyle, Pennie to Wash Porter 11-4-1875
Doyle, Sue to J. K. P. Harrell 6-16-1868 (no return)
Dozier, C. to W. L. McCulloch 10-1-1866 (10-4-1866)
Dozier, Jane to John Cook 7-23-1862 (7-24-1862)
Dozier, Lucy F. to J. A. Pope 12-23-1868
Drane, Louisa to R. B. Wilkinson 5-16-1878 (5-17-1878)
Drave, Mittie E. to John C. Harris 10-18-1866 (no return)
Draw, Ellen to Richard Oakly 1-29-1875 (1-31-1875) B
Drummond?, Virginia D. to James Stricklin 7-5-1869 (no return)
Drummonds, M. F. to J. A. Self 11-11-1873 (11-15-1873)
Dudley, Anne to Nelson T. Pratt 6-18-1879 (6-19-1879)
Dudley, Eliza J. to W. H. Clemmons 3-17-1874
Dudley, Mary K. to Henry Jones 9-2-1873
Duglas, Martha to Robert Fuller 10-31-1867 (12-5-1867)
Duke, Amanda B. to G. F. Bowman 5-13-1867 (5-14-1867)
Duke, Mary C. to William Carter 9-28-1869 (9-29-1869)
Duke, Mary to Richard Madding 12-23-1870 (no return) B
Duncan, A. B. to L. A. Slater 1-4-1864 (no return)
Duncan, Katharin to Crofford Taylor 5-16-1865
Duncan, Lou to Joshua Burnam 11-15-1865 (11-16-1865)
Duncan, Nancy C. to J. H. Briggs 5-24-1875
Duncan, Sarah T. to Joseph H. Evans 4-21-1868 (4-23-1868)
Duncans, Hattie to Richard Hand 7-3-1878 (no return)
Duncen, Cyntha to W. D. Harris 1-18-1868 (1-22-1868)
Dunevant, A. A. to B. F. Wynne 3-5-1873 (3-6-1873)
Dunevant, Frances C. to Henry L. Harrison 12-3-1878 (12-4-1878)
Dunevant, Lavina to A. T. Ferguson 9-18-1879
Dunevant, Mary Ann to John Burkett 9-13-1877
Dunevant, Mary B. to L. H. Bass 2-9-1874 (2-11-1874)
Dunevant, Paralee to John Prichard 12-27-1877
Dunivant, Martha A. to J. D. Powell 3-15-1864 (3-16-1864)
Dunlap, Amanda to Thomas Dillingham 8-5-1870
Dunnegan, Septimus to Albert Treadwell 1-31-1874 (2-8-1874)
Dunnevant, M. T. to J. G. Wynne 2-6-1868
Dunston, Rebecca to Henry Abbott 1-10-1871 (1-13-1871)
Dunvegard?, Ellen to Daniel Liggin 1-26-1867 (no return)
Durden, Pocahontas to John A. Brown 3-12-1879 (3-16-1879)
Dyer, M. E. to J. C. Lasater 7-28-1873 (7-31-1873)
Eady, Mendie to W. F. Lamar 11-12-1870 (11-15-1870)
Earle, M. J. to A. C. Bowen 2-21-1871 (no return)
Earle, Sallie to T. J. Harvey 12-30-1878 (12-31-1878)
Early, Martha to Alfred Shelton 2-27-1867 (3-5-1867)
Easley, Lucinda to Jo Battle 7-18-1878
Eason, Elizabeth to A. J. Foster 7-29-1865 (8-1-1865)
Eason, Louisa to James G. Mays 12-16-1861 (12-18-1861)
Echols, Altonetta to John Henderson 3-17-1866 (3-22-1866)
Echols, M. J. (Mrs.) to John McAfee 5-20-1874
Echols, Margaret to Robt. Purcell 9-20-1879 B
Echols, Mary J. to J. Lanier 7-24-1867
Echols, Mary to Thomas A. Bledsoe 8-31-1876 (9-1-1877?)
Echols, Sallie to John W. Kellow 11-22-1877
Echols, Sarah P. to Noah Leggit 7-11-1862 (7-13-1862)

Edwards, Amanda to Wash Topp 12-28-1870 (12-29-1870)
Edwards, Amanda to Wm. Brown 12-19-1867
Edwards, Dora to Edwin Degernett 2-18-1878 (2-21-1878)
Edwards, Eliza F. (Mrs.) to Isaac Burrell 12-23-1872 (no return)
Edwards, J. E. to Nathaniel Mills 12-30-1873
Edwards, Jane to Henry Mason 3-12-1877
Edwards, Mary to W. F. Spraggins 5-5-1877
Edwards, Mima to Alfred Winberry 11-3-1869
Edwards, Mollie to J. W. Thompson 2-23-1876
Edwards, Nannie to Henry Clay Boyd 6-28-1867 (6-29-1867)
Edwards, P. E. to Jane E. Lane 3-12-1872
Edwards, Rachel C. to H. M. Phillips 9-24-1870 (no return)
Edwards, Sarah E. to Henry W. White 12-2-1861
Edwards, Sarah to H. C. Tevilla 11-28-1868 (11-30-1868)
Edwards, Sarah to Jim Fielder 5-14-1880 (5-16-1880)
Eeson, Rachael to Jeptha O. Sorrell 3-28-1865
Ellington, E. A. to James H. Perry 12-4-1871 (12-6-1871)
Ellington, M. J. to Bethnell Garner 10-18-1864
Ellis, Almedia C. to Nat. A. Mills 11-6-1866 (11-7-1866)
Ellis, Amandy to W. L. Glidewell 12-7-1869 (12-8-1869)
Ellis, Charlotta to W. N. Jones 12-15-1870
Ellis, Etherline to J. D. McCorkle 1-6-1879 (1-8-1879)
Ellis, M. L. to J. T. Ellis 2-2-1874 (2-3-1874)
Ellis, Margaret to Henry Kirk 8-21-1867 (8-22-1867)
Ellis, Mary Ann to R. S. Crow 11-28-1870 (11-29-1870)
Ellis, Nancy to Duncan D. Taylor 10-14-1868 (10-15-1868)
Ellis, Sarah A. to A. F. Ray 1-6-1863 (1-8-1863)
Ellis, Susan A. to Thomas Lambert 5-12-1863 (5-17-1863)
Enoch, Eliza H. to George W. S. Graves 7-31-1867 (8-1-1867)
Enoch, Jamy to James Rose 1-10-1870 (1-11-1870)
Enoch, M. A. K. to John S. Taylor 12-23-1865 (12-27-1865)
Enoch, Nancy Ann to Henry Pierce 9-15-1869 (no return)
Enochs, F. E. to William Taylor 10-8-1872 (10-9-1872)
Enochs, Lizzie to John Townsend 12-29-1873 (12-30-1873)
Enochs, Lou to Pate Thomas 1-3-1878
Enochs, M. T. to Ben C. Wadlington 9-24-1877 (9-27-1877)
Enochs, Malinda to George Phillips 8-23-1879 (no return)
Enochs, Malinda to Thomas Willis 2-23-1872 (2-24-1872)
Enochs, Sarah T. to Sam A. McKnight 10-27-1873 (10-28-1873)
Enochs, Sarah to Perry Carter 5-23-1871 (5-25-1871)
Eskew, Cordelia to Daniel Bodkin 11-21-1876 (11-22-1876)
Espy, Nancy to William R. Helen 3-20-1862
Essary, Bettie J. to Jesse A. Brown 9-23-1868
Estes, Rachel to A. S. Anderson 10-14-1879
Etheridge, Nancy T. to Washington Williva 8-12-1862
Eudaly, Fannie to E. R. Johnson 12-22-1875
Eudaly, Mary to Frank Colbert 12-12-1874
Eudaly, S. J. to J. D. Carter 1-1-1873
Evans, Betty to Thomas Hudson 1-5-1867 (no return)
Evans, Ida to Enoch Osborn 12-24-1869 (12-26-1869)
Evans, J. M. to W. C. Fitzhugh 1-9-1878 (1-10-1878)
Evans, M. A. to N. T. Lassiter 1-10-1866
Evans, Mary Jane to W. C. Crossnoe 12-13-1870 (no return)
Evans, Nancy to F. N. Forshee 5-13-1866
Evans, Nancy to Jessup? Grimm 11-14-1877
Everett, Julia C. to J. M. Lucas 12-22-1875 (12-23-1875)
Faine, Victoria to Needham B. Bairfield 5-2-1870
Fakes, Sallie to Will R. (Dr.) Hayes 12-18-1878
Farmer, Mary J. to T. T. Reddick 3-30-1864 (no return)
Farmer, Sarah A. to Robert A. Cheny 9-18-1861 (9-20-1861)
Farrer, N. E. to D. M. Chamberlain 3-10-1868 (no return)
Faulkner, Cornelia to George Alexander 1-26-1874 (1-28-1874)
Faulkner, Martha (Mrs.) to Barnabas Edwards 11-9-1872 (11-10-1872)
Faulkner, Martha to Wm. H. Harrison 10-26-1870 (10-27-1870)
Featherston, Adaline to J. H. Waldren 2-12-1873 (no return)
Featherston, E. J. to J. S. Robbins 10-31-1877 (no return)
Featherston, E. L. to J. W. Hall 3-8-1870 (no return)
Featherston, M. E. to S. E. Milam 12-4-1873
Featherston, Martha to Charley Sawyer 1-1-1874
Fedrick, Mary Ann to Jas. C. Enscow 4-27-1863
Ferguson, A. A. to G. W. Hawkins 10-6-1868 (no return)
Ferguson, Amanda to George Anderson 10-15-1873 (10-16-1873)
Ferguson, America to William Fowlkes 6-29-1871
Ferguson, Ann to Henry Strother 12-24-1868
Ferguson, Harriet L. to E. E. Hawkins 2-12-1867 (2-13-1867)

Ferguson, Ida M. to A. T. Harrell 12-23-1867
Ferguson, Lucinda to Jerry Fowlkes 10-4-1873
Ferguson, Martha A. to Alfred Reddick 2-10-1866 (no return)
Ferguson, Martha M. to W. R. Bentley 12-14-1860 (12-19-1860)
Ferguson, Mary Louisa to Thomas F. Ledsinger 9-27-1865
Ferguson, Mary to Jack Parker 1-10-1880 (1-18-1880)
Ferguson, Matilda to John Mabin 3-15-1879
Ferguson, Matilda to Pleasant Terry 12-14-1864
Ferguson, Montie to James A. Foster 5-11-1875
Ferguson, P. I. to K. H. Bentley 2-25-1861 (no return)
Ferrell, Jane C. to David C. Bullard 2-4-1867 (2-5-1867)
Ferrell, Sarah Jane to Andrew Cart 10-11-1870
Ferrell, Sarah Jane to Andrew Hart 10-11-1870 (10-12-1870)
Ferril, Josie to James A. T. Neal 10-14-1874 (10-19-1874)
Ferrill, Ellen to J. K. P. Holland 8-19-1869
Ferrill, Frances C. to Levi H. Pitt 9-30-1868 (no return)
Ferrill, Lucy E. to T. B. Lane 11-18-1878 (11-20-1878)
Ferrill, Lucy to Osborn Thomasson 12-27-1880 (no return)
Ferrill, Margaret A. to Jesse Dixon 2-19-1879 (2-20-1879)
Ferrill, Martha Jane to Stephen Sawyer 4-17-1873 (no return)
Ferrill, Queenie? to Henry Patterson 12-18-1879 (12-25-1879)
Ferrill, Sarah to M. L. Bledsoe 5-16-1874 (5-17-1874)
Ferrill, Tennie to Andrew Boose 5-18-1876
Fielder, M. S. to S. F. Haley 10-26-1867 (no return)
Fielder, Myra V. P. to Francis M. Johnson 9-8-1863 (no return)
Fields, Ann to George Coleman 9-14-1869 (no return) B
Fields, Della to Henry Word 12-25-1879
Fields, Linnie to Sam A. Williams 11-23-1876
Fields, M. F. to A. C. Heddin 5-27-1869 (no return)
Fields, Mary to Lee Ferguson 10-24-1876
Fields, Morean to Green Douglass 4-1-1878 (4-3-1878)
Fields, Sallie to Guy Grimm 3-18-1873 (3-19-1873)
Fields, Susan to Wm. Spence 1-15-1868
Finch, Jane to A. J. Hall 8-16-1873 (8-18-1873)
Finch, Lucy E. to Fountain E. Hughes 11-12-1863
Finch, Sallie A. to George Wilborne 1-5-1876
Finley, Ida F. to S. M. Drummonds 12-21-1870
Finley, Jennie to R. M. Bledsoe 2-1-1877
Finley, M. E. to T. J. Richardson 3-6-1873 (3-5?-1873)
Finley, Martha E. to C. A. Dupre 11-27-1865
Finley, S. L. to J. W. Ledbetter 3-27-1873 (no return)
Finly, Sarah A. to Joseph Sanford 11-2-1867 (11-3-1867)
Fisher, Jane to M.? J. Williams 9-3-1867 (no return)
Fisher, Mary E. to Robert Sanford 7-1-1869 (7-4-1869)
Fizer, Lizzie to Haywood Ruff 1-4-1877 (1-5-1877)
Flack, F. to B. A. Carroll 3-11-1874
Fletcher, Jane S.? to Frank Ferguson 5-1-1865 (5-4-1865)
Flowers, Mary to Thomas Ray 10-9-1861 (10-12-1861)
Floyd, Mary Jane to J. D. Ferrill 7-3-1866 (7-5-1866)
Fly, Ann to Dell Gilliam 1-1-1874
Foard, Mary to M. (Rev.) Whittle 1-3-1863 (no return)
Foggerson, S. A. to J. H. Parnell 9-8-1860 (9-11-1860)
Follis, Mary J. to W. C. Fitzhugh 9-29-1869 (9-30-1869)
Fonshee, Mary H. to James Black 9-26-1867 (no return)
Forbes, Lucy to W. B. Simons 4-27-1872 (4-28-1872)
Forester, Cinthia to W. A. Sanders 3-14-1879 (no return)
Forshee, Nancy J. to R. P. Wade 11-12-1868
Foster, A. M. to W. H. Yates 6-27-1860
Foster, Fannie to Gantry Parr 10-16-1879
Foster, Jane (Mrs.) to J. T. Dalton 4-27-1872 (4-28-1872)
Foster, Jane to John Clayton 1-10-1874 (1-11-1874)
Foster, Louisa to Jerry Maggard 7-14-1869 (no return)
Foster, Lucinda to Jo Fowlkes 9-22-1877 (9-25-1877)
Foster, Lucy to Charles Ferrill 12-24-1873 (12-25-1873)
Foster, Martha A. to A. W. Henry 11-22-1865
Foster, S. F. to H. H. Scruggs 7-15-1870 (7-18-1870)
Foster, Susan to Jo Moore 1-21-1880 (1-22-1880)
Foust, Ann to Jackson Smith 12-14-1872 (12-26-1872)
Foust, Elva to Ben Graham 11-28-1878
Foust, Malinda to Isaac Maddrey 12-21-1868 (no return)
Foust, Melvina to Berry Simmons 4-8-1875
Foust, Milly to Matt Bradshaw 8-14-1872
Foust, Rebacca A. to Calvin Baxter 12-25-1866 (12-26-1866)
Foust, Ruth to Matt Bradshaw 12-27-1869 (no return)
Fowlkes, Agg to Jo Jones 5-8-1869 (no return)

Fowlkes, Alice to Boss Ledsinger 4-26-1876 (4-27-1876) B
Fowlkes, Amanda to Walter Scott 1-6-1866 (no return)
Fowlkes, Amelia to Lot Brown 1-24-1879 (1-26-1879)
Fowlkes, America to Dallis Smith 12-8-1873 (no return)
Fowlkes, Angaline to Dick Smith 1-26-1867 (1-27-1867)
Fowlkes, Ann to Pleas Smith 1-2-1871 (1-8-1871)
Fowlkes, Annie to Thomas Horton 1-13-1874 (1-14-1874)
Fowlkes, Belle to Miller Moore 9-15-1877
Fowlkes, Bettie to H. A. Tyler 4-1-1868 (4-2-1868)
Fowlkes, Cheney to Bailey Walker 6-22-1872 (6-30-1872)
Fowlkes, Deliah to James Oliver 12-27-1871 (12-28-1871)
Fowlkes, E. E. to H. T. Pursell 12-9-1873
Fowlkes, Eliza to Frank Moore 1-6-1872
Fowlkes, Eliza to James Barnes 3-1-1877
Fowlkes, Eliza to James Johnson 10-5-1880
Fowlkes, Embra to N. Coker 2-7-1867
Fowlkes, Emma to Daniel Woods 1-6-1872 (no return)
Fowlkes, Emma to Pompey Smith 2-16-1879
Fowlkes, Fannie to Morris Louder 1-30-1879
Fowlkes, Fanny to Jerry Pitts 2-2-1867
Fowlkes, Florence to John Doak 3-3-1880
Fowlkes, Judy to Allen Fisher 5-13-1874 (5-15-1874)
Fowlkes, Letheann to Archer Walker 12-25-1877 (no return)
Fowlkes, Lizzie to Jerry Marchant 7-6-1867
Fowlkes, Louisa to Polk Jones 7-6-1867 (7-7-1867)
Fowlkes, Louisa to Richd. Gleason 12-29-1880 (not executed)
Fowlkes, Loula to Charlie Becket 9-22-1880 (9-23-1880)
Fowlkes, Lucinda to Henry Cowles 7-17-1869 (no return)
Fowlkes, Lucy to Scott Anderson 1-28-1880
Fowlkes, Luella to Ben Parr 3-22-1877
Fowlkes, M. F. to Robt. W. Drane 12-2-1874 (no return)
Fowlkes, Malinda to Wesley Howard 5-26-1871 (5-25?-1871)
Fowlkes, Mary to Louis Dunavant 4-28-1869 (no return)
Fowlkes, Millie to Nelson Alston 8-31-1871
Fowlkes, Mollie to Thomas Jones 1-13-1876
Fowlkes, Parthena to Toler Cook 1-24-1874
Fowlkes, Sarah to Wm. Hudgens 5-22-1880
Fowlkes, Tabitha to F. M. Hambrick 11-15-1866 (no return)
Fowlkes, Z. F. to H. A. Fowlkes 10-29-1872
Fox, Jane to Ed Jackson 7-28-1875 (7-29-1875)
Franklin, Frances C. to Joseph G. Huie? 7-28-1868 (7-29-1868)
Franklin, Mary E. to Jo Baird 6-5-1866 (1?-6-1866)
Frazier, Emma (Mrs.) to W. H. Fowler 7-11-1874 (7-12-1874)
Frazier, Mary C. to J. S. McCorkle 8-23-1871 (8-24-1871)
Frazier, Mary J. to Thos. J. Mays 1-4-1879 (1-5-1879)
Frazier, Mary to Robt. L. Harper 11-19-1860 (11-27-1860)
Frazier, Sarah to Lee Tipton 10-10-1874 (10-19-1874)
Freeman, Ann to Theo. Pitts 5-10-1864 (5-12-1864)
Freeman, Delila to Alfred Reddick 2-2-1869 (no return)
Freeman, N. J. to J. H. Davis 10-5-1874 (10-6-1874)
Frith, M. W. to Eli Johnson 12-23-1868 (12-24-1868)
Frith, Martha to Champ Lankford 2-13-1872 (2-14-1872)
Frost, Julia to Rufus Henderson 9-7-1867 (9-12-1867)
Frost, Lou to Henry McGarg 1-14-1879 (no return)
Fuller, Amanda J. to Gilbert Cozart 12-2-1867 (12-3-1867)
Fuller, Amanda to Marion Pitt 9-2-1867
Fuller, Candice to Louis Fowlkes 2-6-1878 (2-7-1878)
Fuller, Eliza A. to W. Enochs 2-20-1861
Fuller, L. C. to William H. Campbell 2-4-1863 (2-5-1863)
Fuller, L. J. to T. M. Jackson 12-19-1874 (12-20-1874)
Fuller, Laura to Thomas M. Fain 3-19-1878 (3-29-1878)
Fuller, M. C. to William Jackson 2-15-1865 (2-16-1865)
Fuller, Mary E. to Sherrod Johnson 12-29-1869 (12-30-1869)
Fuller, Sarah E. to George W. Hill 11-13-1866 (11-15-1866
Fuller, Stacy A. to W. T. Gwaltney 4-28-1869 (no return)
Fuller, Sue M. to J. C. Vann 10-28-1868 (11-29-1868)
Fullerton, Margaret to Elisha Jenkins 12-28-1870 (12-29-1870)
Fullerton, Sarah E. to M. A. Simpson 3-6-1877
Fultcher, Nancy C. to W. R. Privett 4-17-1875 (4-20-1875)
Fumbank, Eliza to Allen Edney 9-23-1869 (no return)
Fumbank, Jane to David Fowlkes 9-8-1866 (no return)
Fumbanks, Bettie to John Smith 3-11-1880
Fumbanks, Lucretia to Mose Smith 2-14-1878
Fumbanks?, Martha to Jacob Cobb 8-8-1860 (8-9-1860)
Fuqua, M. L. to Henry T. Kirk 3-19-1878

Gabrel, Angeline to L. Deason 5-17-1870 (5-19-1870)
Gallaher, Elizabeth to J. Y. Crocker 7-7-1868 (no return)
Gallaher, M. J. to H. Banks 10-31-1874 (11-3-1874)
Gallion, S. A. to W. L. Carter 3-6-1871 (3-7-1871)
Gamble, S. J. to William Bledsoe 11-28-1877 (11-29-1877)
Gamble, W. E. to John Bledsoe 9-8-1877 (9-9-1877)
Gammon, Fatitia to Jas. Gammon 5-15-1863 (5-17-1863)
Gammon, L. R. to R. J. Smith 2-6-1869 (no return)
Gammon, Mary E(liza) to Thomas J. McGinnis 1-24-1866 (1-25-1866)
Gammons, Ann to M. R. Vire 12-21-1866 (12-27-1866)
Gammons, Beckie to William Sledge 7-15-1879 (7-16-1879)
Gammons, Elizabeth to H. S. Walker 12-14-1870 (12-15-1870)
Gammons, Lavenia to David Fautner 8-16-1864 (no return)
Gammons, Louisa to James M. Farris 4-29-1867 (no return)
Gammons, Margaret A. to Presley S. Beak 3-6-1861
Gammons, Mollie to J. F. Pyles 2-17-1875 (2-18-1875)
Gammons, Nancy A. to Frank E. Gammons 4-29-1867 (no return)
Gammons, Sarah to Robert Sledge 3-8-1879 (3-9-1879)
Gannon, Fannie to H. J. Mason 11-7-1871 (11-9-1871)
Garner, Martha E. to James R. Mills 3-5-1872 (3-7-1872)
Garner, Rebecca to F. T. Hines 9-19-1870 (9-21-1870)
Garrett, Elizabeth V. to Thos. J. Griffin 12-20-1870 (no return)
Garrett, Grisom E. to John C. Adams 6-6-1866 (6-7-1866)
Garrett, Mary to James Craig 1-8-1867 (1-13-1867)
Garrison, C. A. to William D. Taylor 8-7-1878 (8-8-1878)
Garrison, Elizabeth to L. Gallaher 10-25-1860 (no return)
Garrison, Harriet to William E. Troy 5-27-1862 (no return)
Garrison, Marinda to Benj. A. Crisp 2-16-1870 (2-17-1870)
Garrison, Martha to E. W. Brinkley 12-13-1860
Garrison, Sina to Jack Cox 5-1-1869 (no return)
Gaskins, Malinda to George Tripp 6-4-1879 (6-22-1879)
Gauldin, Bettie to Andrew Harris 9-30-1868
Gauldin, Maggie to Fillmore Ferguson 9-29-1875
Gauldin, Martha to Elisha Jackson 12-25-1871 (no return)
Gause, Leanor to Henry Jordan 2-28-1868 (no return)
Gay, Mattie to E. A. Oquinn 7-28-1874 (7-30-1874)
Gentry, M. A. to J. M. Webster 1-10-1872
Gentry, Susan to W. C. Stephenson 1-12-1876
Gibson, Anna to W. J. Bryant 3-11-1868 (no return)
Gibson, Maggie to W. J. Bryant 10-28-1871 (10-29-1871)
Gibson, Mary to G. A. Wicks 1-4-1875 (1-5-1875)
Gibson, Mattie J. to W. H. Mangrum 1-16-1866
Gibson, Sarah J. to James W. Chambers 1-22-1867 (1-23-1867)
Gibson, Susan M. to William H. Thompson 8-1-1863 (8-2-1863)
Giles, Elizabeth to R. B. Saunders 10-1-1866 (10-2-1866)
Giles, Puss to L. C. Harvell 3-7-1865 (3-8-1865)
Gillaland, Lyd A. to Edward Williams 1-30-1861 (no return)
Gillis, M. J. G. to John B. Avey 12-27-1871
Gillis, Mollie to David C. James 1-16-1867
Gillis, S. E. to D. H. Stephens 3-11-1875
Gillis, S. M. C. to A. B. Peery 4-4-1871 (4-6-1871)
Gleaves, Harriet to R. S. Crow 1-17-1872 (1-18-1872)
Glenn, Elizabeth to Wm. Dillingham 10-10-1878
Glevur?, Lizzie to Henry Taylor 11-30-1872 (12-1-1872)
Glisson, Catherine to Caswell C. Mifflin 1-21-1871 (1-22-1871)
Goin, Fannie to Nelson Bland 1-4-1876
Goin, Susan to Shack Oldham 3-16-1880
Goings, Nancy to Edmond Shirley 5-2-1878
Gold, Finey to A. J. Barrett 1-24-1874 (1-25-1874)
Gold, Mary E. to W. E. Connell 11-11-1871 (11-12-1871)
Golden, Lethe E. to Isham James 8-24-1868 (no return)
Gooding, J. L. to J. M. Pope 1-19-1878 (1-20-1878)
Goodloe, Susan to William T. Woods 11-28-1862 (12-?-1862)
Goodman, Malinda J. to Joseph Harrell 7-22-1861 (no return)
Goodman, Martha to Paul G. Clement 1-11-1865 (no return)
Goodman, Mary E. to J. T. Burnett 1-17-1871 (1-18-1871)
Goodric, Amanda to John Devenport 5-14-1870 (5-17-1870)
Goodrich, Elizabeth A. to Levin Thomas 3-7-1861
Goodrich, Jane to James Turner 12-23-1864
Goodrich, Missouri to John Oaks 7-9-1873
Goodwin, Lizzie V. to J. H. Goodwin 1-26-1869 (1-28-1869)
Gowan, Malissa C. to James F. Webb 7-31-1878 (8-1-1878)
Grace, Callie to Richard Thurmond 8-28-1877 (8-29-1877)
Grace, Ellen to J. R. Palmer 10-5-1876 (10-7-1876)
Grace, Mollie to W. A. Webb 8-22-1877

Graves, Rachel E. S. to W. S. Enoch 7-31-1867 (8-1-1867)
Graw (McGraw?), M. A. S. to John H. Tarrant 9-24-1866 (9-25-1866)
Grayum, Lavina to William Warmack 8-17-1870 (8-29-1870)
Green, Abby to William Thompson 4-6-1870 (4-7-1870)
Green, Evelyn to S. Frank Brock 2-24-1866
Green, J. P. to W. H. Woods 10-2-1869 (10-6-1869)
Green, Jennie to Leonard Waggoner 12-13-1878 (12-18-1878)
Green, M. E. to John N. Green 11-11-1875
Green, Mary F. to James R. Hall 11-17-1868 (11-18-1868)
Green?, Ellen to W. H. R. Tiner 10-29-1867
Greenwood, C. B. to Jerome B. Peery 5-8-1869 (no return)
Greer, Ellen to J. L. Cunningham 12-17-1868 (12-24-1868)
Gregory, L. E. to A. J. Grills 11-14-1871
Grier, Mary C. to Wm. C. Gregory 2-27-1865 (3-1-1865)
Grier, S. E. to Charles Robertson 9-20-1876
Griffin, Cynthia to J. M. King 10-12-1865
Griffin, Harriet to Peter Mitchell 1-6-1874 (1-7-1874)
Griffin, Louisa to Henry Griffin 12-27-1866
Griffin, M. L. to R. T. Hill 12-21-1870 (12-22-1870)
Griffin, M. R. to T. H. Thornton 1-16-1878
Griffin, Martha to Toney Parks 12-17-1879 (12-18-1879)
Griffin, Mary Jane to Thomas J. Peel 1-6-1874 (1-7-1874)
Griffin, Sarah C. to Saml. L. Pleasant 10-11-1870 (no return)
Griffin, Sarah C. to Samuel L. Gleason 10-11-1870 (no return)
Grills, Dicey E. to J. F. Snow 10-31-1873 (11-4-1873)
Grimm, Bettie to Elijah Grimm 1-10-1876 (1-12-1876)
Grimm, Bettie to Richard Mann 2-8-1876 (no return)
Grimm, Letitia to Fernando Dunevent 5-19-1875 (5-20-1875)
Grimm, Mourning to Gay Grimm 9-26-1877 (no return)
Grimm, Polly to Hampton Smith 12-6-1877
Guinn, Harriet to B. R. Simpkins 10-2-1863 (10-5-1863)
Guinn, Katie to Emmett Hobbs 1-1-1879 (1-15-1879)
Gurganus, Runinia to Elijah H. Shelton 9-29-1865 (10-1-1865)
Gurganus, S. A. M. to J. W. Shelton 8-26-1867
Gurgett, M. A. to R. N. Dennis 10-25-1879 (10-26-1879)
Gwaltney, Frances to S. J. Self 12-5-1860 (no return)
Haggart, Mary F. to John McCracken 1-21-1862 (1-23-1862)
Halbrooks, Mary A. to John Stephens 8-11-1863
Hale, Agnes to Henry Weakley 8-1-1877
Hale, Bettie to Silas Beckett 1-3-1877 (1-4-1877)
Hall, A. L. to C. A. G. Taylor 9-19-1867
Hall, Candis M. to T. J. Sanders 11-19-1860 (11-20-1860)
Hall, Elizabeth to J. L. Ralls 9-5-1865 (9-7-1865)
Hall, Elmira to Andy J. Campbell 3-3-1877 (3-4-1877)
Hall, Eolino to George Baldrige 12-20-1866 (12-29-1866)
Hall, Frances M. to A. R. Montgomery 12-14-1864 (no return)
Hall, Frankie (Mrs.) to W. S. Hines 2-12-1873
Hall, H. (M.?)J. to J. R. Prichard 3-2-1878 (3-7-1878)
Hall, H. I. to B. S. M. Stalcup 1-19-1871
Hall, M. A. E. to Richard Fletcher 12-20-1865 (12-24-1865)
Hall, M. A. to W. R. G. Crow 1-7-1867 (1-8-1867)
Hall, M. E. to D. C. Lively 1-8-1868 (1-9-1868)
Hall, M. F. to R. H. Michell 8-5-1868 (no return)
Hall, Mary to James Weakly 5-22-1867
Hall, P. E. to J. T. Boon 10-5-1869
Hall, S. J. to Asa M. Davis 5-17-1873 (5-18-1873)
Hall, S. J. to N. A. Edwards 12-21-1864 (no return)
Hall, Sadie to Z. T. Reynolds 1-7-1879 (1-9-1879)
Hall, Sarah to John Pope 12-21-1878 (no return)
Hallet, N. B. to Z. N. Morris 2-19-1866 (2-20-1866)
Halliburton, Ann to Joseph Reynolds 1-6-1875 (1-7-1875)
Halum, Miley to W. T. Pace 9-18-1866 (9-20-1866)
Hamilton, Amanda to James R. Hurd 11-2-1869 (11-4-1869)
Hamilton, C. J. to H. S. Burnside 1-8-1875 (1-12-1875)
Hamilton, F. A. to W. P. Shofner 3-18-1873 (3-23-1873)
Hamilton, Josie to Daniel Davis 8-16-1878 (8-21-1878)
Hamilton, M. J. to J. W. Ellis 2-15-1870 (2-16-1870)
Hamilton, R. L. to T. F. Parnell 11-30-1869 (12-3-1869)
Hamilton, Rebecca A. to J. N. Ellis 8-26-1868 (8-27-1868)
Hamilton, S. E. to M. R. Pace 12-17-1878 (12-19-1878)
Hammel, E. S. to J. F. Murray 12-20-1870 (12-22-1870)
Hampden, M. J. to J. B. Ward 9-7-1872 (no return)
Hampton, Emiline to Calvin Anderson 2-25-1870 (no return)
Hampton, M. J. to W. S. Davis 5-16-1874 (5-19-1874)
Hampton, Mary E. to Ben F. Prichard 12-21-1872 (no return)

Hampton, Mary L. to John T. Lane 1-30-1872
Hampton, Rebecca to Warren Hall 11-10-1877 (no return)
Hancock, M. E. to Charles Coleman 3-31-1879 (4-1-1879)
Hanks, Mary Jane to Wm. Elliott 11-30-1864 (no return)
Hardican, E. F. to J. M. Lemons 2-8-1870 (no return)
Hardican, L. C. to Roy Gaskin 3-5-1873 (3-10-1873)
Hardican, Margaret H. to Thomas Lemmons 3-3-1862 (3-4-1862)
Hardican, Martha to H. B. Williams 10-19-1863
Hardie, Sarah L. to Allen Fenlen? 9-5-1870 (9-6-1870)
Hardin, Mary to Jack Davidson 5-29-1866 (6-30-1866)
Hardin, Sarah A. to S. P. Hawkins 4-5-1870 (4-6-1870)
Hardison, Louisa to W. N. Robertson 1-15-1879 (1-16-1879)
Hardison, Sallie J. to J. W. Clarke 1-26-1874 (1-27-1874)
Hare, M. J. to A. B. Hamilton 2-6-1871 (2-7-1871)
Harmon, Sarah T. to Thomas Woods 1-11-1862 (1-12-1862)
Harper, F. E. to F. P. Smith 7-22-1876 (7-23-1876)
Harper, L. E. to T. J. Pierce 1-23-1872 (1-24-1872)
Harrell, Mary E. to Robt. A. Haley 10-17-1860
Harris, Ada to Henry Connell 5-18-1876 (no return)
Harris, Adaline to James Talley 4-29-1876 (4-30-1876) B
Harris, Amanda A. to George Brimm 12-25-1871
Harris, Amanda to Isaac Canada 9-6-1879 (9-7-1879)
Harris, Ann Eliza to Richmond Turpin 9-22-1863 (9-23-1863)
Harris, Anna L. to James C. Roe 2-20-1867 (no return)
Harris, Arthena to Sam Alexandra 6-11-1870 (6-10?-1870)
Harris, B. J. to A. E. Moore 12-24-1872 (12-25-1872)
Harris, Densi to John Scott 4-23-1870
Harris, E. M. to J. D. Carroll 1-14-1861 (1-15-1861)
Harris, Eadie to Allen Campbell 1-21-1873 (1-3?-1873)
Harris, Ella to Alex Horton 6-6-1874 (6-11-1874) B
Harris, Emma to Aleck Saunders 8-22-1874 (9-22-1874)
Harris, Emma to J. P. Walker 10-29-1873
Harris, Fanny to Dennis Parker 12-28-1868 (no return)
Harris, Frances to Nathan Smith 4-19-1870 (no return)
Harris, James to J. B. Neal 4-7-1879
Harris, Jane to Willis W. Slayton 11-20-1860
Harris, Lou to John W. Wilson 10-21-1867 (no return)
Harris, Louisa A. to Samuel J. Jones 10-26-1869 (no return)
Harris, Lucinda to Lafayette Haskin 12-30-1878 (1-18-1879)
Harris, Lundy? to John McCoy 1-22-1878 (1-23-1878)
Harris, M. E. to Andrew S. Parks 7-8-1868 (no return)
Harris, Martha to Harry Grimm 6-30-1876
Harris, Martha to Richard Haskins 8-19-1874 (8-20-1874)
Harris, Millie to Polk Howard 12-26-1872
Harris, Minerva to W. W. Bruce 5-25-1861 (5-30-1861)
Harris, Nancy to William Mulherin 4-22-1875
Harris, Puss to Champ Peak 12-11-1876 (no return)
Harris, Rachel to Will Woods 4-5-1879 (4-7-1879)
Harris, Sallie to Albert Jones 10-10-1877 (no return)
Harris, Sallie to Booker Howard 4-2-1873 (3?-2-1873)
Harris, Susan to Jasper Cozart 1-13-1866
Harris, Tishie to A. Bradshaw 12-28-1870 (12-29-1870)
Harrison, Alice to A. L. Love 12-12-1870 (12-15-1870)
Harrison, Eliza Rebecca to James M. Bandy 3-22-1879 (3-23-1879)
Harrison, L. C. to H. S. Walker 12-24-1862 (1-8-1863)
Harrison, M. E. to J. Thomas Talley 12-24-1873
Harrison, Mary to Lawson Parrish 5-20-1873 (5-25-1873)
Harrison, Nannie to John M. Rogers 4-26-1879 (4-27-1879)
Harrison, Sally Ann to A. B. Williams 1-4-1866
Harrold, Malinda J. to James Parks 7-29-1867 (no return)
Harrold, S. W. to Jeremiah Jones 2-20-1867 (no return)
Hart, Elizabeth to David M. Craig 11-26-1860
Hart, F. M. to J. T. Wheeler 1-14-1879 (1-15-1879)
Hart, H. M. to T. D. Peek 3-5-1873 (3-6-1873)
Hart, M. J. to J. E. Wheeler 2-17-1872 (2-18-1872)
Hart, Mary to Wm. Elmore 6-3-1863
Harton, Fannie to Charles B. Bloomingdale 7-31-1871
Harton, Louanna to E. W. Smith 2-10-1874 (2-11-1874)
Harton, Rebecca L. to W. N. Taylor 11-14-1870 (11-15-1870)
Harvell, Missouri to W. M. Scallions 5-17-1869 (5-18-1869)
Harvey, S. B. to W. T. McCutchen 7-28-1873 (7-31-1873)
Harwell, Indiana A. to John Wesley Bell 4-2-1877 (4-4-1877)
Harwell, Margaret to Daniel Miller 12-30-1868 (12-31-1868)
Harwell, S. E. to R. A. Sawrie 11-4-1868 (no return)
Haskin, Louis to John Miller 11-7-1867

Haskins, Ann to George Walton 7-14-1877 (7-15-1877)
Haskins, Eddy Carter to Samuel H. Williams 12-23-1874 (12-24-1874)
Haskins, Elizabeth to Joseph Williams 6-11-1879 (6-12-1879)
Haskins, L. M. to R. D. Harris 12-21-1869 (no return)
Haskins, Millie to Thomas Humphreys 2-10-1874 (2-12-1874)
Haskins, Rhoda to Lewis Fowlkes 7-8-1871 (no return)
Hassell, Dinkie to Joseph F. Roberts 3-3-1875
Hassell, Louisa T. to Richmond Turpin 6-13-1864 (no return)
Hassell, Margaret J. to James B. Parrish 8-20-1868 (no return)
Hassell, Mary A. to W. H. Ball 4-1-1867 (4-3-1867)
Hastings, Savannah to W. S. Simmons 8-30-1879 (9-1-1879)
Hawk, Jane to A. G. Pierce 5-2-1866 (5-3-1866)
Hawkins, Ann to B. T. Bibb 11-11-1867
Hawkins, Rebecca J. to John C. Brashears 9-3-1867
Hawkins, S. J. to D. F. Taylor 1-7-1879 (1-8-1879)
Hawkins, Sarah C. to E. W. Chapman 9-13-1867 (no return)
Haynes, Eliza C. to W. W. Haynes 5-3-1870
Haynes, Sarah A. to Franklin Greer 10-11-1862 (10-12-1862)
Headden, Mary M. to W. H. Hendricks 7-24-1877
Headen, Martha M. to Wm. W. Wright 1-16-1871 (1-18-1871)
Hedden, S. E. to James C. Green 11-18-1862 (11-19-1862)
Hedin, Lutitia Mahala to John D. Alexander 9-1-1863 (no return)
Helms, Lucind to John W. Atkins 1-30-1865
Henderson, Caroline to James Miller 12-27-1866 (no return)
Henderson, Laura to J. P. Bowen 10-4-1870 (10-6-1870
Henderson, Lotta to John Porter 3-18-1873 (no return)
Henderson, M. Emma to Robert A. Roe 1-23-1867 (1-24-1867)
Henderson, Martha A. to George Duke 2-7-1865
Henderson, Millie to Zach Badgett 10-15-1880 (10-24-1880)
Henderson, Narcissa J. to William D. Powell 12-3-1861
Hendren, Jane to James McGuire 11-22-1878
Hendricks, H. E. to W. H. Cope 8-12-1872 (no return)
Hendricks, Harriet to W. L. Wyatt 3-1-1871 (10-4-1871)
Hendricks, Margaret M. to B. W. Teater 10-30-1867 (no return)
Hendricks, Martha A. to H. A. Reed 7-15-1878 (no return)
Hendricks, N. L. to J. W. Trout 12-24-1876 (12-26-1876)
Hendricks, S. A. to J. H. Chitwood 11-27-1878 (11-28-1878)
Hendrix, M. E. to John Boyd 1-30-1866 (1-31-1866)
Hendrix, S. J. to W. L. Wilcox 10-22-1867 (no return)
Henry, Ann to Frank Brown 12-27-1866 (no return)
Henry, Isabela to William Dearmon 8-18-1863 (no return)
Henry, Julia A. to B. F. Smith 2-22-1869
Henry, M. F. to J. Z. McAlister 2-7-1872
Henry, Mary A. to W. K. Simpson 12-29-1869 (12-30-1869)
Herald, Elizabeth to Thomas Canady 11-26-1877
Herald, Susan to W. Woods 3-6-1878 (3-7-1878)
Herril, Martha to Jessee B. Baker 3-16-1876
Herron, Margaret to Isaac Jackson 4-28-1860 (4-29-1860)
Herron, Mary Ann to George Jackson 9-20-1860
Hibbitts, Sarah J. to Patrick Y. White 2-6-1866 (2-7-1866)
Hicks, Catherine to John McCulloch 10-25-1865 (10-26-1865)
Hicks, E. C. to F. A. Collins 1-27-1879
Hicks, M. C. to W. R. Hobday 11-25-1874
Hicks, Sallie to W. P. Keenan 4-18-1878 (4-19-1878)
Higgin, Mary to Henry Driscol 12-27-1866 (12-28-1866)
Hill, Annie to James D. McClerkin 4-19-1877
Hill, N. T. to Alex Rogers 9-24-1869 (9-28-1869)
Hill, T. P. to D. A. Smith 12-18-1868 (12-21-1868)
Hilliard, Fannie to J. H. Speight 11-10-1873 (no return)
Hinds, Billie to O. B. Dixon 12-11-1878
Hines, Frances E. to Marcus Sewell 10-25-1875 (10-27-1875)
Hinson, M. J. to W. T. Galliher 2-6-1872 (2-9-1872)
Hitchcock, Jennette to S. A. Thorp 5-16-1866 (5-20-1866)
Hobday, M. F. to A. S. Berry 8-4-1877 (no return)
Hobsen, Martha to J. H. Mitchell 9-12-1870 (9-13-1870)
Hobson, Lizzie to D. M. Stephens 1-14-1878 (1-16-1878)
Hodge, M. S. to W. N. Murray 12-17-1873
Hodge, Nicey to Robert Smith 8-11-1868 (no return)
Hodge, Susan to Louis Sales 12-27-1876 (or 12-28?)
Hoge, Sofrona to Silas Skipper 5-2-1865 (5-3-1865)
Holland, Julia Ann to John B. Duckworth 1-18-1875
Holland, Manerva to J. H. Dillon 4-7-1870 (no return)
Holland, Martha F. to James A. Hathway 11-27-1862 (11-30-1862)
Holland, Mary P. to John G. Bell 1-6-1862 (no return)
Holland, S. C. to J. G. W. Akin 9-4-1876 (no return)

Holland, Sarah C. to D. M. Gwaltney 5-13-1861 (no return)
Holland, Sarah to Anely Thompson 11-27-1860
Hollins, Fannie to E. L. Brassfield 1-28-1868 (1-29-1868)
Hollis, S. A. to J. G. Hardin 5-9-1878 (5-12-1878)
Holmes, Nora to Granville Harris 12-22-1880 (12-23-1880)
Holmes, Sidny to John Bailey 10-14-1875 (10-15-1875)
Hommel, Margaret M. to Edward Willis 12-31-1860 (1-1-1861)
Hood, Amanda S. A. to George W. Hendricks 2-10-1864 (no return)
Hood, Delia (Mrs.) to Thomas McCounts 1-7-1874 (1-24-1874)
Hood, Frances R. to W. D. Dalton 6-14-1879 (no return)
Hood, Sarah M. to Etheridge Staggs 1-11-1877
Hood, Tresa Ann L. to Henry McBride 5-30-1879 (6-1-1879)
Hook, P. E. to W. R. Dodd 10-10-1868
Hooper, Mollie E. to Geo. T. Hurt 2-20-1873
Hooper, Tennie to Harrison Robertson 12-25-1872 (12-26-1872)
Hopkins, Martha to James Gibbs 3-27-1869 (no return)
Hopper, Laura A. to B. F. Young 3-20-1878 (3-21-1878)
Hopper, Martha to James W. Barrett 2-16-1870 (2-17-1870)
Hopper, Ulissus to J. T. Barrett 6-26-1873
Horton, Harriet F. to John A. Kirkpatrick 7-29-1863 (8-2-1863)
Horton, Martha to Alexander Smith 9-24-1872 (9-25-1872)
Horton, Mary Elizabeth to J. R. Neil 9-25-1877
Horton, Rebecca to Pierce Moore 9-20-1873
Horton, Reddie to Peter McDonald 1-17-1878 B
Horton, Retta to Henry Jones 10-14-1876 (10-15-1876)
Hosey, Emily to B. P. Dyer 10-4-1879 (10-7-1879)
Hoskins, Julia Ann to Jacob Cantlin 2-12-1875 (2-25-1875)
Hoskins, L. R. to W. M. Branch 6-18-1875 (6-21-1875)
House, M. C. to John Foreshee 5-28-1867
Howard, Latitia to Jordan Moore 8-13-1866 (no return)
Howard, Lonesome to E. H. Troutt 1-28-1870 (1-29-1870)
Howard, Lucy J. to T. F. Simpson 10-13-1873 (10-14-1873)
Howard, Martha to H. Cowles 12-31-1874
Howard, Mary A. to Dick Smith 12-24-1866 (12-29-1866)
Howard, Mary A. to Stephen Howard 4-21-1860 (4-24-1860)
Howard, Minerva P. (Mrs.) to Riley Privett 10-31-1865
Howell, Charlotte to Thomas Brassfield 2-18-1868
Howell, Mary E. to Henry Leonly? 4-20-1867 (4-22-1867)
Howell, Sallie to Joseph Deal 8-16-1866
Howell, Susan P. to S. K. Jackson 12-14-1870 (12-15-1870)
Howell?, E. C. to W. T. Goodwin 1-10-1870 (1-12-1870)
Hudson, Nannie to Wm. Jordan 3-26-1880
Huffine, Malinda to Alse L. Pope 11-28-1877 (11-29-1877)
Huffine, Margaret Jane to B. G. M. Cole 12-14-1876
Huffine, Sarah C. to H. T. Pope 12-4-1878 (no return)
Hufstettler, F. E. to A. J. Blackmore 8-21-1875 (8-23-1875)
Hufstettler, Margaretta A. to James L. McCoy 7-21-1874 (7-27-1874)
Hufstettler, Mary J. to A. M. Green 6-22-1874 (6-23-1874)
Huggins, Alice to Balaam Emerson 10-25-1876 (no return)
Hugueley, C. R. to D. J. Scoby 5-5-1863 (5-6-1863)
Huguely, Margaret M. to W. B. Scoby 2-8-1862 (2-12-1862)
Hull, E. M. to George A. Tower 7-6-1870
Hull, M. E. to A. P. Brewer 3-27-1877 (3-29-1877)
Humble, V. A. to P. L. Scott 5-22-1879 (6-7-1879)
Humphrey, Jesse to J. S. Colvin 9-25-1878 (9-26-1878)
Humphreys, Nancy J. to W. F.? Vinyard 12-24-1868 (no return)
Hunt, M. E. to R. M. Arnett 5-13-1873
Hurley, A. J. to G. A. Scott 2-19-1878 (2-21-1878)
Hurley, Elizabeth to Wm. James 5-18-1863 (5-20-1863)
Hurley, M.E. to John C. Pate 8-3-1872 (no return)
Hurley, Nancy to James Howard 2-1-1870
Hurt, Fannie to Geo. T. Johnson 11-29-1877
Hurt, Frances to J. T. Higgason 1-13-1868 (1-15-1868)
Hurt, Martha A. to Solomon Cook 2-25-1861
Hurt, Martha E. to George T. Baker 9-27-1865 (9-28-1865)
Husband, Lavina to T. J. Lockhart 7-1-1875 (no return)
Husbands, S. T. to G. B. Pierce 9-18-1874 (9-20-1874)
Hutson, Barbara A. to S. D. Bates 1-24-1877 (no return)
Hutson, Jane to Alex Tipton 2-20-1878 (no return)
Ivey, Mary to C. R. Dunn 4-6-1878 (4-7-1878)
Jack, Mary C. to James A. Wallace 11-11-1862 (11-13-1862)
Jackson, A. M. to J. T. Avants 1-23-1872 (1-28-1872)
Jackson, Alice to J. M. Woodsides 8-23-1875 (8-25-1875)
Jackson, B. Z. to M. C. McCormack 9-23-1879 (9-24-1879)
Jackson, Charlotte L. to R. P. Wade 12-20-1867 (12-28-1867)

Jackson, Charlotte to George W. Norman 4-30-1860
Jackson, Elizabeth to J. P. Spencer 9-19-1878 (9-20-1878)
Jackson, J. L. to J. E. White 3-15-1877
Jackson, J. L. to J. E. White ?-?-1877 (no return)
Jackson, Jane to Jesse Guinn 1-1-1879 (1-2-1879)
Jackson, Jennie to J. G. Swanner 10-26-1871
Jackson, Laura to J. B. Jennings 10-23-1868 (no return)
Jackson, Lou to Robt. Jones 4-24-1877 (no return)
Jackson, Louisa to W. L. Hampton 7-1-1867 (7-2-1867)
Jackson, M. O. to M. J. Butler 4-3-1877 (4-4-1877)
Jackson, Mattie Ann to J. W. Olive 10-31-1878
Jackson, Nancy to James W. Lewis 11-14-1878 (11-17-1878)
Jackson, Sarah to James H. Beakley 2-19-1876 (2-20-1876)
Jacock, Margaret C. to J. N. Nunn 1-30-1867 (1-31-1867)
James, Ellen to C. C. Mifflin 1-8-1870 (1-9-1870)
James, Emma to John W. Curby 7-23-1874
James, Evaline to Charles Jackson 11-23-1877 (11-24-1877)
James, Katie C. to W. H. Jones 12-22-1874 (12-23-1874)
James, Martha to Joel Pugh 8-24-1863 (8-25-1863)
James, Mary L. to R. M. Winberry 1-3-1871 (1-5-1871)
James, Mattie E. to W. B. Finley 12-29-1877 (12-30-1877)
James, Mollie to Joel E. Light 12-12-1878
James, Sally to J. K. (Dr.) Huey 4-7-1869
Jarrett, Malinda R. to James D. Pike 8-22-1872
Jarrett, Nancy J. to Stephen A. Via 7-19-1871 (no return)
Jelks, Tennessee to Geo. Nash 2-23-1880 (2-25-1880)
Jenkins, M. J. to W. B. Lacy 9-18-1867 (9-19-1867)
Jenkins, Susan to G. W. Simpson 11-29-1876
Jennings, Lucy S. to J. T. Fields 11-8-1876
Johnson, A. E. to W. L. Shaw 12-24-1870 (12-25-1870)
Johnson, Abigial? to Balsam Wynne 3-2-1867
Johnson, Amanda I. to William Spradlin 4-3-1876 (4-12-1876)
Johnson, Bettie to James E. Brooks 7-9-1878 (no return)
Johnson, C. A. to W. R. Patterson 12-23-1867 (no return)
Johnson, E. C. to James A. Parker 4-25-1872
Johnson, Eliza to Henry Winchester 3-7-1874 (3-11-1874)
Johnson, Elizabeth to Wesley Williams 11-19-1869 (11-21-1869)
Johnson, Emiline to J. N. Thurmond 9-11-1873
Johnson, Emily to John Smith 2-5-1878
Johnson, H. H. to W. S. Forsyth 6-11-1873 (6-15-1873)
Johnson, J. E. to F. A. Slater 10-17-1874 (10-18-1874)
Johnson, Jane to Jerry Skipper 12-4-1865
Johnson, Josephine to Moses Walker 9-12-1866 (9-27-1866
Johnson, Julia Ann to William Searcy 5-1-1869 (no return)
Johnson, L. V. to M. V. (Mo?) Bettis 11-21-1866 (no return)
Johnson, M. A. to James S. Massey 5-10-1860
Johnson, M. J. to J. Z. Ledsinger 12-2-1868 (no return)
Johnson, M. L. E. to S. J. Welch 8-18-1870
Johnson, Malinda to Boston Fielder 12-21-1868 (12-30-1868)
Johnson, Martha to Luke Williams 11-23-1870 (11-24-1870)
Johnson, Martha to Wade Hampton 1-29-1877
Johnson, Mary N. to George W. Ivie 2-11-1867 (2-13-1867)
Johnson, Mary to Thomas Skipper 7-4-1860
Johnson, Mattie to Joseph Brooks 10-28-1862 (no return)
Johnson, Phillip to Ben Topp 2-21-1868 (2-22-1868)
Johnson, Sallie R. to R. T. Chambers 6-8-1878 (6-11-1878)
Johnson, Sarah to Tom Parker 4-17-1869 (no return)
Johnson, Sarah to William Skipper 12-25-1860
Johnson, Susan J. to O. A. Jones 1-28-1868 (1-29-1868)
Jones, Abba to J. S. Howe 6-22-1866 (6-24-1866)
Jones, Ada to Robert Trew 8-26-1870 (8-29-1870)
Jones, Alice to John Dumas 10-2-1873 (10-4-1873)
Jones, Amanda to David Armstrong 4-16-1873 (4-17-1873) B
Jones, Amelia C. to R. E. Parnell 10-28-1868 (no return)
Jones, Amelia to W. C. Chronister 10-17-1860 (10-8?-1860)
Jones, Arteny to Mit Baxter 2-17-1871
Jones, Bettie E. to W. T. Walker 7-25-1877
Jones, Bettie to Joseph Bacon 3-22-1875 (3-24-1875)
Jones, C. A. to A. H. McKee 12-11-1867 (no return)
Jones, C. F. to William Whitlock 3-6-1874 (3-7-1874)
Jones, Canda to Jesse Parks 5-17-1867 (5-18-1867)
Jones, Catharine to D. C. Nixon 4-7-1864
Jones, Catharine to Henry Bell 5-25-1867
Jones, Charlotte to singleton Britt 6-20-1876 (6-22-1876)
Jones, Eliza to Henry Enoch 7-18-1868 (7-19-1868)

Jones, Emeline to Jas. A.? Craw 3-23-1864 (no return)
Jones, Emma to Lewis M. Rogers 7-8-1878
Jones, Frankie to Armstead Grayson 7-4-1876
Jones, Hannah to Neid? Parker 7-29-1876 B
Jones, Katie A. to W. H. Biggs 7-25-1877
Jones, L. E. to William R. Spoon 7-20-1878 (7-21-1878)
Jones, L. J. to Wiley B. Parnell 4-19-1873 (4-20-1873)
Jones, Lizzie to Raphe Douglass 12-26-1879
Jones, Lola to T. S. Talley 6-20-1878
Jones, M. A. to J. W. Gaulden 12-20-1864 (12-21-1864)
Jones, M. E. to W. H. Cowell 2-26-1872
Jones, M. J. to C. H. Smith 9-24-1869
Jones, Mabel to Lafayette Pitts 12-11-1867 (12-12-1867)
Jones, Margrett E. to James Henry White 2-8-1870 (2-9-1870)
Jones, Marina Jane to William Self 2-12-1873 (2-13-1873)
Jones, Martha A. to E. D. Hudson 5-8-1877 (5-14-1877)
Jones, Martha Helen to Elijah Snow 5-10-1862 (5-18-1862)
Jones, Martha to Jesse Harris 7-18-1868
Jones, Martha to Sam Parks 6-8-1867 (6-9-1867)
Jones, Mary Jane to Mose? Walker 7-23-1873
Jones, Mary to W. H. Watson 11-27-1871 (11-28-1871)
Jones, Milly to Richard Parks 2-1-1867 (2-2-1867)
Jones, Mollie to M. Tansil 1-13-1874
Jones, Nancy to John Richardson 8-20-1868 (no return)
Jones, Rachel to Esquire Welch 6-19-1877
Jones, S. E. to J. G. Meadows 10-10-1870 (no return)
Jones, Sarah to David Shepley 2-27-1878 (2-28-1878)
Jones, Susan Anna to J. B. Taylor 12-27-1876 (12-28-1876)
Jones, Susie to A. R. Biggs 11-30-1870 (12-1-1870)
Jones, V. A. to W. A. Peery 1-31-1872
Jordan, Emma to H. C. Scott 1-8-1878 (1-10-1878)
Jordan, M. E. to E. G. Harris 10-15-1879 (10-21-1879)
Jordan, Mary to Israel Snead 11-17-1874 (11-18-1874)
Joslin, Martha E. to James Bain 4-18-1878 (4-21-1878)
Jostling, S. J. to T. N. Gill 3-12-1870 (3-13-1870)
Joyner, Winnie to Liss Light 5-6-1875
Justice, Fannie to Nelson T. Davis 4-8-1872 (4-10-1872)
Justis, Bettie C. to W. A. Fuller 1-17-1877
Justis, Mollie J. to John T. Fuller 1-17-1877
Kee, Louisa to Geo. W. Law 2-27-1873
Kelley, Maria (Amanda?) T. to W. J. F. Dobbs 3-3-1873
Kellow, Emma to T. L. Plummer 12-13-1876 (12-14-1876)
Kellow, S. E. to Wm. W. Moore 11-11-1874 (11-12-1874)
Kelly, S. J. to James E. Polston 12-20-1866
Kelly, Susan M. to S. A. McKnight 2-28-1865 (3-1-1865)
Kenady, Ruth Ann to James Holland 1-14-1865 (1-15-1865)
Kennady, N. E. to R. C. Dickey 10-10-1872
Kent, Celia A. to Fred L. Anthony 1-1-1877 (1-2-1877)
Kent, Harriet Liller to Louis H. Silsby 4-28-1860 (4-29-1860)
Kent, M. A. to J. M. Poarch 2-29-1876 (3-1-1876)
Kent, M. E. to B. P. Hobday 2-29-1876 (3-1-1876)
Kerley, Minerva to D. V. McKinney 10-30-1862
Kerley, Sarah J. to B. A. Johnson 10-9-1860
Key, Mary to John Gentry 8-22-1865 (8-23-1865)
Kidd, Mary V. to W. R. Mitchell 1-26-1878 (1-28-1878)
Killet, Sarah P. to George W. Lane 9-3-1863
Killet, Sarah to Thomas E. Hall 2-16-1871
Kimbrel, Mattie E. to James F. Lillard 5-13-1876 (5-14-1876)
King, A. C. to C. G. Johnson 7-2-1866 (7-3-1866)
King, A. J. to J. W. Morris 9-23-1873 (9-24-1873)
King, Alice Z. to W. W. McCoy 9-13-1871
King, Amanda J. to J. D. Reynolds 3-30-1875 (4-1-1875)
King, Ann E. to W. S. Scott 1-28-1874 (1-29-1874)
King, Bettie to J. F. Mills 9-29-1871 (10-3-1871)
King, E. A. to James F. Troy 8-25-1866 (8-26-1866)
King, Eliza to Thos. J. Reynolds 10-26-1872 (10-27-1872)
King, Lillian C. to Seth L. Thornton 12-3-1867 (no return)
King, M. A. to S. L. Thornton 11-18-1874 (11-19-1874)
King, M. C. to A. J. Crow 10-14-1872
King, M. E. to M. R. Lewis 9-10-1875 (9-12-1875)
King, M. J. to W. F. Holland 11-18-1867 (11-19-1867)
King, Margaret to Richd. Davenport 8-31-1867 (9-13-1867)
King, Martha Ann to Henry Winchester 12-24-1867 (12-25-1867)
King, Martha J. to W. S. Walker 8-12-1869 (8-13-1869)
King, Martha to John L. Brockman 12-27-1865 (12-28-1865)

King, R. A. to T. H. Franklin 11-9-1869 (11-10-1869)
King, S. D. to A. J. Morris 7-1-1878 (7-2-1878)
King, Sallie to Albert Overton 12-25-1874
King, Saluda J. to W. T. King 6-24-1869
King, Sarah O. to John W. Love 12-23-1862
King, Viny M. to John Whittington 10-30-1865 (10-31-1865)
Kinley, V. A. to J. L. Humbles 12-18-1872 (12-19-1872)
Kirk, Ann Eliza to Jackson D. C. Cobb 1-30-1861
Kirk, Ellen J. to E. H. Green 9-6-1860
Kirk, M. E. to T. M. Hobday 12-18-1876 (12-19-1876)
Kirk, Martha V. to Danl. W. Heath 12-21-1864 (12-22-1864)
Kirk, Mary L. to Henry W. Baker 1-20-1863 (1-22-1863)
Kirk, Melissa H. to A. J. Heath 11-15-1869 (11-16-1869)
Kirk, Susan to A. L. Williams 11-18-1874 (no return)
Knight, Mary C. to Wm. McDowell 9-16-1871 (9-17-1871)
Knight, Mattie to D. H. Reynolds 8-23-1873 (8-24-1873)
Knight, Sarah J. to W. H. Moseley 5-5-1870
Knowles, Martha C. to J. W. Newnam 12-5-1877 (12-6-1877)
Knowles, Mary E. to James G. Thomason 11-13-1878
Lack, E. C. to Anthony Duke 12-11-1866 (no return)
Lacy, Nancy R. A. to Matt Rambo 10-16-1866 (10-20-1866)
Lacy, Nancy to Butten Jones 8-13-1860
Lamb, Martha L. to N. H. Corley 6-23-1871 (6-27-1871)
Lambert, S. A. to A. C. Hendricks 9-21-1875 (9-30-1875)
Landford, Emily to Eldridge David 1-31-1872 (2-1-1872)
Landis, Lula to M. L. Harton 12-4-1877
Landrum, Matilda A. to William Brown 8-5-1873 (8-15-1873)
Landrum, Mattie to W. W. Heughan 7-27-1877 (8-2-1877)
Landrum, Sarah M. to John B. Wright 3-28-1877 (3-29-1877)
Lane, E. A. to J. M. Robertson 12-24-1878 (12-26-1878)
Lane, Martha to Hiram Eady 5-29-1868
Lane, Mary to Jefferson M. Ridens 9-21-1862
Lane, R. Candace to J. B. Echols 1-19-1876
Lanier, Amanda to Benjamine Whitis 2-5-1861 (2-20-1861)
Lanier, Frances to David Brewer 2-27-1861 (no return)
Lanier, Jane to George McGaughey 2-21-1873 (4-21-1873)
Lanier, Lucinda to Ben Haskins 12-25-1877 (12-26-1877)
Lanier, Missouri J. to Lemuel T. Lucas 11-6-1867 (no return)
Lanier, Polk to W. M. Johnson 1-1-1872 (no return)
Lanier, Ritta to Richard Reddick 12-7-1868 (no return)
Lanier, Sarah L. to Wm. A. Hodge 10-17-1876
Lankford, Adelphi A. to Madison James 12-25-1869 (12-26-1869)
Lankford, Eliza J. to John M. James 4-15-1877
Lankford, Frances S. to S. C. Robbins 11-17-1877 (11-18-1877)
Lankford, Sarah C. to J. A. Kenley 9-3-1878 (9-4-1878)
Lanningham, Catharine to Jefferson Brown 5-27-1873
Lanningham, Minerva to Charles Clay 7-2-1873 (7-3-1873)
Lasiter, N. J. to B. P. Dyer 10-25-1876 (10-26-1876)
Laster, Columbia E. to John P. Hall 4-11-1877 (4-12-1877)
Laster, Marinaan to Joseph Ray 8-29-1871 (8-30-1871)
Laster, Mary E. to J. L. Chrisman 10-31-1871 (11-3-1873?)
Latham, Virginia H. to W. F. McCoy 10-19-1876
Latta, Lucy to J. G. Seat 10-18-1871
Latta?, Kate to T. C. Gordon 6-24-1879 (6-25-1879)
Lattimore, Sarah A. to Jack Gammons 1-13-1868
Lauderdale, Lucy Jennie L. to William Carroll Doyle 7-25-1860 (no return)
Lauderdale, Mary A. to John S. Reffington 11-18-1868
Lawhorn, F. E. to W. C. Williamson 1-20-1863 (1-21-1863)
Lawhorn, M. A. to J. F. Stalkup 1-27-1870 (1-28-1870)
Leach, M. A. to Charles H. Alston 11-6-1867
Leath, T. C. to L. H. Jackson 1-11-1873 (1-12-1873)
Ledbetter, Mary G. to D. A. Robertson 9-19-1866 (9-20-1866)
Ledbetter, Nannie to J. M. Drummon 2-10-1870
Ledbetter, Rosa Lee to W. J. Prichard 2-13-1878
Ledsinger, A. O. to J. A. Fowlkes 6-3-1869
Ledsinger, Alice to Wyatt Smith 4-13-1871 (4-14-1871)
Ledsinger, Catharine to James Newton Wynne 9-24-1869 (no return)
Ledsinger, Cynthia A. to Tobe Wicks 12-27-1875
Ledsinger, Dora to Peyton Burkley 5-11-1878 (5-15-1878)
Ledsinger, Eliza to James Stewart 12-28-1870 (12-29-1870)
Ledsinger, Ellen to Jack Segraves? 12-27-1877
Ledsinger, Emma to Henry Haskins 9-24-1872 (9-26-1872)
Ledsinger, Lucinda to Samuel Enochs 3-20-1873
Ledsinger, Maggie E. to H. T. Grant 9-2-1873

Ledsinger, Mary to John Jordan 5-14-1878 (5-15-1878)
Ledsinger, Penny to Charley Ruff 12-19-1867
Ledsinger, Phillis to Lee Davis 1-25-1877 (no return)
Ledsinger, Z. F. to G. A. Fowlkes 4-4-1865 (4-6-1865)
Lee, Jane to Joseph Deberry 8-5-1868 (no return)
Leech, Dora B. to Stephen Pierce 12-30-1869 (no return)
Leetch, Marian A. to Thomas V. Forisher 6-9-1864
Leggett, Susan to A. M. Smith 12-15-1868 (no return)
Leight, Mollie P. to Preston M. Tipton 2-6-1878
Lemmon, H. Ann to J. F. Bookout 12-31-1860 (1-1-1861)
Lemmons, Lena to Wily Baker 12-17-1873
Lemon, Amanda to Simpson Meredith 11-13-1867
Lemons, S. M. to Wm. Bowen 10-1-1867 (10-2-1867)
Leonard, R. F. to A. F. Hall 1-9-1878 (1-10-1878)
Leroy, Mary Ann to George W. Yeargin 12-30-1862
Leroy, Mary Ann to John Sawyer 6-26-1871
Lewis, Lizzie to J. M. Buckingham 3-23-1874 (3-24-1874)
Light, Anna to Joseph Sawyer 6-8-1870
Light, Artelia to Thomas Johnson 9-9-1875
Light, Chanie to Alfred Hollis 12-5-1878 (no return)
Light, Dinkie to Lee Wells 10-26-1871
Light, Emma to Alex Harris 2-19-1880 (no return)
Light, Emma to George Johnson 9-16-1870
Light, Emma to Wilson Lovelace 7-10-1880 (7-11-1880)
Light, Helen to Jack Connell 5-4-1875 (5-5-1875)
Light, Jane to John F. Connell 2-17-1871 (2-18-1871) B
Light, Margaret to Henry A. Robinson 4-5-1876 (4-6-1876)
Light, Mary Ann to Henry Ray Walker 6-5-1866
Light, Mary E. to Thos. R. Moore 5-20-1869
Light, Mary to Jack Ferguson 6-27-1866
Light, Mollie to Charley Moore 12-25-1877 (12-27-1877)
Light, Nancy to John Wesley Lock 7-29-1868 (7-30-1868)
Light, Nannie to Austin Connell 10-6-1880
Light, Nielli to Callis Jordan 12-16-1874 (12-17-1874) B
Light, Pettie to J. F. Johnston 1-27-1869 (1-28-1869)
Light, S. A. to C. L. Claiborn 12-30-1872 (12-31-1872)
Light, Sallie A. to P. L. Tipton 10-3-1874 (10-4-1874)
Light, Scrappie E. to Parsha L. Fowlkes 11-12-1874
Light, Tennessee to Isaac Fowlkes 4-17-1877
Linton, Margaret V. to W. F. Lamar 11-12-1870 (11-15-1870)
Linton, Margaret to Cyrus Dunn 11-12-1870 (11-15-1870)
Litte, Mary Jane to Wm. J. Reynolds 2-5-1862 (no return)
Little, Frances E. to Beng. Palmore 5-16-1863 (no return)
Little, Susan Lane to Henry Temp Reece 1-5-1865 (1-7-1865)
Livingstone, Josephine to George Statum 10-25-1877
Locke, Alice to Bascom Wright 7-28-1875 (no return)
Lockhart, Nannie to Tecumseh Lanier 10-27-1874
Love, Ada B. to D. M. McKenzie 12-4-1869 (12-7-1869)
Love, Hattie F. to Homer McKenzie 12-12-1870 (12-17-1870)
Love, L. D. to Homer McKenzie 11-26-1877
Love, Martha L. to W. J. Clendening 2-4-1867 (2-5-1867)
Lovelace, Anna M. to Wen. D. L. Duncan 9-26-1867
Lovelace, Claudia to J. W. Tinsley 3-21-1877
Lovelace, E. F. to S. C. Sorrell 7-29-1868 (no return)
Lovelace, F. A. to H. G. Putman 1-23-1870 (1-25-1871)
Lovelace, Fannie S. to C. T. Nash 5-27-1867 (5-30-1867)
Lovelace, Rachel to Moses Thacker 12-21-1868 (no return)
Lovett, L. B. to R. L. Jetton 9-2-1879 (9-10-1879)
Lovett, M. A. to J. W. Wall 9-28-1868 (no return)
Lovett, Susan to J. L. Davis 10-1-1866 (10-10-1866)
Lovit, Rebecca to W. J. Glassgow 10-10-1871 (10-12-1871)
Lowe, M. Amanda to Geo. D. Sollis 2-1-1879
Lowe, Sarah A. to J. M. Bradley 5-25-1873 (5-21?-1873)
Lucas, M. L. to John R. Griffin 9-3-1867 (no return)
Lucas, S. E. to J. G. Brantlen 2-28-1871 (2-29?-1871)
Lumley, Bettie to J. B. Smith 7-27-1872 (8-1-1872)
Lumley, Lucinda to J. M. Turner 1-31-1877 (2-1-1877)
Lumley, Rebecca to J. H. Henry 1-1-1872 (1-4-1872)
Lumley, Susannah to N. C. Pritchett 2-20-1879
Lunsford, Arenia to Thomas F. Nixon 5-30-1868 (no return)
Lyon, Sarah E. to Elias Heddin 8-3-1866 (8-7-1866)
Lyons, May F. to Isaac Spencer 5-11-1874
Lyons, Nancy A. to John Lyon 5-6-1861 (5-9-1861)
Macomb, M. S. to Thos. H. Webb 9-4-1867 (no return)
Maddra, Mollie to Hezekiah Strother 7-18-1873 (10-31-1873)

Maddrey, Malinda to Stephen Sanders 1-4-1877
Madry, Mary to Andrew Smith 12-26-1867
Magary, Clarissa Ann to Marion Boone 12-25-1871 (12-27-1871)
Magary, Lenora to Thomas Ledbetter 4-4-1872 (no return)
Maggard, Harriet to Jeff Williamson 1-20-1872 (1-21-1872)
Maggard, Julia to Peter McDaniel 8-26-1869 (no return)
Maggard, Martha to Jacob Foster 9-7-1870 (no return)
Mahan, Rebecca A. to Jo. Fletcher Smith 7-25-1867 (no return)
Mahan, Serena Isibella to Joel H. Pursell 11-3-1862 (11-4-1862)
Mahon, Angaline to Rupert Smith 5-10-1867 (5-11-1867)
Mallory, M. L. to S. C. Meadows 12-22-1870 (no return)
Mallory, Mollie to J. M. Moore 1-6-1868 (1-8-1868)
Malory, Sally to W. F. Harwell 3-17-1865 (3-21-1865)
Mangrum, Mary to William Brown 1-19-1867 (1-20-1867)
Mangrum, Nannie to Lucius Brown 11-18-1869 (11-21-1869)
Manley, Charity to James Smith 12-26-1870 (12-28-1870)
Manley, M. C. to W. A. Stone 10-17-1874 (no return)
Manning, Addie to James Brown 7-16-1868
Manning, Jane to J. W. Jones 4-10-1861 (4-11-1861)
Manning, Martha to O. Heath 8-17-1867 (8-18-1867)
Mansfield, Armenia to Benj. Reddick 1-30-1866 (1-31-1866)
Mansfield, Malvina to Phillip Smith 7-4-1867
Marchant, M. E. to F. C. Baker 9-18-1866 (9-19-1866)
Marchant, Susn to W. T. Davis 10-15-1868
Marcum, Fannie T. to William W. Olds 11-16-1876 (11-29-1876)
Margall, Julia to John Davis 7-26-1873 (7-27-1873) B
Martin, Charity to Andrew Jackson 3-21-1878
Martin, Hattie (Mrs.) to W. A. Thomas 12-26-1870
Martin, Lucinda to Henry Barnett 1-2-1877 (1-3-1877)
Massey, Cora I. to J. S. Lockhart 12-10-1873 (12-11-1873)
Massey, Jennie to James H. Darden 12-9-1872 (12-12-1872)
Matheney, Belle to J. H. Parmenter 2-19-1876 (2-20-1876)
Matheny, Alice to Abner Tom Scott 4-8-1879
Matheny, Manerva to William Logan 3-12-1861 (3-14-1861)
Matthews, Nancy to Hiram Light 4-2-1874
Mauldin, Eliza to Isaac Pursell 5-25-1867
Maury?, M. E. (Mrs.) to Thos. E. Fisher 9-1-1866 (9-2-1866)
Maxwell, Callie to G. P. Tinsley 5-7-1873 (5-8-1873)
May, Everett to James Fielder 2-28-1874 (3-1-1874)
Mayall, Julia to John Davis 7-26-1873 (no return) B
Mayo, Jane to William Pettus 12-30-1880
Mays, Lethe Jane to William H. Brent 4-30-1860 (5-1-1860)
Mays, Margaret to Lee Ferguson 8-10-1874
Mays, Mary B. to James T. Eudaley 11-19-1862
Mays, Nellie to William Femzer 12-7-1872
Mays, Sylvia to Alex Williams 2-15-1877
McAfee, Sarah E. to J. A. White 7-5-1869 (7-7-1869)
McAlilley, M. R. to J. W. Harrison 2-26-1879 (2-29-1879)
McBride, Eliza to W. R. Crow 1-12-1870 (1-13-1870)
McBride, Lucy F. to Wat Dotson 9-26-1867
McBride, M. L. to R. M. Reed 12-9-1874
McBride, Mary to Thomas E. Tansel 10-12-1871
McBride, Sarah E. to Stephen S. Thompson 5-25-1867 (5-27-1867)
McCalister, Emily to Miles Manly 10-19-1867 (10-20-1867)
McCarroll, T. S. to J. H. Modlin 2-16-1875 (2-17-1875)
McClusky, Emiline to Hardy Williamson 12-4-1867 (12-5-1867)
McCombs, Rosa P. to J. R. Chamberlain 2-1-1877
McCorkle, A. L. to E. P. Pope 11-5-1873 (11-6-1873)
McCorkle, E. J. to J. L. Cawthon 2-19-1877 (2-21-1877)
McCorkle, Elizabeth J. to Henry W. Reeves 12-19-1861
McCorkle, Ellen to Monk Smith 10-27-1875 (10-28-1875) B
McCorkle, M. L. to J. T. Gregory 5-24-1864 (5-25-1864)
McCormack, H. A. to J. E. Shelton 12-22-1875
McCoy, Lou to T. J. Fitzhugh 2-28-1877 (2-29?-1877)
McCoy, Pinckney A. to M. N. Gowan 1-2-1877 (1-4-1877)
McCoy, Sarah V. to John Fitzhugh 10-20-1875
McCracken, C. J. to J. J. Gray 11-2-1870 (11-4-1870)
McCracken, M. E. to G. W. Mills 5-22-1869 (no return)
McCrackin, Ella to N. L. Bowman 4-24-1875 (4-28-1875)
McCrackin, Mattie to M. H. Higdon 2-14-1874 (2-18-1874)
McCrackin, Polly to James M. Walls 9-11-1861 (no return)
McCulloch, Adalaide to W. H. Marlow 11-20-1877
McCullough, Lucy to A. R. Pace 8-20-1875 (8-22-1875)
McCutchen, Bell to Anthony Perry 3-14-1868
McCutchen, Caroline to Jo B. McCorkle 12-20-1871 (12-21-1871)

McCutchen, Georgia to John Barnes 3-7-1873 (3-25-1873)
McCutchen, Laura A. to A. F. Dickson 11-26-1866 (no return)
McCutchen, Margaret to R. F. Wigfall 7-23-1875 (7-24-1875)
McCutchen, Mary to J. S. Thompson 12-30-1868 (no return)
McCutchen, N. C. to T. E. Blair 7-28-1873 (7-31-1873)
McCutchen, Parlee to Ed Chamberlin 5-16-1872
McCutchen, S. A. to M. V. Akin 9-4-1871 (9-5-1871)
McDaniel, Eliza A. to Daniel Folson 8-26-1869 (no return)
McDaniel, Minerva to Rufus Smith 1-22-1880 (1-21?-1880)
McDavid, Emma to R. R. Nash 10-11-1860
McDavid, Harriet to Thos. (Dr.) Nash 10-22-1868
McDavid, Lucy A. to William N. McKnight 1-16-1864 (1-17-1864)
McDavid, Martha A. to Jos. S. Richardson 1-6-1864 (no return)
McDavid, Mattie to W. W. Edwards 9-14-1870
McDavid, Rebecca A. to Wiley B. Tipton, jr. 10-9-1866
McDearmon, A. F. to Neil B. Rucker 3-13-1873
McDearmon, W. M. to J. P. Smith 12-19-1878
McDon, Elmira to Hiram Dempsa 8-27-1868
McElyea, M. J. to S. C. Pile 9-21-1866 (9-23-1866)
McFarland, Elizabeth to Charles C. Gentry 12-14-1863
McFarland, M. J. to J. T. King 3-24-1874
McFarland, Winnie E. to T. J. Graham 10-31-1874
McFarlin, Anne to J. W. McCoy 3-20-1879
McFarlin, E. J. to L. P. Fitzhugh 10-8-1879 (10-9-1879)
McFarlin, Elizabeth to Ozy Borin 5-19-1870 (no return)
McGarg, Alice to A. M. Frost 12-16-1878 (12-18-1878)
McGarg, Mariah to Wiley Paul 12-30-1878 (no return)
McGary, Sarah to Henry Wood 5-6-1876 (5-7-1876)
McGary, Tennessee to Vincent Smith 12-27-1880 (12-29-1880)
McGaughen, Victoria to Willis Swift 7-26-1873 (8-27-1873)
McGaughey, Victoria to Thomas Mason 12-27-1876 (12-28-1876)
McGaughey, Victoria to Willie Swift 7-26-1873 (no return)
McGaughy, Laura to Thomas Hunt 3-19-1874
McGaughy, Myra to W. W. Walker 7-31-1867
McGill, V. C. to John B. York 10-18-1870 (10-20-1870)
McGinn, Laura A. to Charles Allison 12-3-1866 (12-4-1866)
McGinnis, E. J. to Geo. B. Fuller 9-14-1863 (9-17-1863)
McGinnis, Julia Ann to David Jones 12-15-1866 (12-22-1866)
McGinnis, Maggie J. to Wat B. Sampson 4-9-1861
McIntosh, Josephine to J. W. Cribbs 10-9-1878
McIntosh, Laura J. to W. S. Turner 4-8-1867
McIntosh, Maggie A. to J. W. Cribbs 11-16-1875 (11-18-1875)
McKane, Martha A. to David B. Walker 3-17-1868 (no return)
McKani, Bettie to W. H. Crane 10-19-1874 (no return)
McKee, Elizabeth to A. L. Pace 8-10-1868 (8-11-1868)
McKee, Mary T. to Isaac N. Haynes 8-20-1873 (8-21-1873)
McKee, Mollie to John Green 1-2-1869 (1-3-1869)
McKelley, Margaret A. to John W. Delph 3-25-1862
McKenzie, Ida to John Kohnmann? 12-4-1878
McKinney, Hannah to Charles McSheyn 12-6-1866
McKnight, E. J. to A. C. Harrison 12-15-1875 (12-17-1875)
McKnight, Mary E. to George T. Hurt 7-28-1874
McKnight, Mary L. to John T. Whitson 7-24-1879
McKnight, Rosannah to Noah Parr 12-27-1880 (12-30-1880)
McKnight, Sarah E. to Sam Pierce 10-18-1871 (no return)
McMackin, Josaphine to W. B. Weddington 2-15-1871
McMackin, Leona J. to G. A. Leath 12-1-1874 (12-2-1874)
McMillen, Susie to William E. Chapman 12-20-1870
McNail, Bettie to Will Smith 1-5-1880 (1-15-1880)
McNeil, Jamima E. to Martin A. Green 12-3-1872
McNeil, Minerva to John Chandler 9-8-1877 (no return)
Meadows, Julia to W. M. Smith 6-1-1867 (no return)
Meadows, Manerva E. to James S. Kirkpatrick 4-11-1864
Meadows, Vandelia to A. J. Burkeen 12-21-1870
Menzies, Jane to Beng. Simmons 1-21-1869
Menzies, M. E. to H. Parks, jr. 2nd 10-27-1873 (10-28-1873)
Menzies, Mariah to Wm. Horton 9-14-1868 (9-17-1868)
Merandy, Mary A. to J. H. Meeks 1-14-1868
Merchant, Mary A. (Mrs.) to George W. Muns 12-22-1863
Meter, Sarah E. to James J. Mangrum 8-19-1867 (8-20-1867)
Michaels, Amanda E. to W. L. Knight 12-26-1872 (no return)
Michaels, Frances to T. J. Harris 1-4-1877
Michaels, M. to R. P. Powell 5-4-1872 (5-5-1872)
Michell, M. E. to Isaac W. Lowe 9-4-1872 (9-8-1872)
Mifflin, Lou to James Colbert 6-4-1866

Mifflin, Mary to Archer Mosely 5-9-1874 (5-10-1874)
Milam, E. C. to P. A. Walker 10-16-1866 (no return)
Milam, Louisa to Thos. J. Pritchett 2-4-1863 (2-5-1863)
Milam, M. S. to P. E. Gregson 5-4-1871
Milam, Nancy E. to W. S. Scott 4-8-1868 (4-9-1868)
Miller, Alice to Geo. Sandford 5-18-1878 (5-24-1878)
Miller, Amanda to John R. Nash 11-14-1877 (11-15-1877)
Miller, Annie to J. H. Ward 10-1-1877 (no return)
Miller, H. A. H. to H. H. Phillips 1-15-1866
Miller, Julia to Robert C. Roberts 1-24-1861
Miller, M. E. to W. W. Spain 5-23-1860
Miller, M. L. to J. H. Hardison 8-29-1876 (8-31-1876)
Miller, Mollie to Bird Soward 2-7-1878
Miller, Rilla Jane to Anderson Jones 3-30-1876
Miller, Susan F. to Jackson F. Brothers 1-6-1879 (no return)
Millican, Ann Eliza to J. S. Brinkley 11-7-1867
Mills, Eliza J. to F. G. Ellis 12-1-1866 (12-2-1866)
Mills, Martha to John Dove 8-11-1863 (no return)
Mills, Mary E. to G. G. Cooper 7-27-1875 (7-29-1875)
Mills, Maryline to Amos Woodard 4-30-1861
Mills, N. P. to James A. L. Crow 10-24-1866 (10-25-1866)
Mills, Nancy A. to S. Burch 8-30-1870
Mills, Nannie to W. H. Read 12-20-1877
Minton, S. J. to J. A. Strawn 3-31-1865 (4-1-1865)
Minton, Susan C. to J. M. Hall 7-10-1861 (6-11-1861)
Mitchell, Fannie to Thomas Bates 12-27-1876 (12-29-1876)
Mitchell, Lizzie to Allen Copeland 10-12-1872 (no return)
Mitchell, Lou Ellen to James Campbell 1-26-1877 (1-28-1877)
Mitchell, Millie to Jim Harris 11-1-1879
Mitchell, Rebacca to Lewis Powell 12-26-1866 (12-27-1866)
Mitchner, Eugene to J. W. Stagner 3-2-1878 (3-23-1878)
Mitchuer, H. to Tinzel Wade 1-20-1872 (1-21-1872)
Mobley, Annie W. to A. Eason 1-2-1872
Mobley, Malissie A. to Joseph W. Echols 11-8-1870 (11-9-1870)
Montgomery, Frances to Amaziah Woodside 10-3-1860 (no return)
Montgomery, M. J. to N. L. Robertson 12-2-1871 (12-3-1871)
Montgomery, Sallie J. to W. J. Crenshaw 12-3-1877 (12-4-1877)
Montgomery, Sarah E. to Joseph E. Miller 3-7-1866 (3-8-1866)
Montrose, S. B. to R. L. Hinton 8-22-1860
Moody, Ann C. to Reuben Davis 12-17-1870 (12-25-1870)
Moody, Eliza to Solomon Jelks 10-26-1869 (no return)
Moody, Maryline E. to D. W. Wooley 11-28-1874 (12-1-1874)
Moody, P. F. to J. J. Mills 8-19-1872 (8-21-1872)
Moore, C. A. to Silas Matthews 9-19-1867 (no return)
Moore, E. B. to J. J. Baker 8-24-1867 (8-25-1867)
Moore, Elizabeth F. to Columbus W. Thompson 1-17-1871
Moore, Helen V. to John R. Gammon 11-12-1866 (11-13-1866)
Moore, Jane to Frank Mulherin 4-6-1880 (no return)
Moore, Lou to Haywood Ruff 9-9-1880 (no return)
Moore, M. E. (Mrs.) to T. J. Sanders 9-30-1875 (10-3-1875)
Moore, Mollie F. to M. C. Hamilton 12-18-1876 (12-21-1876)
Moore, Mollie to James K. Polk 12-27-1867 (12-26?-1867)
Moore, O. D. to James Kellow 8-8-1876 (8-9-1876)
Moore, S. E. to C. R. Featherston 9-30-1875 (no return)
Moore, Sarah A. to Thos. W. Tinkle 2-2-1861 (2-3-1861)
Moore, Verginia to Neal S. Harwell 1-17-1871 (1-18-1871)
Moore, W. D. to O. J. Radford 8-2-1871 (8-22-1871)
Morgan, D. A. to T. E. Griffin 1-23-1878 (1-24-1878)
Morgan, Emma to Wesley Smith 8-28-1880 (8-29-1880)
Morgan, H. F. to Elijah Smith 3-2-1866 (3-4-1866)
Morley, Merandy G. to W. F. Nash 7-9-1868 (no return)
Morris, Angeline to S. L. Johnson 11-28-1876 (11-29-1876)
Morris, E. T. to Plesant R. Bessent 12-18-1867 (12-19-1867)
Morris, Mary to M. H. P. Weakley 12-24-1870 (3-15-1871)
Morris, Sarah A. to Isaac Garret 4-10-1867
Moseley, Amanda R. to Thomas Thompson 12-24-1873
Moseley, Ellen to James M. Adams 1-6-1876
Moseley, Ellen to James M. Adams 6?-6-1876? (with Apr 1876)
Moseley, Mattie to Nelson Scott 2-5-1880
Mosely, Sarah F. to James M. Adams 11-7-1872
Mote, M. T. to J. E. Crisp 1-20-1874 (1-21-1874)
Muirhead, Nannie to John L. Duncan 11-5-1877 (11-7-1877)
Mulherin, Amanda to Austin Connell 2-22-1872 (2-23-1872)
Mulherin, Amanda to Bob Clark 6-13-1867
Mulherin, Tete to Alf? Smart 7-3-1877

Munns?, S. E. to S. A. Denney 9-11-1876 (9-17-1876)
Murdough, Mary to William H. Redding 5-4-1863 (no return)
Murphey, A. F. (Mrs.) to W. R. Simpson 11-30-1872 (11-3?-1872)
Murray, Alice to Andrew Johnson 1-10-1877 (1-11-1877)
Murray, Eliza A. to J. N. Waters 6-13-1868
Murray, Jane to W. B. Darden 12-25-1872 (12-26-1872)
Murray, Martha to Caleb Flack 3-11-1874
Murray, Mary to Wm. F. Nunn 10-25-1870 (10-26-1870)
Murray, Missouri to W. C. Blankenship 10-16-1879
Murray, Rebecca J. to G. T. Hay 3-9-1874 (3-11-1874)
Murray, Sarah J. to P. L. Blankenship 6-15-1872 (6-16-1872)
Musgrave, Mariah to Edward Shurley 12-28-1872
Muzier?, Jane to Ed Fizer 4-5-1876
Nance, Jane to Wm. Saulsburg 5-22-1879
Nash, Alice A. to F. M. Williamson 9-16-1868
Nash, Emily to J. N. Nash 8-7-1865 (8-8-1865)
Nash, Emma (Mrs.) to R. C. Coffman 12-3-1872 (12-5-1872)
Nash, Fannie to William Sandford 12-26-1871 (12-27-1871)
Nash, Fanny to Jenning? James 1-22-1867 (1-20?-1867)
Nash, Hattie to L. H. Waters 4-10-1880 (4-18-1880)
Nash, Julia to Shepard Mitchell 12-29-1875 (12-30-1875)
Nash, M. A. to Wm. M. Thurman 3-9-1866 (3-11-1866)
Nash, Martha Jane to T. W. Redding 12-5-1877 (12-6-1877)
Nash, Mary to Isaac Slater 2-19-1867 (3-23-1867)
Nash, Miranda G. to W. N. Taylor 11-25-1878 (11-27-1878)
Nash, Parthena to Danil Porter 11-30-1870 (12-3-1870)
Nash, Rachel to Peter McGarg 3-2-1878 (3-7-1878)
Nash, Susan to Limus Porter 12-28-1872 (2-2-1873)
Neal, Augustine to W. W. Cochran 12-27-1871 (12-28-1871)
Neal, Eliza to Jesse C. North 5-27-1868
Neal, L. A. to Rewben J. Harrington 11-28-1876 (11-29-1876)
Neal, Louisa to John F. Whitman 11-29-1862
Neal, Louisa to Walter Gibbs 2-27-1875 (2-28-1875)
Neal, Naomi L. to J. D. Sinclair 9-26-1866 (9-27-1866)
Neal, Susan E. to William J. Canada 1-15-1873 (1-16-1873)
Neal, Victoria to James L. McDavid 1-29-1868 (no return)
Neeley, Sarah E. to J. A. Hooks 12-18-1871 (12-21-1871)
Neely, Easter to Base Fowlkes 12-12-1871 (12-13-1871)
Neely, Elizabeth F. to A. G. Fumbanks 12-4-1866
Neely, Mary L. to Albert B. Sorrell 4-21-1866
Neely, N. T. to D. A. Freeman 9-2-1871 (9-3-1871)
Neely, Virginia to G. W. Robertson 7-19-1865 (7-20-1865)
Nelson, A. M. to J. H. Williams 12-14-1877 (12-16-1877)
Nettles, Mary Jane to Henry Morgan 6-24-1867 (7-25-1867)
Neules, Nancy A. to G. W. Brunston 2-19-1872 (2-20-1872)
Nichols, Alice to E. S. Therman 10-14-1868 (10-15-1868)
Nichols, Bettie to A. W. Bigelow 11-4-1875
Nichols, Jane to C. J. Walton 5-3-1879
Nichols, Jennie to William D. Spain 7-12-1875 (7-13-1875)
Nichols, Maggie to Jno. L. Martin 5-2-1866
Nichols, S. C. to W. E. Potter 10-8-1867 (10-9-1867)
Niece, Polly to L. H. Yates 12-4-1869 (12-5-1869)
Niece, R. J. to P. W. Anthoney 2-18-1868 (no return)
Nixon, C. J. to F. G. Ellis 3-2-1863 (3-4-1863)
Norman, Martha Jane to John Cannady 1-27-1870 (no return)
Norment, Chincy to John Webster 7-3-1867
Norrington, Amanda C. to Enos Rainey 7-7-1865 (7-15-1865)
North, E. J. (Mrs.) to N. L. Mays 6-27-1874 (6-28-1874)
Norton, Mary E. to Alex Williams 9-3-1867
Norwich, Ida to Allen McCutchen 7-8-1878 (8-1-1878)
Nuirhead, Susan to James Sandford 1-13-1877 (1-14-1877)
Nunn, Amanda to Thos. H. Fuzzle 8-1-1861
Nunn, Bettie to Jessie Reddick 2-15-1868
Nunn, Donie M. to Edward L. Cook 8-27-1878 (8-28-1878)
Oakley, L. H. to H. L. Churchman 7-31-1869 (8-1-1869)
Oakley, R. P. to William Hunt 9-18-1878 (9-19-1878)
Odle, Callie to J. R. Williams 8-22-1870 (8-28-1870)
Odle, Melissa C. to John Wm. Ross 10-30-1875 (10-31-1875)
Odom, Frances to James T. Nichols 6-4-1879
Odom, Nancy L. to J. M. Mays 8-14-1861
Odum, Ann to Adam Swayne 5-11-1867 (no return)
Oldham, Jane to Frank Works 2-10-1872 (2-15-1872)
Olds, Julia to James Belton 1-8-1862 (1-9-1862)
Olds, Martha to Jo. Williams 2-10-1872 (2-19-1872)
Olds, Mary F. to S. J. Bird 12-15-1873 (12-16-1873)

Olds, Sarah F. to David Albrittain 12-15-1869
Olds, Sarah J. to John H. Thornton 12-2-1868
Olive, M. E. to Wm. H. Vaughan 9-10-1872 (9-11-1872)
Oliver, Sallie to Allen Scott 12-20-1871 (12-21-1871)
Oneal, A. to R. M. Ward 10-21-1867 (10-24-1867)
Oneal, M. W. E. to W. H. Royster 7-27-1869 (no return)
Oneal, S. A. to W. D. Featherston 12-20-1865 (no return)
Only, J. P. to J. T. Olds 2-16-1878 (2-19-1878)
Orr, Minerva to J. H. Scarce 9-2-1878 (9-5-1878)
Osborne, Rachel E. to L. D. Dilliard 11-19-1868
Osburn, Caroline to James Smith 11-15-1877
Owen, Theodosia to B. C. Bettis 9-11-1871 (9-12-1871)
Pace, Jennie to J. T. Stockton 9-15-1874 (9-17-1874)
Pace, Lizzie to W. L. Jones 9-19-1877 (9-20-1877)
Pace, Martha C. to Richmond Herrin 10-4-1872 (10-6-1872)
Pace, R. A. to A. J. Ellis 12-18-1876 (12-21-1876)
Page, Mattie to N. W. Sorrell 1-3-1872
Paine, Lucinda to Isaac Reynolds 4-11-1874 (4-12-1874)
Palmer, Betsy to Kelly Murrell 8-16-1873 (8-21-1873)
Palmer, Elsie to Robt. Grace 5-23-1877 (5-24-1877)
Palmer, Harriett to Andy Tatum 12-26-1870 (12-29-1870)
Palmer, M. J. to L. H. Hollingsworth 1-31-1877 (2-1-1877)
Palmer, Malissa to Roland Gaulden 4-3-1878 (no return)
Palmer, S. H. L. to A. H. Smith 12-28-1870
Palmore, Eliza to R. Harris 5-18-1871 (5-21-1871)
Para, Pamela R. to B. P. Peery 12-17-1866
Parker, Ellen to Tex Harris 9-29-1870 (10-1-1870)
Parker, Emiline to J. Z. Leath 8-16-1872 (8-22-1872)
Parker, Eudora to J. B. Tucker 4-1-1879 (4-2-1879)
Parker, I. Etta to Henry C. Perry 9-5-1870 (9-7-1870)
Parker, L. E. to J. H. Harrison 7-28-1875 (7-29-1875)
Parker, Lucy to Green Fowlkes 11-18-1870 B
Parker, M. J. to Albert Johnson 12-25-1878 (12-26-1878)
Parker, Mary to David Stinson 12-28-1868 (12-29-1868)
Parker, Mollie to John Hardin 2-12-1869 (no return)
Parker, Mollie to W. B. (Dr.) York 1-14-1867 (1-15-1867)
Parker, Parthena to Isaac Menzies 10-24-1872 (9?-24-1872)
Parker, Parthena to James Harris 3-5-1874
Parker, Sarah E. to R. T. Ponder 10-19-1872 (10-24-1872)
Parker, Sarah to W. T. Piercy 11-5-1868
Parker, Susan E. to Robert F. Brown 10-18-1865 (10-25-1865)
Parks, L. C. to sM. Thompson 12-10-1872 (12-11-1872)
Parks, Lutie A. to A. B. Tigrett 5-14-1873 (5-15-1873)
Parks, Mariah to William Jackson 11-16-1872 (11-18-1872)
Parks, Martha J. to Lewis Baird 4-12-1871 (no return)
Parks, Mary to Sam Parks 11-20-1877 (11-23-1877)
Parks, Mollie I. to Walter Scott Draper 11-24-1870
Parks, Parena V. to J. N. Wyatt 12-13-1864 (no return)
Parnell, Lucy A. to Wm. Hugely 2-19-1866 (2-20-1866)
Parnell, Margaret to William Boyd 12-13-1862 (12-16-1862)
Parnell, Martha A. to Levi Cothran 4-3-1861 (4-4-1861)
Parr, Edwina? to John Soward 2-24-1876 (no return)
Parr, Lou to Sandy Maggard 1-12-1878
Parr, Mary to J. W. Diggs 2-12-1878 (2-13-1878)
Parrish, Bettie to Wm. Gardner 11-12-1867 (11-13-1867)
Parrish, Emily J. to Benj. F. Farmer 11-6-1865
Parrish, Janettie A. to A. A. Kellow 12-27-1876
Parrish, Lucinda to Murry Saunders 7-15-1867 (7-16-1867)
Parrish, Salina to M. D. Hodge 12-31-1872 (1-1-1873)
Parrott, E. F. (Mrs.) to J. A. Blackburn 2-9-1869 (no return)
Parsley, Nancy S. T. to S. P. Andrews 12-13-1870
Parteet, Cerilla J. to W. J. Weaver 2-18-1869 (no return)
Pate, A. M. to Jefferson Moore 12-26-1868 (no return)
Pate, Ella F. to J. D. B. Tipton 8-15-1874 (8-16-1874)
Pate, M. E. to W. B. Brewer 11-24-1875
Pate, M. J. to H. H. Browder 4-25-1863 (4-26-1863)
Pate, M. J. to Jo Green Ferguson 11-30-1870 (nor return)
Pate, Olive to Crawford Michell 1-22-1867 (1-24-1867)
Pate, Sallie F. to A. P. McCallister 10-20-1869 (10-21-1869)
Pate, Sallie to Bryant Fitzhugh 11-18-1867
Pate, Z. S. to William T. Hunter 11-18-1872 (11-19-1872)
Patrick, Annie C. to Page H. Patrick 1-23-1861 (1-24-1861)
Patrick, L. A. to C. W. Rodgers 12-8-1875 (12-9-1875)
Patrick, Mary to William Williams 4-2-1873 (4-3-1873)
Patterson, Lavinia to Willis Bell 1-27-1876

Patterson, Margaret to Thomas Daniel 2-14-1876
Patterson, Mollie to Orange Whittaker 1-17-1876 (no return)
Patterson, Nancy to Louis Matheny 8-17-1861 (8-31-1861)
Patterson, Sarah A. to Jack Gammons 3-13-1868 (1?-14-1868)
Patterson, Sarah to C. W. Greer 1-13-1874 (1-18-1874)
Patton, R. E. to M. V. Davidson 10-24-1866
Paul, Lizzie to Wm. Harris 2-19-1876 (4-15-1876)
Payne, Elizabeth F. to T. H. Walton 6-23-1862 (no return)
Payne, J. A. to David A. Gardner 2-15-1870 (2-16-1870)
Payne, Susan to J. H. Shelton 10-12-1867 (10-13-1867)
Peacock, Fannie to Nelson Motley 4-24-1875 (3-5-1875)
Peacock, Octavy to Henry Townsend 11-3-1880 (11-4-1880)
Peal, Sarah Ann E. to John C. Bailey 2-3-1862 (no return)
Pearce, Vena to Monroe Jones 12-28-1869 (no return)
Peel, Julia to W. J. Follis 10-31-1871
Peery, Donie to J. Buck Finley 1-13-1874
Peery, Missy to Prince Powell 8-23-1869 (no return)
Peery, Mollie to M. Sherwood 6-12-1869 (6-13-1869)
Peery, N. J. to E. P. Mays 1-24-1878
Peery, T. A. to E. P. Tevilla 11-10-1868
Pell, Ella to T. Lee Wells 2-26-1879
Pell, Martha to David Connell 11-25-1875
Pennington, Nancy Ann to John James 6-22-1878 (6-23-1878)
Pennington, Susan to James A. Rambo 4-25-1861
Peoples, Elizabeth to W. G. Tate 9-20-1872 (9-29-1872)
Perry, E. L. to F. E. Mahon 12-3-1864 (12-13-1864)
Perry, Elizabeth to Jessee Gordan 11-9-1870
Perry, Frances to W. H. Howell 9-3-1869 (9-5-1869)
Perry, Josephine to Ned Manning 7-11-1865 (7-17-1865)
Perry, Julia to Joseph Nunn 12-28-1867 (no return)
Perry, M. L. to J. M. Baulch 11-11-1871 (11-16-1871)
Perry, Mary J. to J. H. Nunn 10-16-1871 (10-17-1871)
Perry, Mozella to Jno. B. Tucker 10-1-1866 (10-10-1866)
Perry, Renie to William Brown 5-27-1871 (6-1-1871)
Peterson, Harriet to John W. Robertson 1-26-1864 (1-29-1864)
Peterson, Pheby to J. W. Robertson 8-26-1861 (8-27-1861)
Petty, J. A. to S. A. Tinkle 6-1-1874 (no return)
Phillips, Eliza A. to Will M. Watkins 9-27-1860
Phillips, Mary A. H. to Thomas Shelton 11-30-1874 (12-2-1874)
Phillips, Mary K. to Charles C. Walton 7-30-1879 (7-31-1879)
Phillips, Provie E. to John H. Guill 6-3-1868 (6-4-1868)
Phillips, S. F. to F. M. Estes 10-13-1875
Pierce, Amanda to S. H. P. Lester 6-14-1875 (no return)
Pierce, Angelina to Peter Sales 1-10-1878
Pierce, Dollie to Wm. Howell 5-24-1869
Pierce, Elizabeth to John Delf 12-30-1872
Pierce, F. E. to W. W. Jordan 12-4-1871
Pierce, Frances E. to Henry Bean 3-19-1862
Pierce, Isabella to Louis Southern 12-?-1865 (12-30-1865)
Pierce, Joanna to Ephraim Dority 12-13-1871
Pierce, Margaret to Roland Gaulden 3-4-1876 (4-12-1876) B
Pierce, Mary Jane to B. A. Powell 10-24-1867
Pierce, Mary P. to John T. Howell 8-19-1867
Pierce, Missouri to J. M. Gold 7-24-1872
Pierce, Mollie to D. A. Shaw 1-16-1872
Pierce, Phillip to Charley Foulkes 10-30-1880 (10-31-1880)
Pierce, Roda to Rupert Jones 10-14-1870
Pierce, Ruth to Jacob McCon 4-15-1873 (4-16-1873) B
Pierce, Sallie to M. R. Hendricks 3-23-1874 (3-24-1874)
Pierce, Susan to D. R. Fields 9-14-1865
Pierce, Susan to Zachariah Quinn 5-9-1867
Pierce, Susannah to Philip Delph 8-2-1879 (8-3-1879)
Pinkston, Jane to William Turner 6-1-1861 (no return)
Pinkston, Rhody J. to J. T. Espy 7-24-1865
Pinnon, Martha E. to W. H. H. Murray 11-23-1876
Pinyan, Ellen to Ben T. Walker 11-3-1877 (11-4-1877)
Pitts, Martha E. to R. F. Viar 8-22-1866 (8-23-1866)
Pitts, Mary A. to W. E. Curtis 7-30-1869 (no return)
Pitts, Mary to Thomas Cotham 2-21-1869 (no return)
Pitts, V. A. to J. J. Hamilton 1-22-1879 (1-23-1879)
Platt, Elizabeth to Duke Baker 2-11-1863
Polston, Dumbilla to J. M. Rodgers 8-14-1876 (8-15-1876)
Pooch, Nancy to Wm. M. Tipton 12-25-1866
Pool, Martha A. to E. Mis? Kelly 12-27-1865
Pool, Martha A. to E. Miskelly 12-27-1865 (12-30-1865)

Pope, D. E. to J. H. Pierce 1-19-1876 (no return)
Pope, D. L. to H. C. Hart 2-15-1876
Pope, Eliza to W. T. Reycroft 6-8-1870 (10-5-1870)
Pope, M. E. to T. F. Ray 1-7-1869
Pope, Martha to Samuel Simmons 9-7-1878 (9-17-1878)
Pope, Mary E. to O. E. Lanier 10-28-1867 (10-29-1867)
Pope, Sarah to James Brewer 2-12-1876 (2-10?-1876)
Porter, Alice to Luke Nash 10-8-1877 (10-9-1877)
Porter, Fannie to Marcus Bowen 12-28-1872 (12-30-1872)
Porter, Frances to Letas Beckett 5-30-1871 (6-1-1871)
Porter, Huldah to Uriah Walker 12-12-1876 (12-13-1876)
Porter, Mahulda to Louis Hill 5-19-1880 (5-20-1880)
Porter, Margaret to Frank McCutchen 12-3-1873 (12-4-1873)
Porter, Mary C. to James H. Wood 10-23-1876 (10-24-1876)
Porter, Susan to Samel Scott 12-24-1872 (12-30-1872)
Poston, Nancy C. to Jacob Burnett 1-8-1867 (1-9-1867)
Poston, Nancy Caroline to Marion Duffee 11-11-1865 (no return)
Poteet, Savannah E. to A. F. Ray 6-22-1877 (6-24-1877)
Potter, Amanda M. to Thos. H. Johnson 12-21-1867 (12-22-1867)
Pounds, Mary J. to James A. Dodd 3-25-1869
Powell, Amanda to Peter Pillow 10-2-1871
Powell, Ann to Willis Ward 12-2-1869 (no return)
Powell, Henrietta to Henry Mitchell 10-19-1877 (10-21-1877) B
Powell, Jane to Phillip King 12-10-1878 (12-11-1878)
Powell, Lenora to Saml. B. Bradshaw 9-15-1863 (no return)
Powell, Nancy to J. G. Bowman 1-5-1870
Powers, M. E. to Calvin Jones 3-8-1870
Powers, Paralee to John W. Curby 8-8-1876 (8-9-1876)
Prato, Louisa to Louis Young 9-17-1868 (no return)
Presgrove, Frances E. to Hiram Purdee 11-17-1863 (no return)
Price, L. E. to T. J. Walker 1-14-1867 (1-20-1867)
Price, Lucra to J. D. Thogmodden 2-19-1867 (3-22-1867)
Price, Mollie to J. A. Atkins 3-23-1869 (no return)
Prichard, Alice to Green Fizer 2-24-1875 (2-26-1875) B
Prichard, Almedia to Wm. A. Boon 1-17-1877 (1-18-1877)
Prichard, Bettie to Hilliard Smith 12-22-1874 (12-23-1874)
Prichard, D. J. to J. W. Norsworthy 12-18-1878 (12-19-1878)
Prichard, Fannie to Haf Haskins 8-16-1873 (8-17-1873)
Prichard, Finetta to B. H. Mitchell 10-19-1876
Prichard, Kisann to W. J. Holland 2-1-1865 (2-2-1865)
Prichard, M. M. to James W. Kent 2-5-1879 (2-6-1879)
Prichard, Mary F. to L. C. Hafford 9-14-1876
Prichard, Mary M. to James House 4-16-1867 (no return)
Prichard, Mollie to Elmore Maddrey 12-12-1877 (12-13-1877)
Prichard, Sarah A. to G. W. Prichard 9-7-1868 (no return)
Prichard, Sarah A. to Joseph D. Keath 11-13-1874 (11-14-1874)
Pritchett, Sarah Jane to Albert Hampton 4-16-1870 (4-17-1870)
Privett, Mary Ann to J. R. Blackbern 10-29-1862 (10-30-1862)
Privett, Nancy to J. T. North 8-18-1877 (8-19-1877)
Pruitt, Cynthia to L. P. Lanier 1-1-1868 (1-2-1868)
Pugh, Fannie to T. B. Berry 5-6-1871 (5-7-1871)
Pugh, Louisa to N. J. Michell 12-2-1869 (12-5-1869)
Pugh, Mollie to C. G. Johnson 2-2-1875
Purdle, Priscilla to Jack Jones 11-13-1875 (no return)
Purdy, Frances A. to Joseph Barker 6-23-1866 (6-28-1866)
Purdy, Mary E. to R. L. Crafton 6-18-1866 (6-22-1866)
Pursell, Emily to S. H. Chitwood 4-16-1867 (no return)
Pyland, Tempa N. to Jackson Cleek 3-23-1868
Radford, A. J. to J. G. Arnold 11-4-1874 (no return)
Radford, Caroline to Alex Mitchell 1-25-1869 (no return)
Radford, M. J. to J. P. Bell 5-16-1867
Radford, M. J. to W. C. Dickey 10-25-1879 (10-26-1879)
Rainey, L. C. to H. M. Taylor 2-4-1875
Rainey, M. F. to W. G. Welch 10-29-1870 (10-30-1870)
Randolph, Angeline to John O. Dillender 2-24-1864
Randolph, Julia to James Shoemake 10-11-1860
Rauls, Malinda E. to S. H. Johnson 7-28-1868 (7-30-1868)
Rawles, Alcenia A. to G. G. B. Patton 1-9-1861 (no return)
Rawles, M. J. to J. W. Marchant 2-9-1876
Ray, Elizabeth to John Burns 3-29-1869 (no return)
Ray, Frances to S. T. Lunsford 5-18-1869 (no return)
Ray, M. S. to H. R. Carpenter 5-11-1878 (5-13-1878)
Ray, Mary to George Williamson 9-23-1865 (9-24-1865)
Ray, S. C. to H. C. Aspray 1-15-1872 (no return)
Ray, Sallie to P. W. Cooper 11-20-1875 (11-24-1875)

Ray, Sudie to Morris Hallum 8-26-1879 (8-28-1879)
Ray?, Susan C. to James E. Polston 6-26-1860
Raybern, Harriet F. to Wallace Evans 8-6-1864 (no return)
Read, Nannie to G. W. Mills 1-9-1877 (1-10-1877)
Reasons, Lizzie to W. W. Whitehorn 7-9-1872 (7-15-1872)
Reaves, M. T. to J. W. Morris 4-14-1879 (4-18-1879)
Reddick, Amanda to Francis Reddick 3-9-1864
Reddick, Disey E. to J. W. Pyland 8-13-1860 (8-17-1860)
Reddick, Luvena to Bob Green 2-1-1870 (no return)
Reddin, Mary J. C. to W. H. H. Morris 7-18-1867 (7-17?-1867)
Redding, Martha Ann to Henry Staggs 12-23-1863 (no return)
Redding, Martha Ann to J. L. Gray 11-22-1865 (11-23-1865)
Redding, N. L. to Thomas J. Dew 10-22-1872
Redding, Sarah S. to Newton R. Prichard 1-1-1866
Redditt, Addie to Jerry Lewis 9-11-1880 (9-12-1880)
Redick, Maria M. to Isaac C. Nunn 12-20-1866 (no return)
Redley, Silla to Porter McCutchen 2-4-1867
Reece, Elizabeth A. to N. Williams 1-9-1871 (1-11-1871)
Reed, E. P. to J. M. James 4-11-1871 (4-12-1871)
Reed, M. A. E. to John H. Lowrance 11-15-1863
Reed, M. to W. A. Wallace 3-9-1863 (3-25-1863)
Reed, Mary to W. M. Hoskins 1-17-1874 (1-18-1874)
Reed, Nancy J. to A. J. Fullerton 9-22-1868
Reed, Sallie Ann to H. B. Pomeroy 1-21-1879 (1-22-1879)
Reed, Sarah Jane to W. J. Davis 11-27-1866 (11-28-1866)
Reese, Sarah to L. H. Evans 9-1-1874 (9-2-1874)
Renfro, Melissa C. to Wm. A. Odle 11-1-1869
Reycroft, Martha A. to Alfred Brewer 2-27-1878
Reynolds, Amanda King to J. R. Eatherly 1-27-1879 (1-29-1879)
Reynolds, Jane to W. M. Hall 8-1-1871 (8-2-1871)
Reynolds, Lucinda to G. G. Harold 2-12-1869 (no return)
Reynolds, Martha E. to Jesse Baker 12-4-1869 (12-5-1869)
Reynolds, Martha J. to Garland Lively 1-29-1866 (no return)
Reynolds, R. E. to W. O. Christie 10-16-1877
Reynolds, Rebecca to Jacob Spencer 1-18-1870 (1-16?-1870)
Reynolds, Sallie to A. A. McGraw 12-31-1872
Rice, Fanny to Mark Bowen 10-13-1866 (10-14-1866)
Rice, Harriet to Charles Ward 2-21-1872 (2-23-1872)
Richard, Nancy A. to J. D. Parker 11-30-1876
Richards, Mary J. to R. B. Parker 12-27-1871 (12-28-1871)
Richardson, Ann E. to James Robertson 9-29-1869 (9-30-1869)
Richardson, Frances to J. V. Trafford 6-11-1870 (6-12-1870)
Richardson, Rebecca to Dock Wood 12-18-1866 (1-20-1867)
Richardson, Susan E. to Charles Davenport 12-17-1873 (12-18-1873)
Richardson, Verginia L. to Jos. H. Smither 10-10-1870 (10-11-1870)
Richie, S. C. to Thomas E. Young 12-22-1877 (12-23-1877)
Richmond, Margaret to John Davis 7-3-1867 (7-4-1867)
Ridens, Dicey to W. H. Simmons 6-17-1869
Ridens, M. M. to D. B. Neal 10-5-1871
Ripley, Willie B. to Thomas S. King 9-11-1877 (9-12-1877)
Rives?, Martha C. to John M. Rainey 7-22-1873 (7-23-1873)
Robbins, Louiza A. to Asberry Webb 9-12-1860
Robbins, S. B. to Mortimer Stephens 1-30-1878 (no return)
Robbins, Susan A. to Henry Brown 8-20-1879 (8-21-1879)
Roberson, Pernissa R. A. to Thomas Black 11-6-1865 (11-7-1865)
Roberts, Amanda to William King 10-27-1879
Roberts, Belle J. to Marvila Lowe 2-25-1878 (2-27-1878)
Roberts, Mary (Mrs.) to J. R. Smith 3-29-1879 (3-30-1879)
Robertson, Alice to Green Montgomery 12-30-1865 (no return)
Robertson, Elizabeth to Irvin Hicks 2-22-1878 (2-23-1878)
Robertson, Elizabeth to John F. Dodd 8-2-1862 (8-3-1862)
Robertson, Eugenie C. to H. C. Churchman 12-16-1872 (12-17-1872)
Robertson, Harriet M. to Robert Kingkaid 1-1-1866 (no return)
Robertson, Harriet to Caleb Ross 3-3-1862 (3-4-1862)
Robertson, Henrietta to Irvin Hicks 8-25-1877 (no return)
Robertson, Jane to Henry Smith 4-8-1861 (no return)
Robertson, Lou to Albert Overton 12-28-1872 (12-31-1872)
Robertson, Marenah to Thomas Acklin 11-9-1870 (11-10-1870)
Robertson, Margaret to John Jones 9-6-1867
Robertson, Martha to Ephraim Powers 10-7-1862
Robertson, Mary E. to James Henry Coker 1-16-1871 (1-17-1871)
Robertson, Verginia to J. H. Burkett 10-6-1870 (no return)
Robertson, Vina E. to W. B. Brooks 2-9-1874 (2-11-1874)
Robertson, Z. A. to B. T. Cowell 7-10-1879 (no return)
Rodgers, C. L. to J. R. Polston 10-31-1878 (no return)

Rodgers, Earnestine to T. J. Henderson 12-23-1870 (12-25-1870)
Rodgers, Sally to William P. Merygin? 10-16-1866 (no return)
Rogers, Amanda to Frank Pillow 9-12-1878
Rogers, Lucy to E. B. Pendleton 10-12-1869
Rogers, M. E. to J. A. Burket 1-23-1878 (1-24-1878)
Rogers, M. E. to N. E. McDearmon 1-15-1872 (1-16-1872)
Rogers, Mary E. to David C. Simons 5-9-1868 (5-10-1868)
Rogers, Nancy to Henry Stanley 8-24-1878 (8-25-1878)
Roney, A. G. to A. H. Gibson 11-1-1879 (11-5-1879)
Rooks, E. S. to W. J. Powell 11-22-1866 (11-25-1866)
Rooks, Nancy to Asbury Early 11-16-1869 (no return)
Roper, Mary E. to W. P. Ripley 2-24-1872 (2-25-1872)
Roper, Sarah E. to J. B. Bradshaw 3-16-1878 (3-17-1878)
Ross, Maggie to James Smith 12-21-1876 (12-24-1876)
Rowden, Elizabeth to Jesse Davis 11-17-1866 (11-18-1866)
Rowly, Amanday to Robert Mangrum 11-16-1867 (no return)
Roycroft, Samarimus (Sue) to R. A. McKee 1-8-1867 (1-10-1867)
Rucker, A. R. to J. M. Chambers 12-18-1872 (12-19-1872)
Rucker, Alvira S. to S. H. McDearman 12-17-1870 (12-22-1870)
Rucker, M. V. to C. S. Chambers 12-20-1876 (12-21-1876)
Rucker, S. A. to J. M. McDearmon 12-22-1874 (12-23-1874)
Rudder, Famie to J. W. Harper 10-16-1878
Rudder, Marian to Stephen McCann 10-29-1874
Rudder, Rosaline to W. H. Rowark 12-4-1867
Ruff, Caroline to Fillmore Tipton 2-28-1877
Ruff, Mariah to William Tipton 10-31-1874
Rumley, Nancy to J. F. McFarland 1-6-1872
Saddler, Martha A. to Robt. S. Clemens 7-16-1860
Saichern?, Martha to Calvin Fowlkes 10-9-1876
Salisbury, Catherine to H. N. Mount 10-18-1866
Salisbury, Mary A. to Jesse S. Robinson 2-20-1867
Salisbury, S. E. to J. C. Farmer 11-6-1876 (11-8-1876)
Salsberry, Frances to Wells W. Hall 1-27-1865 (1-28-1865)
Sampson, Sarah B. to Samuel B. Carson 3-12-1868
Sanders, Josephine to Polk Howard 12-22-1876 (1-24-1877)
Sanders, T. E. to William Kirk 10-18-1875
Sanderson, Elizabeth to W. H. Cotton 4-5-1871 (4-11-1871)
Sandlin, Sallie to A. N. Wright 10-20-1874 (10-22-1874)
Sanford, S. E. to C. D. Jones 8-18-1869 (8-19-1869)
Sargent, Elizabeth to A. N. Moore 6-7-1879 (no return)
Saunders, Ann Eliza to Robert Richardson 8-8-1868 (8-9-1868)
Saunders, L. C. to Samel J. Kellow 10-29-1874
Saunders, Mary R. to W. N. Ditto 10-9-1866 (10-11-1866)
Saunders, Rebecca F. to S. G. Rambo 2-24-1863 (2-26-1863)
Savage, Mattie to W. H. Prichard 12-18-1878 (12-24-1878)
Sawrie, Elizabeth to L. H. Dunaway 2-28-1866 (3-6-1866)
Sawyer, Adeline to Phillip Delph 9-18-1866
Sawyer, Catherine to Wm. Foust 10-23-1867 (no return)
Sawyer, Fanny to R. M. Johnson Benton 12-22-1869 (no return)
Sawyer, Hannah to Daniel Foust 4-16-1872
Sawyer, Harriet to C. J. Fumbanks 2-1-1879 (2-2-1879)
Sawyer, Lucinda to James King 7-29-1880
Sawyer, Marissa to W. H. Gooch 12-20-1869
Sawyer, Martha C. to W. G. M. Cole 2-16-1871
Sawyer, Puss to Phillip Bowling 12-25-1871 (12-27-1871)
Sawyer, R. J. to E. G. Cribbs 11-18-1869 (11-19-1869)
Sawyer, Sarah H. to J. M> Ferrell 12-15-1870
Sawyer, Tennessee to Jimmie Rollins 8-1-1870
Sawyers, Susan A. to Andrew Smith 7-13-1872 (no return)
Scales, Susie T. to Jas. J. Coker 5-2-1870 (5-3-1870)
Scalions, Sarah Ann to Isaac Green Dodd 4-30-1870 (no return)
Scallions, Martha to Henry Evans 8-16-1867 (9-18-1867)
Schoolcraft?, Ella to J. A. Humes 12-31-1870 (1-1-1871)
Scobey, Isabel to Sevraves Jones 1-29-1873 (1-30-1873)
Scobey, M. A. to J. A. Smith 12-11-1878 (12-19-1878)
Scobey, M. A. to J. S. Stockton 12-2-1878 (12-5-1878)
Scobey, M. A. to M. A. Lightfoot 11-4-1875 (no return)
Scobey, Parthena to L. C. Scobey 11-22-1871 (11-24-1871)
Scobey, S. S. to B. F. Pace 11-1-1879 (11-4-1879)
Scobey, Sophia E. to Jesse A. Green 8-1-1877
Scoby, Lucy E. to Saml. E. Huguley 12-13-1864 (12-14-1864)
Scoby, Martha J. to S. H. Moore 12-11-1865 (12-13-1865)
Scoby, Melissa J. to W. W. Haynes 11-19-1866 (no return)
Scoby, P. A. to W. W. Haynes 12-30-1869 (no return)
Scoby, T. A. to Jo. D. Pace 9-7-1869 (9-8-1869)

Scott, T. C. to J. L. Trimble 2-26-1873 (2-27-1873)
Scroggins, Ella to Phillip Rogers 10-14-1880
Scroggins, Matilda to Nash Jones 7-24-1875 (7-25-1875) B
Seals, M. A. to H. M. Thomason 8-14-1869 (no return)
Searcey, Clara to H. W. Dudley 8-10-1875
Searcy, A. A. to a. J. M. Amick 3-16-1875 (3-17-1875)
Self, Deller M. to Levi T. Heath 4-6-1863 (4-8-1863)
Self, N. J. to N. W. McCoy 12-23-1875
Sevier?, Matilda to James Walls 10-24-1866
Shackelton, Jane to John F. Cole 4-3-1866 (no return)
Shackleton, Amanda to Jonathan Nichols 4-28-1866 (no return)
Shackleton, E. S. to James T. Green 6-26-1875 (6-27-1875)
Shackleton, M. E. to J. D. Crawford 1-19-1876
Shackleton, Martha to Alfred T. Nichols 4-26-1870 (4-27-1870)
Shackleton, Mary A. to J. W. H. Oakley 10-24-1871 (10-25-1871)
Shahon, Lizzie to J. S. Moore ?-?-1867 (4-28-1867)
Shankle, Bettie to J. W. Reynolds 9-26-1878 (9-27-1878)
Sharber, Fannie P. to W. N. Porter 8-1-1870
Shaw, M. L. to Phillip McElmurry 6-22-1870 (6-23-1870)
Shelton, E. E. to J. M. Moseley 8-5-1874 (no return)
Shelton, Elizabeth M. to M. D. Pate 12-16-1869
Shelton, M. A. to J. F. Hunter 10-28-1875
Shelton, M. M. to J. A. Walker 10-16-1869 (10-17-1869)
Shelton, Mahala to Charner B. Colvin 12-21-1876 (12-25-1876)
Shelton, Mahala to John H. Moss 1-27-1863 (1-29-1863)
Shelton, Mary to James Warmack 11-28-1873 (12-11-1873)
Shelton, S. A. B. to B. P. Payne 8-17-1866
Shelton, S. E. to G. W. Walker 3-5-1879 (3-6-1879)
Shelton, Susan C. to S. H. Moor 12-30-1878 (1-1-1879)
Sherrod, M. E. to W. S. Payne 12-24-1877 (12-25-1877)
Sherwood, Henrietta to J. D. Pace 11-29-1871
Shipman, M. P. (Mrs.) to E. K. Manning 12-14-1872 (12-15-1872)
Shoemake, Elizabeth to Bowling Adcock 9-26-1860
Shoffner, S. E. to P. T. Kirk 8-13-1866 (8-14-1866)
Shofner, E. A. to W. E. Earley 4-9-1873 (4-10-1873)
Shofner, Fannie to J. D. Pace 10-30-1867
Shumaker, R. A. to W. H. Applewhite 6-22-1870 (6-23-1870)
Sigrary?, Amanda to Green Fowlkes 2-14-1880 (2-16-1880)
Silsby, Alice to John H. Thomas 12-28-1872
Silsby, Hellen to James Donald 1-12-1871
Silsby, Mary to Henry Ward 12-20-1865 (12-24-1865)
Silsby, Millie to Wm. Smith 6-14-1876 (6-15-1876)
Simmons, Laura E. to M. W. Eudaily 6-30-1869 (no return)
Simmons, Polly Ann to John Gibson 2-3-1862 (2-6-1862)
Simms, Amanda L. to Charles A. Tinsley 3-17-1868 (no return)
Simms, Lizzie to W. M. Smith 3-3-1873
Simons, Maggie to W. E. Trout 12-31-1878 (1-1-1879)
Simons, Martha A. to James A. Webber 5-3-1875 (5-4-1875)
Simons, S. J. to J. M. Ripley 1-24-1876 (1-26-1876)
Simpson, Eliza C. to E. J. Kiger 12-24-1874
Simpson, Elizabeth to John M. Childress 1-12-1871
Simpson, Frances to F. M. Waters 1-1-1870 (1-3-1870)
Simpson, J. A. to D. M. Loving 2-28-1868 (no return)
Simpson, Martha to Jonathan Mills 12-28-1878 (12-29-1878)
Simpson, Mary J. to Albert Watson 11-20-1868 (11-22-1868)
Sims, Polly A. to George Kirk 10-23-1871
Sinclair, Eliza to Henry Stevens 3-8-1870 (no return)
Sinclair, M. Alice to J. L. Daniel 11-25-1869 (11-30-1869)
Sinclair, Nannie B. to J. F. Osborn 10-1-1867 (no return)
Singletary, C. C. to M. D. Anderson 5-18-1863 (no return)
Singleterry, M. J. to T. F. Simpson 9-16-1868 (9-26-1868)
Singleton, A. F. to W. M. Bradley 10-23-1866 (10-24-1866)
Singleton, Caroline (mrs.) to William Mann 7-19-1873 (7-20-1873)
Singleton, Ellen to H. H. McClure 5-17-1867 (5-18-1867)
Singleton, Jane to Ransom Hamilton 7-2-1870 (no return)
Singleton, Mattie to D. Brock 3-29-1875
Skepper, Sarah F. to John Goodrich 12-27-1864 (no return)
Skipper, Ella to Green North 10-7-1867
Skipper, Julian to Christian J. Barger 6-30-1860 (7-1-1860)
Slayton, Elizabeth to R. S. Hudspeth 12-25-1867 (12-26-1867)
Slayton, Martha A. to Richard Crichfield 1-21-1868
Slayton, Mary E. to Jesse Bailey 9-26-1868 (9-27-1868)
Slayton, Sarah to Alfred Childers 12-23-1867
Slayton, Sarah to T. E. Lewellyn 3-6-1876 (3-8-1876)
Smith, Amanda to Andrew Bishop 1-27-1869

Smith, Amanda to Jeff Goforth 8-5-1879 (8-7-1879)
Smith, Ann Eliza to Flem Dunevant 12-16-1876 (12-21-1876)
Smith, Ann to Jefferson Pierce 8-27-1868
Smith, Annie to Andrew Johnson 7-12-1873 (7-13-1873)
Smith, Bettie to R. S. Fain 1-17-1872
Smith, Caroline to W. A. Pitts 10-23-1860
Smith, Caroline to Wiley M. Hicks 12-24-1866 (12-25-1866)
Smith, Carrie to Toney Moore 3-26-1874 (3-28-1874)
Smith, Darcus to J. W. Saunderson 5-4-1872 (5-5-1872)
Smith, Dortha A(labama) to Benj. F. Williams 12-12-1865 (12-13-1865)
Smith, E. F. to J. S. Hall 12-7-1868 (12-8-1868)
Smith, Eliza to Hesikiah Strother 10-4-1880 (10-17-1880)
Smith, Fanie (Mrs.) to Alse Garrett 9-12-1866 (9-13-1866)
Smith, Fannie to Levi Shepherd 4-10-1873 (4-11-1873)
Smith, Fannie to Richard Woodson 2-12-1874
Smith, Frances to Asa Bradshaw 2-28-1871 (3-3-1871)
Smith, Frances to Miles Floyd 11-30-1865
Smith, Frances to Wm. Spence 2-22-1878 (2-23-1878)
Smith, Isabella to Dan Simmons 3-17-1875 (3-18-1875)
Smith, Joella to James Dorsey 1-14-1869
Smith, Josephine to Matthew Dumas 2-16-1874
Smith, Josie to J. I. Fenn 2-7-1872
Smith, Julia Ann to James Hall 1-29-1872 (no return)
Smith, Julia P. to George A. Coon 12-9-1874
Smith, L. E. to J. T. Pace 7-22-1873 (7-24-1873)
Smith, L. M. T. to F. M. Nelson 11-22-1877 (11-25-1877)
Smith, Lucy A. to Robt. L. Doak 1-20-1862 (no return)
Smith, Lucy to Alex Tipton 6-3-1879
Smith, Lucy to James Fowlkes 12-1-1870 B
Smith, Lucy to Minor Wood 1-20-1869
Smith, M. E. to F. E. Scobey 12-11-1878 (12-12-1878)
Smith, M. E. to James F. Sudberry 11-25-1873 (no return)
Smith, M. F. to J. S. Thompson 8-12-1867 (8-13-1867)
Smith, M. F. to J. W. Echols 12-26-1876 (12-27-1876)
Smith, M. J. to J. H. Tipton 4-12-1871 (no return)
Smith, M. J. to J. P. Troy 9-14-1863 (9-15-1863)
Smith, Martha E. to Geo. Brimen 12-28-1878 (no return)
Smith, Martha T. to William S. Wright 6-26-1863 (7-2-1863)
Smith, Mary A. to W. A. J. Walker 9-7-1870 (no return)
Smith, Mary to Alex Connell 5-27-1871 (5-28-1871)
Smith, Mary to Thomas Wells 2-17-1866 (2-18-1866)
Smith, Mein? to Henry Johnson 11-30-1878 (12-1-1878)
Smith, Miss ____ to Jacob McCoy 4-2-1874
Smith, Mollie to George Smith 8-8-1878
Smith, Nancy to M. W. Hood 2-24-1877 (2-25-1877)
Smith, Nancy to Nick Moore 10-28-1880
Smith, Nancy to Taylor Fowlkes 8-14-1868 (8-16-1868)
Smith, Rebecca to J. F. Smith 1-3-1867
Smith, Rebecca to Manuel? Frosh 3-2-1878 (3-3-1878)
Smith, S. T. to J. F. Black 8-4-1876 (8-5-1876)
Smith, S. V. to N. B. Tarrant 1-4-1870 (1-5-1870)
Smith, Sallie to Joseph Banker 11-15-1872 (11-17-1872)
Smith, Sarah A. to Z. T. Akin 10-7-1863 (no return)
Smith, Sarah to Lemuel Day 9-12-1871 (9-13-1871)
Smith, Sophia to Andrew Jackson 10-12-1870
Smith, Susan Jane to Zach Dozey 8-5-1879 (8-7-1879)
Smith, Susan to Joseph Baird 2-25-1871 (2-26-1871)
Smith, Tennessee to Bedford Smith 11-7-1878
Smith, Tennessee to Robert Parker 12-17-1879 (no return)
Smithwick, Prudence to N. L. Doer? 8-20-1860 (8-22-1860)
Snell, H. C. to M. D. L. Pate 7-21-1874 (7-22-1874)
Snow, Elizabeth to H. L. Harwell 12-21-1875 (12-22-1875)
Snow, Isabella S. to V. M. Benham 7-27-1867
Snow, Sarah to Albert Jones 8-13-1860 (no return)
Sorrell, Fannie to Wm. D. Tarkington 4-3-1878 (4-4-1878)
Sorrell, Helen to Isiah Lea 12-27-1862 (1-3-1863)
Sorrell, Hellen to Chas. Clay 10-6-1864 (no return)
Sorrell, Mary to W. C. Eason 1-1-1873
Sorrell, P. A. to T. G. Neely 2-20-1866
Sorrell, S. M. to W. A. Flowers 3-19-1867
Southern, Martha to Albert Fowlkes 12-28-1866
Southern, Susan to James H. Cooper 6-28-1870
Soward, Josephine to Julian Parr 12-23-1875
Spain, Emily to L. C. Benns 12-6-1871 (12-7-1871)

Spain, Helen to L. C. Bemis? 12-6-1873 (12-7-1873)
Spain, Jane to James B. Southerland 10-29-1860 (no return)
Spain, Lizzie to J. B. Thompson 2-25-1878 (2-27-1878)
Spain, Margaret E. to Powell S. Taylor 7-18-1867
Spain, Mary E. to James F. Wilkinson 3-19-1878 (3-25-1878)
Sparkman, Julia A. to John T. Wilson 7-13-1867 (7-14-1867)
Spence, Clary to William Tipton 5-8-1879 (5-9-1879)
Spence, Margaret to Jack Anderson 6-2-1866
Spence, Mary to Alex Tipton 5-30-1866 (6-2-1866)
Spence, Mollie to Richard Smith 3-16-1878
Spence, Palmira to Robt. H. Ferguson 10-7-1863
Spence, Sarah A. to A. L. Tancel 6-18-1868
Spence, Susan to Randle Light 8-11-1866
Spence, Tennessee to Robert Rodgers 1-1-1880
Spence, Tennessee to Samuel Barnett 8-11-1866
Spoon, Lucy to A. B. Canada 12-20-1875 (12-21-1875)
Spoon, Tiressa to James Forbes 9-9-1876 (9-15-1876)
Spurriers, Hellen to J. G. Richards 2-11-1879
Staggs, Clem to G. A. Smith 4-20-1876
Staggs, Eliza C. to Giles F. Moody 10-2-1867 (no return)
Staggs, Joseph Isabella to R. D. Stull 1-30-1877
Staggs, Sallie to John Roper 10-10-1863 (11-3-1863)
Stalcup, Harriet A. to W. M. Ballentine 12-6-1867 (no return)
Stalcup, Margaret to J. F. Andrews 6-22-1872 (6-21?-1872)
Stalkup, A. R. to S. R. Williams 10-17-1878 (10-18-1878)
Stallcup, Mary Ann to William A. Bailey 7-21-1863 (no return)
Stallcup, Millie to R. W. Dickey 11-23-1871
Stalling, L. F. to J. K. P. Reddick 12-19-1866 (12-20-1866)
Stallings, Ann to W. B. Nash 1-7-1867 (no return)
Stallings, Harriet to M. V. B. Reddick 10-26-1860 (10-27-1860)
Stallings, M. E. to W. M. Dean 3-6-1878 (3-7-1878)
Stallings, Paris to Peter Byassee 4-8-1871 (4-9-1871)
Stanley, Sarah to Jo. Saunders 2-8-1869 (no return)
Starrett, S. E. (Mrs.) to Noah Green 3-13-1873
Stedman, Cynthia to Ben Williams 11-16-1870 (11-18-1870)
Steen, Mary J. to S. A. Ferrell 2-18-1865 (no return)
Steen, Sarah F. to James M. Yates 3-29-1866 (no return)
Stegall, Margaret to William Pierce 9-9-1862
Stegall, Martha to John Taylor 2-2-1864 (2-3-1864)
Stephens, Anna to B. H. Sullivan 2-23-1876
Stephenson, Emma to Ephraim Frazier 2-1-1868 (2-2-1868)
Stevens, Alice to Green Turnage 8-23-1872 (8-25-1872)
Stevens, Amanda to Matthew Routly 12-1-1866
Stevens, Ella N. to John M. Pierce 4-29-1876 (4-30-1876)
Stevens, Fannie to Geo. E. Scott 4-28-1874
Stevens, Fannie to Zach Watkins 10-11-1876 (10-12-1876)
Stevens, Georgia A. to J. M. Brackin 4-10-1878
Stevens, Georgia to Frank W. Luscumbe 9-10-1872
Stevens, Kate to WM. Kerr 4-6-1869 (no return)
Stevens, Mamie to Jo. E. Sharp 11-6-1878 (11-7-1878)
Stevens, Mary L. to M. M. Marshall 2-24-1879
Stevens, Nancy to Jonas Murphey 11-1-1871 (11-2-1871)
Stevens, Sarah to Nathan McCoy 5-8-1880 (5-9-1880)
Stevenson, Nancy J. to T. P. Chronister 1-7-1868
Stevenson, Ozella to J. F. Pierce 3-2-1875
Steward, Juntha J. to Joseph Turpin 12-5-1860 (12-26-1860)
Stewart, Bettie J. to J. L. Hampton 2-26-1869 (no return)
Stewart, Elizabeth to J. H. Johnson 6-17-1878
Stewart, Letty to Albert Simmons 12-24-1873 (12-25-1873)
Stewart, Matta to John Ledsinger 12-31-1872 (1-1-1873)
Stewart, Nancy E. to B. F. Wimberley 4-27-1868
Stewart, Viney to Mik Foust 3-5-1868
Stillman, Mary Ann to Rufus King
Stinnett, F. R. to Andrew Parks 4-13-1875 (4-15-1875)
Stith, M. L. to Oscar R. Robbins 10-11-1869 (10-12-1869)
Stokes, Malvina to L. A. Robertson 12-22-1862 (12-23-1862)
Stone, Dennis to W. L. Wright 10-16-1865 (10-18-1865)
Stone, Ella G. to Thomas E. Boaz 11-19-1872
Stone, Tennie to J. T. C. Palmer 11-17-1876 (12-19-1876)
Strahorn, L. J. to Franklin Perry 12-23-1867 (no return)
Straine, Elizabeth to S. D. Prichard 12-5-1864 (12-7-1864)
Strange, Amanda J. to Janus M. Stricklen 3-10-1868
Strawn, Julia to Joseph D. Haynes 11-20-1860 (11-21-1860)
Strawn, Stacy S. to W. T. Pace 12-29-1865 (12-30-1865)
Street, Bettie to S. T. Johnson 5-30-1879 (no return)

Stricklin, Liza to Armstead Grayson 4-2-1867
Stricklin, Nancy to Alex Wayson 1-15-1878
Striclin, Mariah O. to W. S. Warren 2-19-1869 (no return)
Strother, Eliza E. to C. Nicholas 10-21-1871 (10-22-1871)
Strother, Elvira to William E. Roberts 12-24-1869 (no return)
Stucken, Martha J. to James Warren 11-22-1860
Stults, N. E. to G. F. Jones 1-25-1876 (1-26-1876)
Sudberry, F. E. to James Saulsbury 12-30-1871
Sudberry, Jane to King Green 1-1-1878
Sudberry, Nancy to Henry Ranser 1-3-1866 (1-20-1867)
Sudberry, Tabitha to John Barr 1-3-1871 (1-4-1871)
Sudbury, N. E. to S. J. Yates 11-14-1866
Sulivan, P. A. to M. C. Ross 9-22-1863 (11-16-1863)
Sumerow, C. L. to Chas. F. Herring 10-27-1875
Summers, E. M. to D. L. Green 12-22-1873
Swain, Sallie to George W. Jones 9-21-1871
Swann, Darcus (Mrs.) to R. Staggs 4-3-1871 (4-9-1871)
Swanner, Amanda to John Travis 12-12-1877
Swanner, Ann to John C. Davis 6-25-1879 (6-28-1879)
Swanner, Bell to J. L. Pugh 12-11-1877 (12-12-1877)
Swanner, Efarilla to George W. Willis 12-23-1863 (no return)
Swayne, J. A. to J. W. Davis 1-9-1879
Swift, Adrienne to J. S. Hawkes 11-21-1878
Swift, Amelia to Sam Haskins 4-30-1874 (5-1-1874)
Swift, Mary A. to P. W. Groves 11-13-1863 (11-18-1863)
Swift, Minerva to Peter McDaniel 4-2-1874
Swift, Nancy A. to William Edwards 7-29-1870 (8-1-1870)
Tague, Nancy A. to C. N. Kay 2-8-1872
Talley, Amanda to Scott Overton 12-21-1874 (12-30-1874) B
Talley, Eliza to William Searcy 7-24-1875 (7-25-1875) B
Talley, Elizabeth to James W. Wright 5-14-1861
Talley, Julia to Millard Southern 4-6-1878 (4-7-1878)
Talley, Mariah to George Peacock 3-24-1870 (no return)
Talley, Mattie to Nelson Shaw 1-27-1880 (no return)
Talley, T. S. to Osborne Strong 12-27-1876
Tansel, Pocahontas to James W. Edwards 3-12-1866
Tarkington, J. T. to Wilson A. Bunnell 7-31-1863
Tarkington, Mary E. to Pleasant Tipton 11-3-1868
Tarleton, Marian to Sylvester Robbins 3-5-1879 (3-6-1879)
Tarrant, L. A. to J. W. King 7-9-1878 (7-10-1878)
Tarrant, L. A. to M. L. King 7-18-1876 (no return)
Tarrant, M. F. to D. E. Fuller 9-8-1869 (9-9-1869)
Tate, Adaline to J. L. Cochrill 1-30-1877 (1-31-1877)
Tatum, Ann B. to G. W. Webb 8-12-1868 (8-20-1868)
Tatum, M. A. to S. A. Chitwood 8-29-1866 (no return)
Taylor, A. M. to J. S. Rodgers 11-23-1869 (11-24-1869)
Taylor, Fannie to A. R. Swindle 2-6-1873
Taylor, Frances E. to John H. Hay 9-13-1867 (no return)
Taylor, Lou to R. H. Halliburton 8-31-1870 (9-1-1870)
Taylor, M. C. to W. H. Burgess 12-14-1876
Taylor, M. M. to S. H. Ball 1-5-1876
Taylor, Margaret E. C. to James N. Taylor 10-16-1866 (10-18-1866)
Taylor, Polly to Jno. A. Cunningham 9-10-1861 (no return)
Taylor, R. J. to J. A. Laster 1-9-1869 (no return)
Taylor, Sarah J. to W. J. Stallcupp 4-10-1869
Teat, Neettie to T. H. Cook 6-13-1874 (6-14-1874)
Teater, Margaret M. to Robt. H. Thomas 7-27-1878 (7-28-1878)
Telford, M. S. to W. H. Hood 3-3-1862 (3-5-1862)
Templeton, F. J. to H. M. Dickey 12-8-1869 (12-10-1869)
Templeton, M. C. to J. C. Holt 4-3-1865 (4-5-1865)
Tevilla, M. to M. F. Campbell 1-11-1871
Thacker, H. E. to M. H. Goodloe 9-5-1870 (no return)
Thacker, M. E. F. to R. J. M. Byrn 3-27-1862 (no return)
Tharpe, Mary E. to B. B. Carr 3-22-1876 (no return)
Thedford, Mary to Samuel M. Dunn 9-19-1879 (9-30-1879)
Thedford, Mrs. to G. W. Harper 7-22-1874 (no return)
Thetford, E. P. to W. A. Williams 10-11-1877
Thetford, Fannie B. to Henry H. Hollinsworth 5-13-1876 (5-14-1876)
Thetford, L. R. J. to J. D. Askridge 8-10-1875 (8-11-1875)
Thetford, Lenora J. to Solomon S. Hall 3-25-1868 (no return)
Thetford, Margaret to James Daniel 8-16-1875 (8-18-1875)
Thomas, Elizabeth to William Shaw 1-17-1863 (1-22-1863)
Thomas, F. G. to John Fonville 1-8-1863 (1-12-1863)
Thompson, Amanda to Richard P. Gibson 8-17-1867 (no return)
Thompson, Eliza to Nathan C. Smith 5-17-1871 (5-18-1871) B

Thompson, Lucinda to G. E. Spence 10-1-1867 (no return)
Thompson, Lucinda to Robert Couch 12-24-1872
Thompson, Lucinda to T. H. Aiken 10-29-1868 (no return)
Thompson, M. E. to J. A. Moore 1-14-1868 (1-15-1868)
Thompson, M. to James H. Goodrich 7-6-1870
Thompson, Martha A. R. to Jarret Thompson 5-15-1865
Thompson, Mary E. to J. S. Ward 1-27-1868
Thompson, Mindie? to W. O. Childress 6-13-1879 (6-15-1879)
Thompson, Phoeby to Samuel Herrin 9-26-1866 (no return)
Thompson, Sarah E. to Danl. Roads 4-6-1863 (4-8-1863)
Thornton, Susan to Richard Harris 1-30-1877 (1-31-1877)
Thurmon, S. M. to A. Canada 8-20-1868 (8-23-1868)
Thurmond, E. F. to Hosea Boren 3-20-1878
Thurmond, Fannie to J. D. Glisson 12-23-1876 (1-4-1877)
Thurmond, Hasentine to Jackson Stricklan 2-18-1871 (2-19-1871)
Thurmond, Nancy A. to P. W. Hart 9-11-1873
Thurmond, Roberta (Mrs.) to Jethro King 4-30-1879
Timmes?, D. A. to W. M. Vail 12-19-1878
Timms, N. J. to J. W. Daniel 12-15-1874
Tinsley, May to F. C. Espey 1-20-1875 (1-22-1875)
Tipton, A. C. to C. Doherty 10-15-1868
Tipton, Agnes V. to V. G. Wynn 12-20-1865
Tipton, Cenus? to Bowlin Adams 12-15-1870 B
Tipton, E. R. to A. W. Tarkington 1-5-1867 (1-7-1867)
Tipton, Fannie to Edward Fizer 7-23-1874 (no return)
Tipton, Fannie to Louis Barnett 1-3-1877 (1-4-1877)
Tipton, Lavenia to James Atkins 2-14-1872 (2-4?-1872)
Tipton, Margaret to Pierce Moore 2-25-1871 (2-26-1871)
Tipton, Mattie E. to H. T. Tipton 2-20-1866
Tipton, Queen to John W. Lauderdale 11-3-1870
Tisdale, Ellen T. to Richard S. Biggs 10-17-1874 (10-18-1874)
Tisdale, M. A. to Martin Pierce 12-5-1871 (no return)
Todd, Annie to William A. Trotter 4-29-1861 (5-2-1861)
Todd, M. A. to J. R. Clemmons 12-29-1875
Todd, M. Amanda to A. Horton 11-26-1874
Todd, Missouri to Joseph C. Pinner 4-20-1870
Todd, Nancy to G. R. Gooch 7-26-1865 (7-27-1865)
Toombs, P. to W. F. Rawles 8-27-1872
Topp, Matilda to John Simpson 6-1-1867 (6-10-1867)
Treadaway, M. M. to W. Riley Peel 2-22-1873 (2-25-1873)
Trout, J. A. to W. G. Hearn 6-5-1873
Trout, Polly to J. H. Smith 10-4-1871 (no return)
Troy, M. to J. R. Whittenton 8-26-1869 (8-27-1869)
Tucker, Dollie to Willis Smith 10-19-1870 (10-10?-1870) B
Tucker, E. C. to J. B. Trout 3-25-1867 (2?-28-1867)
Tucker, E. R. to J. L. Banks 9-18-1872
Tucker, Eliza to Doc Price 12-29-1870 (no return)
Tucker, Ella (Mrs.) to John Webb 12-24-1866 (12-25-1866)
Tucker, Harriet to Harry Grimm 1-3-1872 (1-4-1872)
Tucker, Jennie to Isaac A. Harris 12-24-1873 (12-25-1873)
Tucker, Judy to Ned Dearmore 2-8-1877
Tucker, Laura to Alex Beaumont 8-11-1870
Tucker, Laura to Geo. Bradshaw 11-25-1875
Tucker, Lucy A. to Alfred M. Harper 11-5-1867 (no return)
Tucker, Lucy E. to Dossey Harrell 12-22-1862 (12-23-1862)
Tucker, Lucy to Major F. Cook 4-28-1880
Tucker, Lucy to William Bell 11-7-1878 (no return)
Tucker, M. A. to A. B. (Dr.) Haskins 5-19-1873 (no return)
Tucker, Martha F. to John F. Ray 8-5-1862 (8-19-1862)
Tucker, Mary Ann to Robt. R. Bogguss 9-6-1875 (9-9-1875)
Tucker, Nannie to George Rogers 8-7-1874 (8-12-1874)
Tucker, Noon? to Peter Connell 8-9-1877
Tucker, Sarah J. to Samuel Morrow 10-1-1860 (10-10-1860)
Tucker, Sarah to Granville Taylor 12-25-1877 (12-27-1877)
Tucker, Zenobia? to Dave Baxter 2-1-1877
Tumage, Malvina to Rufus Henderson 3-16-1871 (3-19-1871)
Turnage, Ann to Amos Grimm 4-7-1877 (4-9-1877)
Turnage, Dinkie to Umphrey Law 4-16-1872 (4-18-1872)
Turner, Annie to William Waddy 12-23-1871 (12-24-1871)
Turner, Lovey A. to M. A. Hall 1-25-1869 (no return)
Turner, Margaret E. to M. A. Robbins 1-5-1876
Turner, Martha to Charles Weaver 11-26-1860
Turner, Mary to J. J. Owens 11-11-1876 (11-14-1876)
Turner, Sarah C. to Andrew Hart 4-16-1860
Turney, J. E. M. to R. W. Mitchell 2-10-1875 (2-19-1875)

Turnley, Viola to W. W. Sorrell 10-23-1877 (10-24-1877)
Turrentine, M. E. to J. W. Trout 12-20-1866 (12-23-1866)
Twilla, Margaret Ann to John B. McIntosh 1-24-1878
Twilla, Victoria to Sid Anderson 7-16-1870 (7-17-1870)
Vail, Elosie? to John Pew 7-28-1869 (7-30-1869)
Vail, Harriet R. to Nathaniel W. Warren 4-2-1864 (4-4-1864)
Vail, Sarah C. to E. H. Sandlin 3-3-1870
Vails, M. E. to M. L. Grugett 12-16-1874
Van Eaton, N. B. to D. C. Franklin 10-20-1879 (10-21-1879)
Vaughan, Hellen to M. P. Enochs 9-22-1874
Vaughan, Mary J. to W. H. Jobes 10-17-1874 (10-18-1874)
Vaughan, Susan to James Armstrong 3-20-1871
Via, Barbara F. to H. C. Hodge 1-22-1878 (1-24-1878)
Via, Polly to R. L. Shaw 12-10-1874
Viah?, Mary F. to J. B. M. Stevenson 1-3-1866 (no return)
Viar, Melissa E. to Thomas Viar 11-16-1865 (no return)
Vick, Nannie to Geo. W. Church 9-5-1870 (9-11-1870)
Vinson, Alice to W. H. Hampton 12-25-1872
Vinson, Eliza to Frank Fowlkes 11-27-1875
Vinson, Nancy to James Wilson 4-23-1872 (4-24-1872)
Vire, Narcissa to Joseph Harrison 5-15-1866 (5-16-1866)
Wade, Eliza to Washington Lillard 11-6-1873
Wagsted, Deevy to Moses Nichol 5-25-1860 (no return)
Waits, Eliza E. to John J. Gant 12-22-1875 (12-23-1875)
Walker, A. C. A. to A. J. Pierce 1-6-1864
Walker, Addie to Thomas C. Ferrill 1-11-1866
Walker, Alice to Dallas Mahon 1-28-1868 (2-10-1868)
Walker, Arabella C. to W. W. Simmons 10-23-1861 (no return)
Walker, Barbary to P. M. Tipton 11-16-1865
Walker, Charita to Dennis Smith 1-18-1871 (1-19-1871) B
Walker, Delia to David Woods 12-6-1879 (12-8-1879)
Walker, Eliza to Dave Foster 12-16-1876 (12-24-1876)
Walker, Idella to G. W. Reynolds 3-6-1876 (3-8-1876)
Walker, Kisa to Polk Howard 1-26-1870 (no return)
Walker, M. A. to A. C. Walker 8-3-1869 (8-4-1869)
Walker, M. E. to John W. Massey 3-1-1879 (3-5-1879)
Walker, M. L. (Mrs.) to Daniel S. Tucker 2-19-1872 (2-20-1872)
Walker, Margaret to Bryant White 3-24-1870 (no return)
Walker, Martha A. C. to Leonard Baker 1-10-1872 (1-11-1872)
Walker, Martha to Wm. Turner 5-12-1869 (no return)
Walker, Mary B. to W. B. Smith 2-6-1861 (2-7-1861)
Walker, Mary M. to Asa A. Atkins 12-14-1874 (12-15-1874)
Walker, Mary R. E. to J. M. Young 9-4-1876 (9-6-1876)
Walker, Mary to J. S. Chamberlain 11-22-1877
Walker, Mary to W. H. Macon 9-28-1871
Walker, Nancy E. to A. L. Ray 11-5-1860 (11-6-1860)
Walker, Rachel to Isaac Thomas 12-27-1876
Walker, Sarah to Henry Foster 12-11-1880 (12-17-1880)
Wallace, Elizabeth to W. T. Kidd 12-31-1878 (1-1-1879)
Wallace, Mayville to William Prock 8-12-1861 (8-13-1861)
Wallace, Nancy J. to G. S. Milam 3-15-1865
Wallace, Rebecca to Frank G. Sampson 2-6-1868
Wallace, Susana to J. A. Wallace 3-25-1873 (3-27-1873)
Wallae, Adaline to Mose Fowlkes 9-4-1876
Wallan, L. Evaline to R. T. Golden 8-22-1866 (8-23-1866)
Walls, Ella to Ethelbert L. Pierce 11-21-1872
Walsin, Fanni A. to S. McDavid 10-1-1867 (10-2-1867)
Want?, Mamie J. to J. Cas Tipton 6-5-1870
Ward, Asenith to John E. Davis 10-12-1868 (10-14-1868)
Ward, L. C. to T. M. Patterson 1-4-1870 (1-5-1870)
Ward, M. E. to M. A. Avrett 11-6-1868 (11-8-1868)
Ward, M. J. to T. R. Akin 12-9-1874 (12-10-1874)
Ward, Martha to James Jones 9-2-1870 (9-6-1870)
Ward, Mary Jane to John Richardson 6-26-1867 (no return)
Ward, Mary to Aaron Lanier 9-26-1866 (no return)
Ward, Matilda to James Evans 1-6-1869
Ward, Mollie to Amos Bumpass 6-18-1870 (6-19-1870)
Ward, Sallie P. to C. A. Goodlow 5-14-1868 (5-16-1868)
Ward, Sarah to John B.? Bailey 9-24-1864 (no return)
Ward, Susan to Aaron White 11-30-1878 (12-1-1878)
Warpole, Martha to Amos Faulkner 12-21-1863 (no return)
Warre, S. M. to James Chambers 10-12-1868 (12-13-1868)
Warren, Amanda to Alec. Bowlin 8-30-1862 (9-1-1862)
Warren, Elizabeth to W. J. Griffin 11-7-1866 (no return)
Warren, Mariah (Mrs.) to J. R. Cerley 12-28-1872 (12-31-1872)

Warren, Martha J. to Nathan L. Davis 10-7-1869
Warren, Nancy Ann to M. M. Palmore 7-25-1871 (no return)
Warren, Nancy to R. W. Sumrow 1-7-1867
Warren, Perry? to Ben Jamin Oakley 8-12-1867 (no return)
Warren, R. P. to M. W. Smart 7-15-1879 (7-17-1879)
Warren, Sallie C. to William A. Jetton 11-23-1874 (11-24-1874)
Warren, Susie A. to Nathaniel C. Oneal 9-22-1879 (no return)
Warren, Zylpha to G. W. Dozier 2-18-1873 (2-19-1873)
Waters, Mary Ann to Ephraim Powers 8-7-1876 (8-9-1876)
Waters, Sarah to Wm. Underwood 12-14-1877 (12-20-1877)
Watkins, Amanda to William Strickland 5-8-1875 (5-9-1875)
Watkins, Fannie to George W. York 4-18-1870 (no return)
Watson, Ellen to J. W. Phelan 10-27-1875
Watson, L. J. to J. R. Griffin 9-3-1872 (9-5-1872)
Watson, Martha J. to Newton P. Watkins 2-6-1869 (no return)
Watson, Martha to J. W. Rodgers 7-22-1879
Watson, Mary Jane to Mark Tyler 5-12-1879
Watson, Nancy to Wm. Whitlock 1-19-1867 (1-21-1867)
Watson, Tennessee to John S. Rook 10-2-1861
Wayson, Margaret to W. F. McBride 4-2-1877 (4-3-1877)
Wayson, Mary E. to William Cate 11-30-1872 (12-4-1872)
Weakley, Ella A. to John F. Doyle 9-17-1861 (9-18-1861)
Weakley, M. A. to B. N. Fryer 11-28-1864 (11-29-1864)
Weakley, Mary K. to W. L. Watkins 2-14-1866
Weakly, Isabella T. to Martin L. Sloan 3-9-1868 (3-10-1868)
Weakly, Jane to Allen Finley 12-7-1865
Weatherington, L. F. to C. A. Smith 2-24-1879 (2-27-1879)
Weatherington, M. F. to H. J. Pace 12-9-1874 (12-10-1874)
Webb, Joella to Dennis F. Sawyer 8-15-1872 (8-16-1872)
Webb, Lou to Willis Gauldin 1-21-1870 (1-31-1870)
Webb, Louisa A. to Pleasant Via 11-14-1876
Webb, Manie G. to Hamilton Parks, jr. 10-5-1878 (10-7-1878)
Webb, Martha to John Bennett 6-28-1871
Webster, Emiline to Daniel Walton 1-20-1872 (2-1-1872)
Webster, Flora to Levi T. Shorter 3-31-1868 (no return)
Weever, Randa to John E. Anderson 6-21-1870
Wessen, Amand J. to John C. Murray 12-19-1860 (12-20-1860)
Wesson, F. E. to J. W. Oslin 12-20-1871 (12-21-1871)
Wesson, Mary E. to John E. Vernon 9-22-1871 (9-25-1871)
Wesson, Mildred to J. S. Meredith 7-19-1871 (7-25-1871)
West, M. O. T. to J. F. Tilman 6-10-1879 (6-11-1879)
Westbrook, T. J. to A. J. Pierce 12-11-1869 (12-12-1869)
Wethen, Elizabeth to Lewis V. Read 11-27-1867 (11-28-1867)
Wethington, Mary to W. P. Davis 9-27-1869 (9-28-1869)
Wheeler, M. A. to M. G. Reasons 11-17-1877 (11-21-1877)
Wheeler, Margaret to M. C. Reasons 2-9-1878
Wheeler, Nannie to John W. Harton 7-31-1869 (8-1-1869)
Wheeler, Sarah A. to F. H. Thompson 8-14-1860 (no return)
Wherry, Dolly to Sain A. Tansil 5-7-1875
Wherry, M. A. to A. J. Grugett? 1-15-1874
Wherry, M. E. to J. L. Calton 9-26-1874 (9-27-1874)
Whit, Harriet to John Pennington 12-13-1862 (12-14-1862)
White, A. G. to J. P. King 12-18-1878
White, Alice to W. H. Applewhite 12-25-1874 (no return)
White, Annie to J. M. Jackson 4-29-1868 (no return)
White, Caroline to William R. Dodd 10-30-1861
White, Eliza to B. Milam 1-7-1879 (no return)
White, Eliza to Redmond Jefferson 4-18-1872 (4-22-1872)
White, F. J. to James R. Green 12-6-1875 (12-7-1875)
White, Fannie to Lewis Washington 5-17-1877
White, Jennie A. to James J. Smith 11-6-1876 (no return)
White, Lucy to Charlie Young 10-21-1870 (1-22-1871)
White, Lucy to Jim Reagan 5-25-1877 (5-27-1877)
White, M. A. to J. J. Johnson 12-2-1868 (12-3-1868)
White, Nancy A. to H. N. Johnson 10-15-1866 (no return)
White, Paralee to W. W. Fedrick 5-5-1863 (5-6-1863)
White, Sarah F. to David H. Jones 1-16-1863 (no return)
Whitley, Callie to J. W. Arnett 5-13-1873 (5-14-1873)
Whitson, Eliza Jane to Robert F. Wood 12-23-1869 (no return)
Whitson, Judy Ann to Frank Smith 1-17-1877
Whitson, Mariah to John Dunevant 12-12-1871 (12-13-1871)
Whitson, Millie to Craig Perry 1-17-1877
Whitt, M. F. to J. H. Burnham 12-21-1870 (12-22-1870)
Whitt, Soprona E. to J. W. Williams 5-8-1869 (no return)
Whitteman, Emily to A. J. Boling 12-6-1865 (12-10-1865)

Whittemore, Emily to A. J. Boling 12-6-1865 (12-10-1865)
Whittenton, Elzira to E. Johnson 8-2-1869 (12-28-1869)
Whittenton, H. D. to Z. T. Gleaves 12-20-1871 (12-21-1871)
Whittenton, M. E. to M. J. Rankin 1-30-1867 (2-3-1867)
Whittenton, Martha to Sam Johnson 6-3-1869 (no return)
Whittington, Eliza to Tom Johnson 2-19-1868 (no return)
Whitworth, Ann to Henry Petty 8-21-18682
Wiggins, M. J. T. to John R. Dodson 5-21-1878 (5-23-1878)
Wilbosern, Sidonia to Joseph Bair 5-22-1860
Wilkins, C. C. to J. H. Cribbs 11-11-1868
Wilkins, Elizabeth A. to Francis S. Lacey 7-9-1862
Wilkins, Fannie to Frank Burton 12-2-1875
Wilkins, Jane to G. W. Jackson 6-10-1876 (6-11-1876)
Wilkins, Josephine to A. P. Powell 1-14-1874 (no return)
Wilkins, M. F. to D. P. Ferrill 2-22-1866
Wilkinson, Margaret E. to D. F. Taylor 6-2-1879
Wilkinson, S. E. D. to J. Cozart 10-2-1871 (10-3-1871)
Williams, Almira to Albert M. Odel 9-17-1866 (no return)
Williams, Amanda to David Green 12-21-1866 (12-22-1866)
Williams, Annie to H. T. Spraggins 1-25-1879 (1-26-1879)
Williams, B. B. (Mrs.) to R. E. Bogle 5-13-1871 (5-14-1871)
Williams, Bell to George Millard 11-12-1873 (11-13-1873)
Williams, Belle to J. W. McFarlin 3-20-1879
Williams, C. S. to G. L. Brandon 11-6-1872
Williams, Callie to James Smith 1-8-1874
Williams, Catharine to Joel M. Pugh 1-22-1879 (1-23-1879)
Williams, Elizabeth to James Burns 11-1-1879 (11-2-1879)
Williams, Emiline to Sandy Smith 7-5-1877
Williams, Emily F. to James M. Mathews 12-16-1865 (12-18-1865)
Williams, Franky to Morris Strong 1-1-1868 (1-2-1868)
Williams, Harriet to James Light 12-16-1875
Williams, Hetta to Jack Connell 12-2-1869 (no return)
Williams, Jane to A. M. Perkins 10-3-1866 (10-4-1866)
Williams, Jane to Elisha Jackson 4-17-1872 (4-18-1872)
Williams, Jane to W. H. Harrison 10-14-1862
Williams, Jennie to John A. Vican 6-6-1879 (6-15-1879)
Williams, M. E. to J. P. Sowers 8-1-1871
Williams, Mahala to James Hill 1-14-1879 (1-16-1879)
Williams, Martha to Henry Hall 3-25-1870 (no return)
Williams, Mary F. to J. E. Hardican 8-17-1869 (no return)
Williams, Mary F. to Nat Wesson 12-24-1867 (no return)
Williams, Mattie to J. W. Wesley 12-25-1874 (no return)
Williams, Nancy to Caswell Worrel 1-2-1866 (no return)
Williams, Nancy to William T. King 4-10-1861
Williams, Parthina to Jesse Hicks 1-9-1867 (1-10-1867)
Williams, Rhody to Daniel Sawyer 5-12-1866 (5-16-1866)
Williams, S. A. to James P. Ethridge 4-26-1873 (4-27-1873)
Williams, S. E. to S. G. Templeton 8-21-1865 (8-22-1865)
Williams, Sarah E. to John R. Prichard 12-24-1864 (12-25-1864)
Williams, Sarah to T. R. Crampley 8-24-1874 (8-25-1874)
Williams, Scelia A. to John A. Sheton 4-22-1865 (no return)
Williams, Susan E. to John Lee 6-1-1867 (6-3-1867)
Williams, Zylphia J. to A. M. Williams 6-24-1873
Williamson, Caroline to S. M. Richards 2-24-1873 (no return)
Williamson, L. J. to F. C. Moore 2-11-1879 (2-12-1879)
Williamson, Mary E. to Flournoy T. Simmons? 12-12-1866 (12-13-1866)
Williamson, Mary J. to Thos. J. Frazier 5-28-1867
Williamson, Mattie to William C. Hutson 1-9-1877 (1-10-1877)
Williamson, Mollie to B. A. Bessent 12-7-1877 (12-8-1877)
Williamson, Pattie to Edward Childress 9-4-1879 (9-7-1879)
Williamson, Prudence (Mrs.) to John A. Mills 12-12-1876 (12-14-1876)
Williamson, Tempe J. to W. R. Simpson 12-16-1874
Willis, Margaret to Nathan Stamps 7-17-1867 (8-10-1867)
Willis, Marian to Dvid Howell? 8-17-1861 (no return)
Wilson, Elvira A. to John A. Johnson 1-28-1863 (no return)
Wilson, Mariah to Thomas Turner 6-12-1878 (6-13-1878)
Wilson, Mary Jane to J. C. Sims 1-31-1865 (no return)
Wilson, R. E. to R. Z. McDaniel 1-4-1869 (1-5-1869)
Winberry, Jamima to W. R. Prewet 10-11-1871 (10-12-1871)
Winberry, Martha to Iram Chadwick 9-17-1870 (9-18-1870)
Winburn, Amanda J. to W. J. F. Dobbs 11-4-1869
Winchester, Ann Eliza to Jim Gray 10-17-1877 (10-20-1877)
Winfred, Mary J. to R. E. Harris 12-8-1869 (12-9-1869)

Winters, Frances A. to L. G. Rasbury 11-7-1862
Winters, L. J. to H. L. McCarroll 1-30-1875 (2-3-1875)
Winters, M. A. to J. H. Modlin 2-16-1875 (2-17-1875)
Wise, Rachel to James Duckworth 2-9-1876 (2-10-1876)
Wiseman, Dora to M. H. Whitten 5-30-1874 (no return)
Wofford, Mollie to J. W. Waldron 1-1-1877 (1-4-1877)
Wood, Amanda to George Steward 1-1-1878
Wood, Amanda to Polk Rodgers 12-27-1871
Wood, C. A. to J. P. Thurmond 2-15-1865
Wood, Emma A. to P. B. Tatum 4-24-1866
Wood, Lucy to John Maggard 12-29-1875 (1-2-1876)
Wood, Mary G. to M. J. Hark 11-8-1877
Wood, Mary to John Anderson 1-27-1867 (no return)
Wood, Nancy E. to W. O. Hobson 4-18-1874 (4-19-1874)
Wood, Patsy to Yancy Henderson 2-26-1870 (no return)
Wood, Susan A. to W. S. Trout 11-20-1866 (no return)
Woods, Mattie to Edward Ellis 4-17-1872 (4-18-1872)
Woods, Mollie to Boss Fowlks 9-25-1879
Woods, Nancy to Miles Mathews 1-16-1871 (1-19-1871) B
Woods, Nora to John Dewitt? 8-30-1877 (crossed out)
Woods, Nora to John Smith 8-30-1877 (no return)
Woods, Sarah Jane to S. A. Greer 9-16-1868 (9-17-1868)
Woods, Susan Ann to J. W. Whichard 3-25-1879 (3-28-1879)
Woodson, Mary to Rufus Pettus 12-23-1876
Word, Sarah to Washington Walker 12-23-1871 (12-26-1871)
Worrels, Mary to John E. Mosely 9-30-1869 (no return)
Worship (Bishop?), E. A. to LaFayette Holland 12-21-1878
    (12-24-1878)
Wright, Amanda to T. H. Brinkly 1-7-1868 (1-8-1868)
Wright, Angeline to Charles Ford 2-13-1867
Wright, E. E. to Columbus L. Nolen 3-9-1874
Wright, Jennie to James W. Whitten 6-16-1874 (no return)
Wright, Mary J. to J. E. Blankenship 11-28-1871 (12-20-1871)
Wright, Mary Jane to Stephen S. Howard 12-9-1863 (no return)
Wright, Mollie L. to S. A. Heddin 10-5-1869 (no return)
Wright, Nancy Ann to Wm. Turfim 2-17-1863 (2-18-1863)
Wright, Rebecca to J. M. Lauderdale 5-4-1869
Wright, Rebecca to James C. Parnell 4-12-1873 (4-13-1873)
Wright, Rebecca to W. T. Trusty 2-7-1872 (no return)
Wright, Sarah J. to A. H. Kirk 10-3-1867
Wright, Senia to Henry Evans 2-25-1868 (no return)
Wright, Susan L. to John A. Floyd 10-12-1861 (10-20-1861)
Wright, Tennessee to J. M. Gleaves 12-21-1876
Wyatt, Amanda to Green Prichard 11-29-1877
Wyatt, Joanna to Martin Fowlks 8-28-1879
Wyatt, Laura to Jerry Prichard 4-2-1877 (4-5-1877)
Wyatt, Margaret to Jack Moore 4-6-1880 (4-8-1880)
Wyett, Becky to Tom Wynne 12-24-1867 (12-26-1867)
Wynne, Angaline to Sam Pierce 3-30-1867 (4-1-1867)
Wynne, Angeline to Edmond Enochs 8-19-1870 (no return)
Wynne, Angeline to Pharaoh Starks 12-23-1879
Wynne, Bettie to John Turner 8-21-1878 (8-28-1878)
Wynne, Clarissa to Allen Johnson 1-4-1873 (no return)
Wynne, Ella to Amos Grimm 1-3-1874
Wynne, Emaline to John T. Whitson 4-4-1861
Wynne, Frances to Miller McKennie 5-20-1876
Wynne, Frances to Thomas Powell 1-8-1880
Wynne, Harriet J. to Jno. A. (Dr.) Williams 3-27-1877 (no return)
Wynne, Jane to Jeff Wynne 12-26-1867 (no return)
Wynne, L. M. to P. J. Flack 12-17-1872
Wynne, Louella to George Sinclair 2-11-1874 (2-12-1874)
Wynne, Louisa to Jo Hicks 3-2-1867
Wynne, Lutitia to Charley Ruff 10-13-1866 (no return)
Wynne, Susan to Bob Clark 1-2-1879
Wyrick, Amanda to James Johnson 12-4-1875
Yancey, Elvie G. to A. W. Howell 10-1-1878 (10-2-1878)
Yarington, Sallie to Eli A. Moody 12-10-1870 (12-11-1870)
Yates, Donie to J. R. Jackson 10-3-1870 (no return)
Yearwod, Katie to J. P. Jones 5-1-1869 (5-4-1869)
You, Nancy to Thomas H. Kellow 1-20-1875 (1-21-1875)
Young, Margaret to Thomas Green 10-18-1869 (no return)
Young, Martha A. A. to John G. Gentry 3-7-1861
Young, Nora A. to David C. Clark 11-22-1877 (11-25-1877)
Yow, Amanda to C. B. R. White 10-20-1874 (10-21-1874)
Yow, Leonie to A. C. Sorrell 9-12-1870 (9-13-1870)

Yowe, M. R. to J. H. Sorrell 12-22-1870
Zarecor?, Jennie to M. H. Dickey 9-29-1875 (no return)
____, ____ to Harrison Britton no date (with Aug 1867)
____, ____ to Thomas Harris 8-24-1866 (no return)
____, ____ to Wash King no dates (with Sep 1875)